Research Methods
in Sport

Active Learning in Sport – titles in the series

To order, please contact our distributor: BEBC Distribution, Albion Close, Parkstone, Poole, BH12 3LL. Telephone: 0845 230 9000, email: **learningmatters@bebc.co.uk**. You can find more information on each of these titles and our other learning resources at **www.learningmatters.co.uk**.

Research Methods in Sport

Mark F Smith

LearningMatters

First published in 2010 by Learning Matters Ltd
British Library Cataloguing in Publication Data
A CIP record for this book is available from the British Library.
ISBN 978 1 84445 261 3
Cover and text design by Toucan Design
Project management by Swales and Willis Ltd, Exeter, Devon
Typeset by Kelly Winter
Printed and bound in Great Britain by TJ International Ltd, Padstow, Cornwall
Learning Matters Ltd
33 Southernhay East
Exeter EX1 1NX
Tel: 01392 215560
info@learningmatters.co.uk
www.learningmatters.co.uk

In memory of Dr James Balmer
A colleague. . . A friend. . . An inspiration

Contents

Chapter 1
The context of sport research

Learning Objectives

By linking your understanding of sport in practice to sport-related research examples, this chapter is designed to help you:

- explain the nature of sport research and describe the characteristics of a scientific approach;
- outline the building blocks of research and establish which approach would link to particular sport-related research questions;
- identify the importance of a research strategy to the overall research framework.

Introduction

Research is the gateway to new discoveries. Discoveries such as new technology to improve the speed of a cyclist around a track, novel training programmes to enhance swim start performance or creative initiatives that evaluate children's enjoyment in sport. Research provides us all with the chance to learn more and acquire new knowledge to help ourselves and others.

This opening chapter of the book *Research Methods in Sport* will provide a brief, but important starting point to help examine the very nature of research within a sporting context. It will introduce the concept of research and provide an important review of the underpinning philosophy to scientific inquiry. By examining a range of sport-related research questions the chapter will uncover the role that the philosophy of science plays in shaping the framework in which we view our sporting research and how such understanding may lead us to the selection of our research strategy.

By further reviewing this research framework, a clear link will be made between the very nature of our sporting problems – that is the questions we wish to answer – and the ways in which we can begin to answer them. By highlighting the need to select the right design and method in the quest to solve our problems, this chapter is considered essential reading before embarking on future chapters throughout the book.

It is not the intention of this chapter to outline the research process in detail or explain how to write your research project. Rather this opening chapter will provide you with an all-important starting point that will help you to understand research methods and their value and then, if you progress to undertaking your own research project, assist you in selecting the most appropriate research strategy. To outline a discourse on the debate about the structure of science or the nature of knowledge is outside the scope of this book; however, where appropriate, you will be made aware of how such debates may impact on your own research activities. It is acknowledged that in simplifying models and examples used to outline approaches to scientific inquiry, terminology may not be aligned with those from a natural and social science background and, therefore, for more in-depth and thorough accounts the reader is directed to the text by Grix (2002).

The nature of sport research

Sport, as an area of study, is unique. In how many other disciplines would you cover as many different subjects as you do in sport? Ranging from the natural sciences such as physiology, chemistry, mathematics and physics to the social sciences such as social psychology, philosophy, pedagogy and coaching, politics, economics and sociology, the study of sport requires a tremendous appreciation of so many different things. By adding to this ergonomics, technology, research methods and all the practical elements involved in studying sport, a wonderfully diverse picture can begin to be painted that highlights the interconnected nature of sport.

With the continual growth of sport from both a participatory and academic study point of view, there is little doubt that to be able to appreciate the complex web of connections researching in sport offers, a plethora of information that informs understanding and builds knowledge must be sought. Whether examining the way the human body responds to physical work in order to develop new strategies to improve athletic performance, evaluating the role sport plays in bringing communities together, or describing how sport has given many people hope and belief following times of personal suffering, it can be liberating for all involved.

This thirst for understanding about sport and its impact on our lives has led to a significant advancement in our knowledge over the last 100 years. From both a natural and social science perspective, the pursuit of knowledge through sport-related research has led to our current level of understanding acted out in the lectures we attend, practical sessions we perform in, journals and textbooks we read and internet pages we scan through.

Reflection Point 1.1

Scientific discoveries allied to sport began in early civilisations through the practices and writings of ancient Greek physicians, such as Herodicus (5th Century BC). With early discoveries relating to physical training and nutrition influencing inquiry through research practice, the emergence of educated scholars keen to develop new knowledge in the area of sport flourished over the course of the next two millennia.

The pursuit of sporting excellence has lead to the emergence of important developments through research to assist athletes and exercisers in their own sporting activities. If we journey back over the last decade or so alone, we can begin to identify, for example, how the appliance of science to sport has enhanced athletes' capabilities to perform. Take the following, for example:

- Training methods, such as hypoxic training, to enhance physiological capacity.
- Pre-event acclimatisation strategies to ensure the athlete's capability to perform in a range of environment conditions.
- Techniques such as ice-bath submersion to aid post-event recovery.
- Differentiated coaching practice that maximises athlete development and optimises performance.
- Technological developments in bicycle design and swimsuit composition to reduce drag and allow the athlete to travel faster.
- Psychological skills training packages (i.e. visualisation and imagery) that can be implemented to prepare athletes for competition.
- Training aids, such as heart rate monitors, ergometry systems, performance profiles, to support advanced preparation for competition.
- Nutritional strategies that offer the exerciser pre-, during and post-exercise fuel supplements to support training and event performance.

Whatever the area of interest, the process of looking back through time and identifying key research milestones presents an opportunity to celebrate the significant impact research has played in the advancement of sport! By doing this it is clear to see that changes in the way sport has been perceived in society and its value to all those that participate has occurred not through chance or luck, but through systematic investigation to discover new knowledge and push the boundaries of what we know.

The importance of research to the area of sport, therefore, is fundamental not just to the advancement of our discipline, but also to our own personal and professional development. Sport provides us with a sense of freedom and release, not bound by the day-to-day hectic lives we now live. We lose ourselves in sport, embracing the rollercoaster of emotions that sport always delivers us. What draws us back to sport time and time again is the need for that fix. Being able to develop and change, improve and compete, offers us the motive to want to continue. Undertaking research as a student should provide us with the same exhilaration, leading us on the same emotional journey, allowing us to develop, change and improve knowledge for the greater good.

Why is research in sport of value?

We are constantly bombarded with research all the time, whether through books, newspapers, television programmes, advertising boards or university lecturers. The discovery of many new things can occur through research and their findings can help make sense of the world. We have all at some point undertaken research, trying to solve problems by working through them in a logical step-by-step fashion. It is often the case, however, that we do not actually recognise the process of finding a solution as research and often take this approach for granted. It is only when we stand back and examine our approach or it's located in a different context, do we begin to identify what research involves and the value it can bring.

It is not uncommon to often use the term 'research' very loosely. Those new to research often perceive that all tasks involve some kind of research; and to some extent this may be true. Many view the mere *gathering* of facts or information as research! By simply reading a few book chapters, a couple of webpages and a vaguely relevant journal article, a conclusion is made that some research has taken place and something new was discovered! An alternative conclusion drawn by many is that the actual practical pursuit of collecting data constitutes research. Asking people about the success of a newly opened sports centre, recording heart rate response during a hockey match or observing a coaching session and noting down negative behaviour alone may be considered research. This process of 'collecting data', carried out in a systematic and accurate way can certainly be viewed as an important part of research, but does not in itself constitute research.

Research allows for the undertaking of information-finding activities; establishing facts and reaching new conclusions. Undertaken in a controlled, critical manner, research allows questions to be asked and then attempts to solve them in a systematic scientific way. Research is about thinking strategically and logically, not haphazardly or irrationally. Research requires planning and organisation, constant reflection and assessment. Creativity and innovation will lead to novel and original approaches, whilst the ability to draw accurate conclusions will show an awareness and attention to detail.

Key Point 1.1

Research has been defined as:

Diligent and systematic inquiry or investigation into a subject in order to discover facts or principles. (Blaxter et al., 2001, p5)

The formal, systematic application of scholarship, disciplined inquiry, and most often the scientific method to the study of problems. (Fraenkal and Wallen, 2003, pG-7)

Systematic inquiry that is characterised by sets of principles, guidelines for procedures and which is subject to evaluation in terms of criteria such as validity, reliability and representativeness. (Hitchcock and Hughes, 1995, p5)

When the term research is used then, the assumption is made that a systematic process has been undertaken that allows for the development and testing of a question in order to arrive at a new conclusion. By reflecting on experience alone, and arriving at some conclusions may not therefore be sufficient enough to be called research. Instead, research aims to combine both experience and reason to create a method of rational inquiry. It is when experience is combined with logical reasoning that the foundation of scientific inquiry is born.

Key Point 1.2

Characteristics of research include:

- a controlled, critical approach conducted in a systematic way;
- information finding that establishes facts and generates new conclusions that are open to public scrutiny and criticism;
- the combination of experience and logical reasoning to generate new facts and principles.

The scientific inquiry of knowledge

Science in its most basic definition is a way of investigating nature and discovering reliable knowledge about it. The scientific approach to discovering new knowledge is distinct from other ways in that it seeks to generate reliable knowledge that is justifiably true. According to the advocates of the scientific method of inquiry other methods of acquiring knowledge, such as personal experience, intuition or authority, may provide what is believed to be true but it may not be justified or reliable. In our own sporting pursuits, we acquire new knowledge through our own sensory experiences, agreement with our team-mates, experts' opinion on television sport shows or by logically reasoning things through.

Although each will provide us with a sense of new knowledge, can we really be confident that the knowledge acquired through these ways is complete and accurate? How do we know that the football pundits are right, or our own sensory experiences are actually complete? Can our own logical reasoning be based on false premises from the start and therefore produce unreliable knowledge? Relying on knowledge that is untrue or unjustified may lead to inappropriate actions. It is therefore thought that by undertaking the scientific method of inquiry, a higher degree of certainty can be gained about knowledge that can be deemed both reliable and justifiably true.

The building blocks of sport research

Our perception of reality, that is to say how we view the world, influences how knowledge is characterised and ultimately legitimised through our research endeavours. The view a researcher holds will have an impact on how research is planned, conducted and evaluated. Therefore, as a junior researcher wishing to undertake a research project in sport, having awareness as to the predominant models provides a foundation for effective practice.

Take the two examples of a sports physiotherapist and a mountain explorer. Some researchers operate in the same way a sports physiotherapist would. The therapist is in possession of some detailed knowledge about the anatomy and physiology of the body, knowing where to find a problem if one occurred. They would know what they were looking for based on facts, know where to look for it and what to expect once they found it. Like the sports physiotherapist, these researchers would work in a linear, step-by-step logical fashion.

In contrast, some researchers more closely resemble that of a mountain explorer, trying to map uncharted territory with little or no prior knowledge of the landscape. They would have the skills to explore but would not know what they were looking for or what to expect if they found something. Whereas the main aim of the sports physiotherapist would be one based on discovery, analysis and prediction, the explorer's main task would be based on exploration, discovery and description.

Key Point 1.3

The steps in scientific research (adapted from Cohen et al., 2003):

Step 1 – Identify a problem, have a hunch, or develop a question.
Step 2 – Formulate a tentative solution or hypotheses associated with the question or problem.
Step 3 – Conduct practical or theoretical testing of solutions or hypotheses.
Step 4 – Eliminate or adjust unsuccessful solutions to evolve or support theory.

These two approaches in some part begin to explain the varying positions researchers take when attempting to discover new knowledge. Different views of social reality in the pursuit of true and reliable knowledge has been discussed and debated for millennia. These philosophical positions sit right at the very centre of any research that is undertaken, because the way reality is viewed dictates 'e approach taken to answer the research question. It is these philosophical approaches to research should form the very building blocks to effective research practice.

Paradigms of research

Philosophy, quite simply, is an individual's or group's belief about something. In the case of research, it concerns the belief of what knowledge is and how it is acquired. How reality is viewed by the researcher shapes their approach to research. In other words, the rules by which they work and the strategies that fit within the rules and beliefs they subscribe to. Because of the diverse nature of sport and the wide range of natural and social science disciplines encountered when sport is studied, it is no surprise that researchers will view reality differently and, depending on the philosophical position they hold, the pursuit of new knowledge through research will take different forms. In other words, the fundamental building blocks of their research will be different.

One way of understanding each philosophical position is to view them as different sets of sunglasses. Each set has different coloured lenses and therefore when put on, the same thing is seen but just in a different way. In essence, when research is conducted, the researcher's philosophical position (that is to say the type of sunglasses worn) will govern the way they view reality. By having awareness as to the different views that exist, the researcher is able to:

- establish a personal philosophical approach to their research;
- understand that of others and recognise the type of arguments being made, and;
- assess each position's influence on a research question and understand its wider social impact.

The philosophy of how social reality is viewed is known as *ontology*. This is the very starting point of all research. For the natural scientist, and those undertaking research in the areas of sport physiology, biomechanics or exercise biochemistry for example, social reality would be viewed from an *objectivist* perspective. Objectivists believe that all social phenomena exist independent of any social influence. Researchers from this ontological position look at 'social facts' for reliable and justifiable truth.

For the social scientist, researching in areas relating to social psychology, sociology of sport or historical aspects of exercise for example, reality would be viewed from a *constructivist* position. They would assert that social phenomena are not independent of social influence, rather are in a constant state of revision and are socially constructed. They search for 'social meaning', being aware that reality is in a state of flux and revision.

It is clear to see, therefore, that from these two competing ontological standpoints, each will impact differently on the way in which the researcher conducts their research. Such world-view, or ontology, has an impact on how we go about discovering knowledge. The act of formulating a research question and then undertaking a process to discover an answer is bound very tightly within an ontological view of reality. Although the student researcher may not be aware, the way in which research is undertaken is governed by a set of fundamental principles about how reality is viewed. For the effective student researcher, linking the question with a philosophical position will enable more constructive debates to emerge, recognising others' point of view, and defending one's own position. Table 1.1 provides clear definitions that show distinctiveness in these key terms.

Branch of science	Natural science (e.g. physiology and biomechanics)	Social science (e.g. sociology)
Ontological view	Objectivism	Constructivism
Belief	*That all social phenomena (behaviour that influences or is influenced by others) and their meanings have an existence that is independent of social actors (the way in which others' actions and reactions modify behaviour) (Grix, 2002; Bryman, 2008).*	*That all social phenomena and their meanings are continually being accomplished by social actors, implying the social phenomena are in a constant state of revision and flux (Grix, 2002; Bryman, 2008).*
Epistemological view	Positivism	Interpretivism
Belief	*Purports to the position that everything is ultimately measurable and applies the methods of the natural sciences to study social reality.*	*Selecting strategies that respect the differences between people and the objects of the natural sciences and therefore requires a grasp of the subjective meaning of social action.*
Methodological view	Quantitative	Qualitative
Belief	*A deductive position that emphasises quantification in collection and analysis of data through the process of precise numerical measurement.*	*An inductive position that emphasises an understanding of human behaviour through methods such as interviews, observations, focus groups, surveys and/or case studies.*

Table 1.1: The branch of science can be summarised into three key hierarchical principles.

If ontology is concerned with how we view the world, *epistemology* is a further branch of philosophy that is concerned with the theory of knowledge. Put simply, epistemology focuses on the knowledge-gathering process and the underpinning assumptions that govern the methods of inquiry. As this book concerns the use of research design and methods in sport research, and recognising that our ontological and epistemological views will have an impact on our research approach, we can start to see how knowing the building blocks of research can impact on our design and associated research methods.

Learning Activity 1.1

If a student wanted to conduct a research project based around the topic of coaching behaviour and player performance they could:

1. Collect some numerical data on coach-to-player ratio and identify whether a low ratio was associated with performance success (i.e. number of games won).
2. Plot the coach's movement patterns in metres during training games and look to identify whether it influences player movement patterns.
3. Observe and record particular phrases the coach uses when talking to the players to assess the impact on players' attitudes towards training and performance.
4. Assess the coach's non-verbal behaviour and link observations to how the players' behaviour alters throughout the session.

Examples 1 and 2 focus on establishing 'social facts', that is to say quantification through measurement of numerical data. Examples 3 and 4 concern 'social meanings', and focus on obtaining subjectivity of response. Based on these approaches, the student will have to decide on their philosophical standpoint – *objectivist* or *constructivist* – and then the corresponding epistemology (i.e. *positivism* or *interpretivism*) and then the methodological position (i.e. *quantitative* or *qualitative*). It is important to remember as a researcher that one is no better than the other; rather each standpoint will lead to a more suitable way of acquiring the knowledge, selecting the approach and drawing more meaningful conclusions.

Methodological approaches to sport research

The two broad methodological approaches to research are quantitative and qualitative. Such approaches are typically split according to whether numerical data is collected or not. Although this is certainly one aspect, there are many other differences that distinguish quantitative to qualitative research approaches. In quantitative research, hypotheses and research questions tend to be based on theories that the researcher seeks to test. Take for example the theory that if we are over-aroused as a performer we under-perform in sport. In this approach the question is derived from the theory and the objective is to test it. In qualitative research, the researcher may generate a theory following some observations or examine an existing theory from difference perspectives (i.e. different coloured lenses). This being the case, each methodology will have its own unique strengths and weaknesses that will impact on the researcher's ability to answer the research question.

Strengths

- Testing and validating already constructed theories about how (and to a lesser degree, why) phenomena occur.
- Testing hypotheses that are constructed before the data are collected. Can generalise research findings when the data are based on random samples of sufficient size.
- Can generalise a research finding when it has been replicated on many different populations and groups.
- Useful for obtaining data that allow quantitative predictions to be made.
- The researcher may construct a situation that eliminates the confounding influence of many variables, allowing one to more credibly assess *cause-and-effect* relationships (i.e. experiment).
- Data collection using some quantitative data collection methods is relatively quick (e.g., self-completion questionnaire).
- Provides precise, quantitative, numerical data.
- Data analysis is relatively less time consuming (using statistical software).
- The research results are relatively independent of the researcher (e.g., statistical significance).
- It may have higher credibility with many people.
- It is useful for studying large numbers of people.

Weaknesses

- The researcher's categories that are used may not reflect other's understandings.
- The researcher's theories that are used may not reflect other's understandings.
- The researcher may miss out on phenomena occurring because of the focus on theory or hypothesis *testing* rather than on theory or hypothesis *generation* (called the *confirmation bias*).
- Knowledge produced may be too abstract and general for direct application to specific local situations, contexts, and individuals.

Table 1.2 Strengths and weaknesses of the quantitative research approach (extracts from Johnson et al., 2004).

Strengths

- The data are based on the participants' own categories of meaning.
- It is useful for studying a limited number of cases in depth.
- It is useful for describing complex phenomena.
- Provides individual case information.
- Can conduct cross-case comparisons and analysis.
- Provides understanding and description of people's personal experiences of phenomena (i.e. the insider's viewpoint).
- Can describe, in rich detail, phenomena as they are situated and embedded in local contexts.
- The researcher identifies contextual and setting factors as they relate to the phenomenon of interest.
- The researcher can study dynamic processes (i.e. documenting sequential patterns and change).
- Can determine how participants interpret 'constructs' (e.g. self-esteem, IQ).
- Data are usually collected in naturalistic settings in qualitative research.
- Qualitative approaches are responsive to local situations, conditions, and stakeholders' needs.
- Qualitative researchers are responsive to changes that occur during the conduct of a study (especially during extended fieldwork) and may shift the focus of their studies as a result.
- Qualitative data in the words and categories of participants lend themselves to exploring how and why phenomena occur.
- One can use an important case to demonstrate vividly a phenomenon to the readers of a report.

Weaknesses

- Knowledge produced may not generalise to other people or other settings (i.e. findings may be unique to the relatively few people included in the research study).
- It is difficult to make quantitative predictions.
- It is more difficult to test hypotheses and theories.
- It may have lower credibility with some people.
- It generally takes more time to collect the data when compared to quantitative research.
- Data analysis is often time consuming.
- The results are more easily influenced by the researcher's personal biases and idiosyncrasies.

Table 1.3: Strengths and weaknesses of the qualitative research approach (extracts from Johnson et al., 2004).

Theory building versus theory testing

It is through the combination of experience and logical reasoning played out in the natural world, that the researcher is provided with an opportunity to conduct research in a diligent and systematic manner. Based on the nature of the question, there are three forms of reasoning: inductive, deductive or a combination of the two.

Reflection Point 1.2

According to Hitchcock and Hughes (1995), a theory concerns the development of a systematic construction of knowledge employing the use of concepts, systems, models, structures, beliefs and ideas in order to make statements about particular actions, events or activities. Built upon one or more hypotheses, and upon evidence, a theory contains logical reasoning and connections between the hypothesis and evidence. Created after observation and testing, theories are designed to explain or predict phenomena. Research attempts to develop (inductive) or test/confirm (deductive) a theory in the quest for new knowledge.

From an inductive perspective, a range of theoretical models has been presented by Abbiss and Laursen (*Sports Medicine*, 2005, 35: 865–98) to explain fatigue during prolonged endurance cycling. In this paper the authors reviewed over 2000 manuscripts addressing the topic of fatigue, out of which a number of theories developed. These include: (i) cardiovascular/anaerobic model; (ii) energy supply/depletion model; (iii) neuromuscular fatigue model; (iv) muscle trauma model; (v) biomechanical model; (vi) thermoregulatory model; (vii) psychological/motivational model; and (viii) central governor model. Through careful analysis of previous evidence, the authors proposed a new 'integrated' theory that combined all existing models into one. Generating new hypotheses allows for the new theory to be tested under a number of conditions (deductive perspective). These may include changing environments, varying distances, different athlete populations or altered physiological states. This way the proposed updated 'integrated' theory of fatigue can be assessed.

Consider a researcher who over the last five years has attended Wimbledon fortnight. For every match observed she noticed that both players always ate bananas at some point during the match. She had observed over 100 matches and based on logical reasoning concluded that all tennis players at Wimbledon must eat bananas. Based on this premise, she inductively constructed a theory that stated all tennis players at other championship competitions must also eat bananas during their matches. To test this theory, she decided to attend the US Open and watch as many tennis matches as possible. Over the course of the first week her theory seemed to be true, until she watched a men's quarter-final. At no point did either player eat a banana. With this being the case, her theory could not be confirmed and she had to make adjustments to accommodate her observations. As illustrated in Figure 1.1, the application of induction and deduction research, either in combination or isolation, provides the researcher with a logical framework to develop and then test theories, concepts and/or ideas.

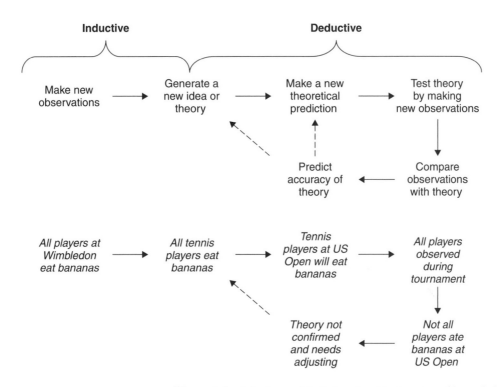

Figure 1.1: A basic model of the scientific inquiry of knowledge that incorporates both inductive and deductive approaches to research.

Inductive approach to research

Theory building begins by using *inductive reasoning*. Inductive research concerns generating theories or ideas from research, that is to say attempting to make some kind of generalisable inference out of observations. So the sport researcher may make a number of observations about crowd behaviour at a number of rugby games, and then start to generate a theory about the way the crowd interact under different match situations. Such theories attempt to make sense of the observations and are produced afterwards (*post factum* or after the facts).

Let's assume a number of observations are made on elite runners' VO_{2max} values and it was observed that all those measured had high aerobic capacities (> 70 ml.kg.min^{-1}). From a theory building approach it can therefore be concluded that "*all* elite runners have a high aerobic capacity" (*the new theory*). In this inductive process, specific observations move to more general statements and theories.

From this position, in order for the researcher to make generalisations and formulate theories, inductive reasoning must confirm to a number of conditions. Firstly, a number of observations must be made to ensure confidence that the generalisable statement applies to all. Obviously this very much depends on the nature of the observations made. You don't need to observe too often that dropping a barbell on your foot results in pain. However, you would not want to jump to the rash conclusion about the aerobic capacities of *all* elite runners having only observed a handful.

Secondly, observations need to be repeated under a large range of conditions. The choice of conditions, however, can be difficult and the question of how many different conditions are needed to make an inductive generalisation can be hard to determine. Because of these factors, generalisations made through induction can lead to conclusions, but only on a degree of certainty governed by the observations made.

Research Focus 1.1

Mankad et al. (*Journal of Clinical Sports Psychology,* 2009, 3: 1–14) investigated the underlying emotional climate of injured athletes within team sport environments. It was hoped that such research would develop a better understanding as to how injured athletes responded to the emotional climate of sport during rehabilitation and the characteristics of their emotional behaviour. The study involved nine male and four female seriously injured athletes from various sporting teams. These athletes participated in a range of sports (i.e. basketball, rugby league, football, water polo and BMX racing) and competed at a high level before receiving injuries. All athletes underwent structured interviews to describe their long-term injury rehabilitation experience. Each was asked to discuss their injury experience from a personal and social perspective, describing emotions, coping behaviours, and interactions within the social environment. As a consequence of the interview data, three themes emerged which focused on: i) emotional trauma; ii) emotional climate; and iii) emotional acting.

The authors' reported that in order for the injured athletes to maintain in-group norms, they engaged in avoidance behaviours, reported suppressing negative affects of fear, used acting strategies to control emotions in public, and thought that such inhibitive behaviours were encouraged within their team environment. Mankad and co-workers summarised their study by concluding that such findings have important implications for the identification and treatment of emotionally destructive behaviours that could potentially delay an athlete's psychological rehabilitation from athletic injury.

Deductive approach to research

Theory testing begins by using *deductive reasoning*. This approach starts with a theory that guides the researcher into making observations that attempt to test the worth of a theory. By applying the theory built from inductive reasoning outlined above the worth of the theory can be tested. The theory developed through inductive research stated that all elite runners have a high aerobic capacity ($VO_{2max} > 70$ ml.kg.min^{-1}). Supposing a new elite runner appeared on the scene; based on the theory they should also have a high aerobic capacity.

So through deductive logic all elite runners have a high VO_{2max} and therefore the new runner must also have a high VO_{2max}. This theory may be challenged, however, as this may not actually be true. The question of confidence begins to arise about the theory. How confident is the researcher that the theory will always be true? The researcher may wish to ask how the theory was derived and how many times has it been tested? The theory that all elite runners have high aerobic capacities ($VO_{2max} > 70$ ml.kg.min^{-1}) will hold true only until another elite runner is found to have a VO_{2max}

value lower than 70 ml.kg.min^{-1}. When this is discovered the theory will then have to be refined and a new one developed. This will then hold true until a time when this is disproved and refined again.

Research Focus 1.2

Lindsay et al. (*Medicine and Science in Sports and Exercise,* 1996, 28: 1427–34) conducted a study to investigate the impact of interval training on athletic performance in highly trained athletes. By replacing a portion of 'aerobic' based training with a programme of sustained high-intensity training (HIT), they wished to investigate the effects of acute, short-term (i.e. 4–6-weeks) intensive training on performance. The study involved eight male performers who undertook a series of exercise tasks within a laboratory setting. Across a period of 28 days, each athlete performed six HIT training sessions, which consisted of 6–8 exercise repetitions each lasting 5 minutes and at an intensity considered high for all individuals. Throughout the 28-day period, assessment tests were also conducted to evaluate physiological performance and a continual profile of their mood states (POMS).

Results showed that as a consequence of the 28-day HIT training programme, a significant difference was found for all performance measures (i.e. time to fatigue during a maximal test, endurance trial over 40-km and their maximal physiological capacity). Interestingly, the authors found no significant difference in athlete mood state over the 28-day period indicating that a sudden change in training intensity over such an acute period of time did not significantly disturb the athletes' emotional adaptation to the intense interval training programme.

In summary, Lindsay et al. noted that the manipulation of athletes' training by replacing 'aerobic' based training with a high-intensity training programme resulted in an improvement of performance in laboratory-based tests ranging in duration from 60 seconds to 1 hour.

When theories are tested, reliable knowledge is sought so that the theory can either be retained as true or refuted as false. By assessing more and more elite runners, the researcher attempts to disprove the theory. It is this very act of trying to disprove or *falsify* that therefore strengthens the theory. The more times the researcher tries to falsify it and can't, the stronger it becomes.

When attempting to test a theory, the researcher must begin by developing statements that are to be tested. These statements are called *hypotheses* and when used in the attempt to retain or refute a theory it is commonly referred to as the *hypothetico-deductive method*. It is this approach that is synonymous with the *scientific method* of research.

By applying deductive, inductive or a combination of both, research therefore prescribes to the notion that questions which are generated lead to the development of clear objectives, which are achieved through a carefully planned and executed *research strategy*. This allows for meaning to be reached from the collected facts, which form a reasoned argument to support the conclusions. Knowledge is then expanded and advanced, which give rise to further research problems.

Reflection Point 1.3

- How is the world viewed? And what can actually be researched? – *Ontology*
- What do we know about what can be studied? – *Epistemology*
- How are we going to acquire what is out there? – *Methodology*
- What plan will be used to acquire what is out there? – *Research design*
- What techniques/tools can be used to collect and analyse what is out there? – *Research methods*

The different types of research

Research starts off by asking some fundamental questions bound within a particular problem or area of interest. It is through these questions asked that the research strategy begins to emerge. Selecting the right strategy will help find the right answer. In the most basic of ways, as described in Table 1.4, the research question will relate to wanting to know, for example, *what* is going on (descriptive), *why* is it happening (explanatory), or *how* may it impact on others (predictive). The questions that are asked (i.e. what, how, when, where and why?) dictate which research approach is necessary to provide a solution to the problem. Such questions will also be wrapped up in an ontological position, so identifying early within the research journey which one the question links to is an important task for any researcher. It may well be the case that some problems may be solved through a quick review of the literature for example, however there may be no logical answer found within the evidence and therefore research must be undertaken to generate new knowledge and understanding.

The research framework

Identifying where and how research design and methods fit into the overall research framework is an important first step in developing a research project. It is not the intention here to cover the research process or provide a step-by-step guide to developing a research project; other books in the series do this well. What is necessary at this stage, however, is to identify where the overarching research strategy, that is to say the design and method, fits into the overall research journey and how the design and data collection methods impact meaningfully on the overall ability to plan, conduct and evaluate the project. Hopefully, Figure 1.2 should come as no surprise, providing a logical and systematic journey through the research process. From the inception of a tentative problem or question to the dissemination of the findings through a report or presentation, the process involves several method-related components that are at the centre of any research project. As outlined in grey, understanding what needs to be established in each of these boxes and making the right and most appropriate decision based on the nature of the question will result in the ability to solve the problem or answer that question.

Type of research	Description	Type of questions that may be asked
Exploratory	Attempts to establish patterns, ideas or hypotheses through the gathering of preliminary information rather than testing or confirming a theory (can lead to explanatory research to provide deeper understanding).	– What is known about the new sport of bossaball (a mix of football, volleyball and gymnastics on trampolines)? – What are the emerging political developments relating to the sport-tourism link in Cumbria? – How do the perceptions of emotional climate among injured athletes impact on their personal and social interactions within a sporting team?
Descriptive	Describes phenomena as it exists, used to obtain data on the characteristics of a particular issue.	– How many football clubs nationally do not have charter standard status? – What are the feelings of older adults (> 65yr) to the introduction of local physical activity road shows? – What are the ground reaction forces on take-off for a group of high jumpers?
Analytical or explanatory	Attempts are made to analyse and explain why or how something is happening.	– How can the number of first-serve errors in tennis be reduced? – Why is the introduction of self-administered training plans found on the internet seen as a threat by professional fitness trainers? – How can a more athlete-centred delivery approach increase retention rates?
Predictive	Attempts to forecast the likelihood of a similar situation occurring elsewhere through generalisation.	– Will the introduction of a new coach lead to higher performance levels throughout the team? – How will the introduction of specific short-term goals impact on motivational levels in junior athletes?

Table 1.4: Research can be categorised into four broad types.

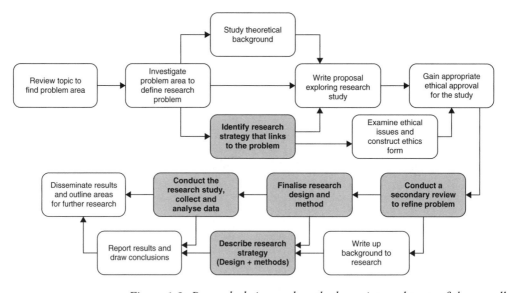

Figure 1.2: Research design and methods are integral parts of the overall research process. As highlighted in the shaded boxes, the research strategy selected will have a direct impact on the ability to draw meaningful conclusions from the data collected.

- *Identifying a research strategy that links to the problem* is an essential early part of the research process. Working thoughtfully through this stage ensures the researcher selects the most suitable research design(s) and method(s) to answer the emerging research question(s).
- *Conducting a secondary review to find a problem* is essentially a research strategy in itself, requiring the researcher to employ a design and method to comprehensively research the literature. This stage is not always necessary and can actually be a research project alone.
- *Finalising the research design and method* provides the researcher with the confidence that the approach is matched to the initial problem. At this stage, pilot study work can be conducted to confirm the research orientation.
- *Describing the research strategy (design + method)* demonstrates understanding as to the approach taken. Correctly describing the strategy allows for others to replicate the research and demonstrates a level of comprehension and communication skill.
- *Conducting the research study, collecting and analysing the data* requires a range of practical and technical skills linked to an underpinning knowledge of the selected strategy. At this stage, inappropriate implementation, evaluation and interpretation can result in invalid, unreliable and unrepresented findings.

A critical approach to research methods

The link between research strategy, that being the design and methods combined, and research question is an important one and can be achieved through a critical approach to research. Adopting a critical approach towards the selection of the research design and associated data collection methods is about accepting nothing at face value, but rather examining the strengths and weaknesses of each in relation to the research question. Each chapter throughout the book has been structured in such a way to aid the development of understanding as to the relative merits and drawbacks associated with each approach. Further to this, each offers a range of valuable practical examples to help guide you through the selection of research approaches.

To adopt a critical approach to research methods, the researcher must be able to evaluate and weigh up different sides of an argument, and be able to draw and evaluate conclusions from logical arguments and data analysis. Critical thinking, therefore, requires background skills such as imagination and creativity, logic and reasoning, conceptual thinking, reflection and feedback. Fisher (2001) noted that the critical-thinking researcher should be able to:

- identify and evaluate assumptions;
- clarify and interpret expressions and ideas;
- judge the acceptability, and credibility, of claims;
- evaluate arguments of different kinds;
- analyse, evaluate and produce explanations;
- analyse, evaluate and make decisions;
- draw inferences and produce arguments.

By applying this approach to the range of research strategies available, the researcher must begin to consider how each provides them with different opportunities to acquire knowledge from the sporting world.

Chapter Review

In this chapter we have considered the importance of research and placed it within a sporting context. We will all at one point or another undertake research in some shape or form. By developing our awareness of the building blocks of research, the philosophical positions that underpin different research approaches, and the varying types of research we may encounter, we can be prepared to start our research journey. In preparation for creating our research question and then selecting the most appropriate research strategy, this chapter will have provided a valuable starting point. By using a range of sport-related research examples throughout this chapter you should now be able to:

- ❏ explain the nature of research within the context of sport and describe the characteristics of the scientific approach;
- ❏ describe the building blocks of research and identify which research type would link to particular sport-related research questions;
- ❏ identify where a research strategy fits into the overall research framework and establish its role within the research process.

(Tick when completed)

Further Reading

Bryman, A (2008) *Social Research Methods*. 3rd edition. Oxford: Oxford University Press.
This broad textbook provides a perfect compendium to this opening chapter. Although not sport-specific, many practical examples simplify often complex passages.

Grix, J (2002) Introducing students to the generic terminology of social research. *Politics*, 22, 175–86.
For students and tutors wishing to grasp the more complex terminology covered in Chapter 1, this paper demystifies often confusing terms through a step-by-step approach to social science research.

Blaxter, L, Hughes, C and Tight, M (2001) *How to Research*. 2nd edition. Maidenhead: Open University Press.
O'Leary, Z (2004) *The Essential Guide to Doing Research*. London: Sage Publications.
Walliman, N (2005) *Your Research Project*. 2nd edition. London: Sage Publications.
Each of the above books extends further the discussions put forward in this chapter, presenting a comprehensive framework on which to base further application. Each is well-presented and accessible to all undergraduate levels.

Chapter 2
Selecting an appropriate research strategy

Learning Objectives

By linking your understanding of sport in practice to sport-related research examples, this chapter is designed to help you:

- explain the importance of research strategy selection;
- describe and define the terms *research design* and *research methods*, exploring the range that can be accessed by the researcher;
- link these key concepts together in a logical and justified manner.

Introduction

Whether playing a round of golf, identifying the roles members of a team play when under pressure, or making a decisive race-winning breakaway, selecting the right research strategy will ensure that time and time again the correct preparation will lead to the selection of the most suitable approach and the desired outcome. The *research strategy* therefore is the logical set of principles that informs the researcher in the process of planning, managing and implementing a single or collection of research methods based on one or more research designs.

In Chapter 1, the two broad approaches to research were reviewed, that being positivistic from a natural science perspective and interpretivistic from a social science perspective. With each approach linked to a set of underpinning assumptions (i.e. paradigms) that impact on the nature of the research question, the selection of the most suitable strategy is a fundamental component to any project. Therefore before unravelling the intricacies of research design and method, the researcher must gain a wider appreciation as to the overarching strategies available. This provides a much more concrete link between the philosophical position of the research and the more pragmatic aspects of data collection and analysis.

Establishing a research strategy

A tennis player is two games away from winning the championship. Up 4–2 in the final set of a five-set thriller, the players return to their seats to work out their individual game plans. Drawing on past experience and evaluating the opponent's strengths and weaknesses, each player works through their options in a logical and rational manner. Based on the objectives of their task, they systematically apply a logical set of principles (*research strategy*) that will shape their decisions. This will allow for a plan to be devised (*research design*). The player who is behind opts to attack the opponent's weakest shot – their backhand – with deep forehand ground shots (their plan). Holding the opponent deep in the court, would then allow for a surge to the net for a volley into the open court (*research methods*).

> ## Reflection Point 2.1
>
> In an excellent book that provides extensive advice on research planning, Blaikie in his text *Designing Social Research* makes a clear distinction between research strategy and other aspects of the research process that are often used synonymously and subsumed under the umbrella term of research methods.
>
> - **Research strategy:** *A logic of inquiry (set of ground rules/principles that shapes the decisions we make when selecting and implementing our research design and methods).*
> - **Research design:** *All aspects relating to the structure or plan by which data collection can occur.*
> - **Research method:** *Execution of the project (incorporating the implementation of instruments, techniques and procedures used to collect data).*
>
> Being able to establish a sense of order to these terms will help in planning the research process as outlined in Chapter 1. Before determining ethics, participant recruitment, protocol/instrument design, etc., the framework or research strategy must be determined and developed in accordance with the nature of the research question.

So the research strategy, which can comprise of one or more designs and one or more methods, is the logical manner by which the researcher shapes the data collection process. Viewing research in such a way allows the researcher to be confident that the strategy selected is best suited to answer the research question. This doesn't always mean that the findings will be what are expected, but it will provide confidence that the process and the logic of conducting the research are achieved in the most suitable way.

Recognising a research project's strategy

Each research project undertaken will inherently have a *research strategy* built within it. It is often the case however that most undergraduate research projects are formed without knowing the strategy selected. The tendency of most is to jump-start into focusing on the research methods, developing questionnaires, constructing treadmill protocols, or structuring and planning interviews, for example. When identifying how to go about collecting data to answer the research question, the immediate concern often is centred on aspects of research construction and implementation, namely deciding on the design and methods and then conducting the study to collect and analyse the data (Chapter 1, Figure 1.2). Although incredibly important aspects of the research process and ones that need time and attention, initial emphasis for the researcher should be on recognising the research strategy.

By identifying this early in the research process, questioned and debated, and arguments built to support the choice, the researcher can be confident that the proceeding selection and evolvement of the design and methods can be built upon a logical framework that fits to the research question being asked. Without such research strategy or overall research orientation, it is difficult to have a clear direction from the start and decide on which design/methods would allow for effective data collection. The act of undertaking research and devising a strategy that is ultimately governed by the research problem will provide the philosophical and practical framework that supports the research process. It is important to recognise that the strategy selected will typically fit firmly into one of the ontological positions (i.e. objectivist or constructivist), the corresponding epistemology positions (i.e. positivist or interpretivist) and the linked methodological positions (i.e. quantitative or qualitative). Understanding these positions early in the research planning will help shape an opinion as to the strengths and limitations of the chosen strategy.

As outlined previously, questions we ask ourselves when deciding on our research approach relate to: i) what does our world consist of, and what constitutes reality (*our ontological position*)?; ii) what do we know about our world and how can we gain appropriate knowledge about it (*our epistemology position*)?; and iii) how are we going to go about acquiring the knowledge that is in our world (*our methodological position*)? Each of these questions will lead us to make decisions that will have a direct influence on the research strategy. As outlined in Figure 2.1, ontological, epistemology and methodological positions can be broadly divided into contrasting paradigms. Each paradigm has its own logic and set of rules, governed by certain principles. Each will, to some extent, dictate the range of research designs and methods that allow for suitable data collection in order to establish knowledge in our world. It is important to recognise working through the figure in a logical direction (from left to right) enables the researcher to approach their design and method selection in a manner than ensures a broad awareness to their selected research positions. The choice of design and method are not an arbitrarily picked range of options, but systematically selected based on the paradigm, that is governed by both the researcher's own position and the research question.

Each chapter within this book has been carefully developed to help the researcher make the right decision based on the type of sport-related question(s) that may need answering. By working through the individual research strategies and their associated design(s) and method(s), the researcher will gain a sense of the philosophical and practice importance of each. In turn, this will aid in the implementation and interpretation of findings within the overall research process.

Problem-led versus strategy-led approaches

It is important to remember that research should always be problem-led and not strategy-led. This means that it should be the research problem that dictates the selection of a strategy, as the researcher should be searching for the most suitable approach to fully answer the question. Although it may be difficult, the researcher must view all approaches evenly without bias towards their own ontological position. It is by taking this approach that will lead to new questions being asked from perspectives and the creation of new opportunities of research that would otherwise be missed.

For the purposes of this book, research strategies have been broadly placed into seven distinct categories that incorporate ontological, epistemological, and methodological positions, as well as appropriate designs and suitable methods. Figure 2.1 provides a representation of the relationship between each position, research design and research methods. Systematic 'literature' review, experimental, correlational, survey, observational, ethnographic and case study research strategies are the most common types of research approaches the sports researcher will encounter throughout the course of studies. In some research projects more than one strategy may be used, but these tend to be larger research studies that begin with an exploratory phase, such as a systematic review or survey strategy, that may be inductive, followed by an explanatory phase, such as experimental research that

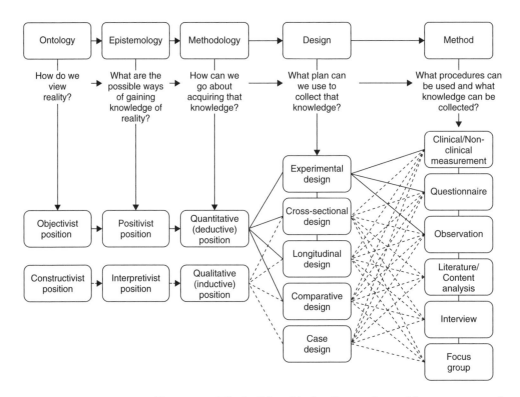

Figure 2.1: The building blocks of research provide a gateway to the design and methods we may choose in order to answer our research question.

would be deductive. The last chapter of the book deals with such 'mixed' approaches and explores ways in which the researcher can approach their research to develop the best approach.

The link between the research question and research strategy

The most important part of research is linking the question that has emerged to an appropriate research strategy. In reality, many research questions fit nicely into one of the seven strategies and the emerging design and methods can be easily deciphered, both by looking back at past research and through logical reasoning. As already mentioned, it is a common mistake to let the tail wag the dog – that is to say that the research strategy shapes the nature of the question. What is fundamental is that the dog wags the tail, so the research question dictates the selected strategy. It is important to recognise that the research question or problem the researcher develops can be answered via a number of different ways. Therefore, reviewing each approach, identifying the linked designs and methods (Figure 2.1), and considering the nature of the data the researcher wants to collect will provide the signpost to the most suitable strategy. The following sections should provide any researcher with a starting point in identifying each strategy and the type of questions that can be answered by each. It is important to remember, however, that some questions can be answered using a number of different strategies that may be applied independently or mixed. The nature of the question therefore will dictate whether one or more approaches are needed.

Systematic literature review research

The purpose of this research strategy is to identify, evaluate and interpret all available research (i.e. primary and secondary evidence) relevant to a particular research question, topic area, or phenomenon of interest. The reasons for undertaking this approach may be to: i) summarise existing evidence concerning a treatment, procedure or technology; ii) identify any gaps in the current research in order to suggest areas for further investigation; or iii) provide a framework in order to give recommendations or guidelines of best practice. Systematic literature reviews are particularly useful when there is uncertainty regarding potential benefits or harm of an intervention, such as the supposed performance-enhancing effect of ginseng or when there are wide variations in practice, such as recommendaed protein intake among strength and endurance athletes. By applying the systematic literature review process to provide emprical answers to focused questions, this strategy may also help in planning new primary research.

   The types of questions that can be answered using this strategy may include:

- What research evidence exists that informs us as to safety guidelines when prescribing exercise programmes to post-operative patients?
- What protocol designs have been applied to evaluate incremental exercise in runners and how does each impact on measurement error?

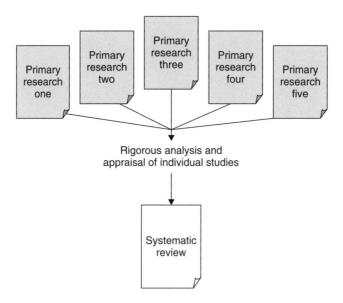

Figure 2.2: The systematic literature review strategy offers an opportunity to answer research questions by using a range of primary research evidence.

- What strategies have been documented that attempt to prevent injury prevalence in adolescent sport?
- What published research is available to generate recommendations for increasing participation in sport?

Research Focus 2.1

In a study by Brunner et al. (*Journal of Aging and Physical Activity*, 2007, 15: 336–48) a systematic literature review was conducted to determine the effects of aging on Type II muscle fibres in human skeletal muscles. In order to develop optimal strategies to prevent functional declines and promote efficient rehabilitation, such research review would aid understanding as to the age-related changes in muscles. The authors performed electronic searches in three widely accessed databases (Medline, PEDro and Science Citation Index) including all cross-sectional and longitudinal studies that were published as orginal journal articles. A range of defined search terms (e.g., aging muscle, Type II fibre, aging skeletal muscle) were used that corresponded with the research question. The focus of the search was on investigations of large limb or trunk muscles in older, healthy human adults who engaged in moderate physical activity. The authors excluded studies examining muscle groups other than large limb or trunk muscles and study populations including patients or subjects performing heavy physical activity. Two reviewers independently evaluated the full text of all retrieved articles using a standard scientific-paper-appraisal form. This form prompted the reviewers to record information regarding the study design, methodological features, analysis, clinical relevance, scientific merit, strengths, and weaknesses of each study. The two reviewers appraised studies for their relevance to the research question and the quality of evidence. All forms were collated and data presented.

Experimental research

The purpose of this research strategy is to compare cases under controlled conditions (e.g., laboratory or fixed environments) in order to establish causality. Causality refers to the relationship between the cause of something and the subsequent effect. Manipulating single phenomena while controlling all others allows the researcher to determine what may cause such effect. By establishing causality, the researcher is able to make generalities in support or refutation of a theory. Therefore, by attempting to establish cause and effect, this deductive approach sets out to test theory. The experimental research strategy fits firmly within the objectivist position and therefore confirms to the objectivity of measurement.

Typically characterised by an 'intervention/treatment' group and a 'control' group, this approach treats situations like a laboratory, attempting to control all confounding factors that may impact on the ability to establish causality. A range of experiment-specific research designs can be chosen and when combined with the large range of data collection methods available within the area of sport, varying approaches can be taken to answer specific research questions that wish to establish cause and effect.

The types of questions that can be answered using this strategy may include:

- What is the impact of a 6-week plyometric training programme of swim start performance in junior swimmers?
- Can an acute 2-week bout of imagery training improve target accuracy in expert pistol shooters?
- Does hypnosis prior to high-dive performance improve concentration and focus in elite competitors?

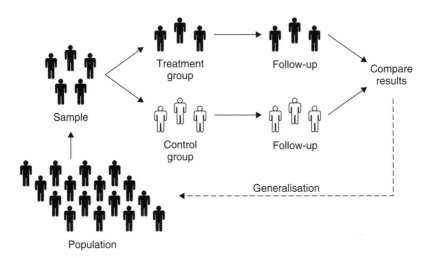

Figure 2.3: The experimential research strategy, as illustrated below with a between-group pre-post test design, establishes causality through the manipulation and control of variables.

Research Focus 2.2

In a study by Rollo et al. (*International Journal of Sport Nutrition and Exercise Metabolism,* 2008, 18: 585–600) an experimental research strategy was selected to examine the effect of a carbohydrate (CHO) mouth rinse on self-selected running speeds during a 30-minute treadmill run. Previous evidence had already supported the positive use of CHO supplemenation to aid endurance performance. The authors wished to further this by examining the notion that even simply tasting a CHO solution might exert a positive influence on the brain and central nervous system, thus eliciting an improvement in performance. Using a randomized, double-blind crossover design, ten endurance-trained runners performed exercise within a controlled laboratory environment. Such fixed setting was to ensure all confounding variables were controlled. Each athlete undertook two 30-minute self-paced runs, prior to and during which they consumed ten bouts of either a 6 per cent CHO or taste-matched placebo mouth wash (i.e. the cause). Each consumption required the runner to rinse the mouth wash for five seconds and then expel the remainder. Throughout the running tasks a range of physiological and performance measurements were continously monitored and recorded (i.e. the effect). The collection of numerical data allowed for a range of statistical assessments to be made on the data.

Correlational research

The purpose of this research strategy is to determine patterns of association between phenomena. In quite simple terms this relates to the mutual relation of two or more things. Numerically orientated, this deductive approach is of value to the researcher who wishes to identify the inter-relationships between measured variables. Sometimes referred to as descriptive research, because it describes existing relationships between variables, the correlational strategy attempts to describe the degree to which one or more quantifable variables relate. Although the degree of agreement between these can be established, a causal link cannot be made. Only a level of association can be determined through the use of statistical techniques. Correlational research can lead to predictions being made based on the strength of the association and has been used to great success in estimating body fat (%).

The types of questions that can be answered using this strategy may include:

- Is there an association between social class and those who attend Badminton Horse trials?
- Is the number of 'aerobic' training miles completed in a year associated with sport-related injuries over the same time period?
- How does the long-term motivation of a sports team associate with the number of wins per session?
- Is there an association between lower limb bilateral strength deficits and the number of falls in elderly women?

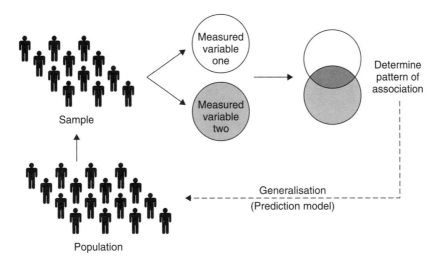

Figure 2.4: The correlational research strategy allows for association to be determined between two or more measured variables.

Research Focus 2.3

In a study by Vila et al. (*Journal of Human Sport and Exercise*, 2009, 4: 57–68) a correlational research strategy was selected to examine the association between anthropometric factors and throwing velocity of elite water polo players. The authors believed that such study would reveal the unique physical and physiological attributes needed to yield successful performance during this important sport-specific task. A total of 22 performers were selected within this cross-sectional design. The authors carried out a range of methods to collect the data. The evaluation of the anthropometric characteristics for each player was made in parameters considered important for the sport. These variables included mass, height, breadth measurements (i.e. wrist, femur, biacromial and humerous), % muscle mass, % body fat, BMI and somatotype. The authors also measured another variable; that being ball velocity. Each player, positioned in a pool 5m away from a target, threw the water polo ball which was recorded on high-speed video camera. With numerical data from each anthropometric variable and the data for ball velocity, the authors conducted statistical analysis to determine the extent to which each anthropometric variable related to ball velocity. The degree of association between the variables provided the authors with an insight into which anthropometric factors related more highly with throwing velocity.

Survey research

The purpose of this research strategy is to describe the characteristics of a population. Whether that be another group, organisation or community, the approach allows the researcher to find out how the population distribute themselves on one or more variables (ie. age, football team preference,

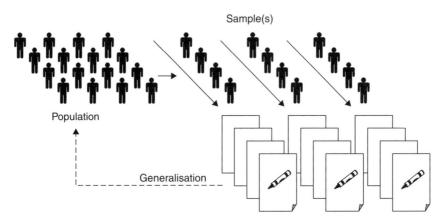

Figure 2.5: *The survey research strategy allows for the collection of data from a large number of cases using methods such as questionnaires.*

attitudes towards school PE, motives, etc). The researcher would generate numerical or non-numerical data from people by way of scores, outcomes, ratings, conditions or opinions through the use of data collection methods such as the questionnaire, interview or observation. The researcher can begin to describe and explain phenomena and attempt to make representations to the wider population. As with other research strategies the population is very rarely studied, instead a sample is surveyed and a description of the population is inferred from what is found out.

The types of questions that can be answered using this strategy may include:

- How effective are community-based well-being initiatives in improving social and emotional health among isolated rural dwellers?
- What is the importance of athlete-centred education to the aspiring elite athlete and how may it support performance development?
- What were the attendee's perceptions of a new 'Active Living' workshop series promoted by a Primary Care Trust?
- What strategies are fitness centre mangers developing and implementing to combat the fall in membership numbers?

Research Focus 2.4

In a study by Brun et al. (*International Journal of Sport Nutrition and Exercise Metabolism,* 2009, 19: 97–109) a survey research strategy was performed to assess information regarding the past and present use of dietary supplements among 164 elite young athletes. A further objective was to identify the supplements used most frequently by the athletes and to assess motives and sources of recommendations, information, and products. In addition, the athletes were asked about their knowledge of the problem of contaminated supplements. Using a cross-sectional design, a total of

228 athletes who participated in an Elite Athlete monitoring programme between September 2006 and December 2007 were provided with a questionnaire regarding their use of dietary supplements. The questionnaires were sent to the athletes by mail with a return rate of 79 per cent. A closed-ended 5-page questionnaire was designed to assess the past and present use of dietary supplements, sport drinks and foods, and other ergogenic aids. In addition, athletes were provided space to list supplements that they could not classify. When necessary, these supplements were classified by experienced nutritionists during data analysis. In a separate question, athletes were specifically asked whether they had ever consumed supplements. Furthermore, information about motives, advice, supplement sources, and knowledge of supplement contamination was assessed using closed-ended questions. To answer these questions, athletes were allowed to choose multiple options.

Observational research

The purpose of this research strategy is to capture, through a range of observational techniques, social behaviour as accurately as possible. The ability of the researcher to effectively use their senses to systematically record observable phenomona or behaviour in a natural real-world setting, allows for the study of people in their native environment in order to understand things from their perspective. Through the systematic inquiry into the nature and qualities of observable individual and group behaviours we can learn what it means to physically and socially function within the world and/or interact with others to form social connections. Away from control and manipulation, the observational research strategy offers a gateway for the researcher to identify how social constructs and inter-relationships within and between people impact on social functioning.

The types of questions that can be answered using this strategy may include:

- What is the nature of the coach–junior athlete relationship in the presence and non-presence of parents?

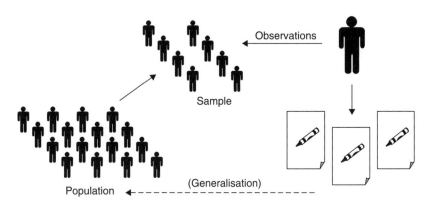

Figure 2.6: The observational research strategy provides a framework to observe behaviour to understand individual and group dynamics within a changing real-world setting.

- What are the movement dynamics of members within a newly built fitness centre and how may this influence placement of promotional material to different user groups?
- What are the actual, rather than reported, warm-up techniques of amateur golfers?
- What behavioural responses do school children exhibit when taught for the first time by a trainee sports coach?

Research Focus 2.5

In a study by Pate et al. (*Journal of School Health*, 2008, 78: 438–44) an observational research strategy was deployed to examine the physical activity levels of children attending preschools. The authors noted the fact that relatively little is known about the physical activity levels of children while they attend preschools or about how activity levels vary across preschools. As preschool-age children often are perceived to be highly physically active the authors wished to empirically examine this perception. For this study, preschools were divided into three categories based on preschool sponsorship and setting. This comparative design involved a total of 539 children across 24 preschools. An observational system for recording physical activity in preschool children was used to measure physical activity in the preschool setting. This recording system involved a '5-second observe interval' followed by a '25-second record interval' for each 30-second observation interval. The observational system assessed physical activity level and activity type (e.g., running, sitting, walking, and riding), social environment (e.g., initiator of activity, group composition), and non-social environment (i.e. child location and activity contexts). Data were collected in 30-minute sessions, and each child was observed for 10–12 sessions. The observation sessions were randomly chosen from the hours that each child attended preschool and were spread across ten days.

Case study research

The purpose of this research strategy is to portray, analyse and interpret the uniqueness of individual units – a person, a class, a family, an event, a situation, an organisation or even a product. Each case should have boundaries – an entity in itself. By capturing the complex contextual nature of the unit within a real-life setting, the researcher is able to present and represent an in-depth, detailed picture of one or more units or cases within their environment using a wide range of data sources. Bound tightly within the constructivist paradigm, the ability to make generalisations sits firmly with the recipient (i.e. the reader of the researcher). Because of the subjective, interpretivistic nature of case study research, generalising any findings should be viewed as approximating future expectations rather than establishing causality or making predictions.

The types of questions that can be answered using this strategy may include:

- What is the impact of a non-charter status football club on coaching provision across a wide age range?
- Does GolfMark improve junior development within a local privately owned club?

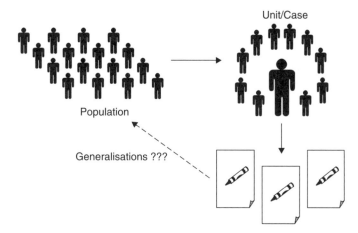

Figure 2.7: The case study research strategy involves collecting data, generally from only one or a small number of cases to provide insight into particular situations and/or experiences.

- What are the physical and mental preparatory strategies of a 'round-the-world' sailor?
- What educational benefit does 'sports day' have within secondary education?

Research Focus 2.6

In a study by Nieuwenhuys et al. (*Psychology of Sport and Exercise*, 2008, 9: 61–76) a case study research strategy was selected to describe the subjective experiences of an elite sailor during competition. It was hoped that such findings would be instrumental in better understanding the implementation of coping strategies during racing. By examining how an elite sailor describes their situational experiences and coping strategies during good and bad races, the authors hoped to develop a conceptual framework as a tool to further explore coping mechanisms in this demanding sport. The case in this study was a 23-year-old male who competed at an international level. Interviewed during two separate sessions, each lasting between 1.5 and 2 hours, the interviewer explored the sailor's performance-related experiences in two races that he had sailed in the past: one considered successful (interview one) and one not so successful (interview two). Each interview was semi-structured in nature and the 'narrative' account of the two races initially provided by the sailor formed the basis of each. Both interviews were recorded and transcriptions were checked for accuracy by the sailor and an independent researcher. Analysis of the data took place in order to identify a range of experiences and coping strategies mentioned by the interviewee.

Ethnographic research

The purpose of this research strategy is to understand and describe a group or culture, accepting that all human behaviour occurs within a context. The word literally means '*writing about people*'

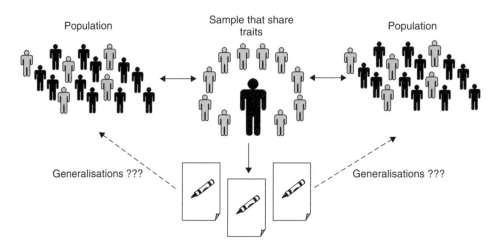

Figure 2.8: The ethnographic research strategy attempts to collect information from an insider's perspective and make sense of the data from an external social science perspective.

and broadly refers to the strategy of studying people for the purpose of describing their socio-cultural activities and patterns. This approach essentially involves descriptive research methods as a basis for interpretation. It represents a dynamic picture about the way of life of some interacting social group and, as a process, is a science of cultural description. Inductive in nature, ethnography differs from other similar approaches (i.e. case study research) in that it attempts to collect information from an insider's perspective and make sense of the data from an external social science perspective.

The ethnography can be written in different styles and formats, typically describing group histories, geography of location, kinship patterns, symbols and rituals, political positionings, educational and social systems, and the degree of contact between the investigated sub-culture and the main culture. Employing methods that range from the literature content analysis of books, newspapers, and electronic materials to individual interviews and observational strategies, the ethnographic approach attempts to gain a true insight from an insider's viewpoint and externalise it to social cultural dimensions.

The types of questions that can be answered using this strategy may include:

- What are the sporting experiences of Eastern European immigrants within inner-city locations?
- How has a change in gender acceptance impacted on women's experience of skateboarding?
- How may a community 'new-age' sports festival alter the perceptions of youth sport among elderly residents?
- Is social status a passport to private golf membership?

Research Focus 2.7

In a study by Atkinson (*Sociology of Sport Journal*, 2007, 24: 165–86) an ethnographic research strategy was selected to explore how a select group of men connected the consumption of sports supplements to the pursuit of 'established' masculinity. Data collection commenced through the researcher's personal involvement as a weight trainer in two local gyms: one, a private club with a closed membership, and the other, a pay-per-entry public gym. The study also built on the researcher's personal knowledge of, and experience with, sports supplements as a long-term (12-year) user and as an endurance athlete. By becoming closely acquainted to a legal supplement taker, the researcher formed connections to 57 men for this case designed study. By highlighting his own insider status as a user in order to encourage participation and deeper conversation, the researcher conducted active interviews to examine the social meaning of supplementation use. Tape recordings were made during every interview, and field notes were taken both during and after. Notes were then transcribed and conceptually analysed. Interviews ranged in length from 45 minutes to 3 hours. Most of the participants were interviewed once, with nine undertaking additional meetings.

What is a research design?

Research design is different from methods by which data are collected. Many research methods texts confuse research designs with methods. It is not uncommon to see research design treated as a model of data collection rather than a logical structure of the inquiry. But there is nothing intrinsic about any research design that requires a particular method of data collection.

(De Vaus, 2001, p 9)

Consider a tournament golfer for a moment. Before they step out onto the course for their round, they would have developed a plan to help them achieve the best score for that day. The player would have a detailed plan of the course layout, where the hazards are situated around each hole, the width of each fairway, the size and shape of each green, undulations and contours, and each flag placement. They would even have an awareness of the general weather conditions for the day. Their plan would also contain detail about how each hole needs to be played, considering where the ball needs to be positioned on the fairway following the tee shot and what parts of the green they want to avoid.

As players function in different ways it would be unlikely that the detail within each of their plans would be exactly the same. They will all show similar characteristics however. Some players, for example, may be naturally more aggressive then others, wishing to take more chances and accept the risks. These players expect unpredictable situations to occur on the course and see this as an inherent aspect of playing golf. Other golfers may be more reserved and calculated. Meticulous in their planning, they like to ensure that their performance is as predictable and replicable as possible, working out exact shots, club selection and distances. Neither of these two approaches is wrong and the plan selected suits the needs of each golfer. By developing a plan before they even go out on the course, the golfers can have confidence that their approach will help optimise their chances of producing their best results.

Developing a design for our research requires the same care and attention as the golfer takes before each round. If the question is to be successfully answered then the design must be well considered before embarking on any data collection. *Research design* refers to the logical and systematic structure or plan by which data collection can take place. Bryman (2008) defines research design as a framework for the collection and analysis of data, supported by the definition of Fraenkal and Wallen (2003) who see the design being a plan for collecting data in order to answer the research question. The design is, therefore, the blueprint for the study, providing the researcher with an overall guide as to how the research methods will fit together and how, when and where the data collection tools and techniques will be implemented.

The design is inextricably linked to the research strategy selected, which is then directly linked back to the ontological and epistemological position held (Figure 2.1). Just as the golfer creates a plan based on their own philosophy to playing the game and their own objectives for the round, the researcher also develops their plan as to their beliefs and the objectives of the research. The plan selected, therefore, sits firmly within underpinning assumptions, governed by the wider ontological viewpoint, but more importantly by the objectives defined – in the case of the golfer, being "how can I achieve the lowest score?" As can be seen in Table 2.1, five research designs allow for a flexible working approach.

How do research methods differ?

Once the golfers have their plans, they can then go out on the course and start playing. Their shot selection will relate back to their original plan and, therefore, dependent on their overall *design* each shot will be different and require technique. The desired outcome for each means that the approach taken will produce slightly different end results and it is likely that these results will be slightly different each time performed. It is how the player is able to implement the skills of using their tools, that is to say their clubs, knowledge, experience and training they have available to them, that will dictate the quality of their play and ultimately the overall score achieved. If the wrong club is selected, technique implemented or decision made (i.e. going off plan), then the desired outcome, that is to say the objectives set at the beginning, will not be accomplished. Selecting a research method in essence is no different. There are many clubs (or methods) in our bag and selecting the right one(s) at the right time, and then being able to use our skill and experience to implement them will dictate the quality and value of the data collected.

It is not uncommon to see many research-related textbooks use research design and research methods interchangeably or confuse the two terms. Research design should be seen as the plan that guides us through the process of data collection, while the research method concerns the approach of how the data will actually be collected. Hitchcock and Hughes (1995) see *research methods* as techniques employed to gather data, consisting of either listening to others, observing what people do and say, or collecting and examining documents which human beings construct. Methods should be viewed as instruments and techniques of research that involve a technical, practical and ethical dimension. As can be seen in Table 2.2 research methods can be categorised into six areas. These

Research design	Description	Research strategy	
		Quantitative	Qualitative
Experimental	A research design that deliberately imposes a treatment on a case in the interest of observing the response. Within this design, a number of experimental conditions can be created (e.g. crossover design, repeated measures design, within-subjects design, between-subject design).	E.g. typically employs numerical data comparisons between an 'intervention/treatment' case with a control case and would require research methods that allow for the collection of objective numerical data.	Not typically employed within this paradigm.
Cross-sectional	A research design that involves collecting data on one or more cases at a single point in time. Collecting quantifiable data in connection with two or more variables allows for patterns of association to be determined.	E.g. can involve collection of numerical data from surveys, observational approaches or literature/ content analysis on a case at a single point in time.	E.g. non-numerical data collected by interviews, focus groups, observation, etc., that relate to a single point in time.
Longitudinal	A research design where cases are assessed at several different time periods. Usually this design is used when interested in how people change over time.	E.g. survey research on a case on more than one occasion or literature/ content analysis relating to different time periods.	E.g. mapping change over time through ethnographic research across periods, interviews on more than one occasion or through literature/content analysis.

Table 2.1: Five research designs that create the plan within the research strategy (extracts from Bryman, 2008).
Continued overleaf

Research design	Description	Research strategy	
		Quantitative	Qualitative
Comparative	A research design that involves studying more or less identical methods on two or more contrasting cases. Making comparisons implies the research can better understand social phenomena between cases/situations.	E.g. survey research where a direct numerical comparison is made between two or more cases, such as cross-cultural research.	E.g. making direct comparisons through ethnographic or qualitative interviews/observations on two or more cases/ situations.
Case	A research design where a case is studied intensively. A case may be individuals, programmes, or any unit, depending on what is to be examined.	E.g. numerically oriented survey research on a single case with a view to revealing important features about its nature.	E.g. applying ethnographic, qualitative interviews, etc. to intensively study a case, being an individual, team or organisation.

Table 2.1: Continued

Research method	Description	Sport-related example
Clinical and non-clinical measurement	Any instrument, technique and/or procedure used within the natural sciences to make accurate objective numerical measurements of phenomena.	Collecting data by performing an incremental exercise protocol on a cycle ergometer to assess sub-maximal and maximal physiological responses.
Questionnaire	Any instrument consisting of a series of questions and other prompts, used for the purpose of gathering numeral and/or non-numerical data from respondents.	Collecting data by administering a series of linked questions to assess mood state during exercise (POMS).
Observation	Any technique, associated procedure and data recording instruments that allow for the systematic recording of observable behaviour of individuals or groups.	Watching and listening to how a coach interacts with a group of beginner swimmers during their first formal poolside lesson.
Literature/content analysis	Any technique and associated procedure that seeks to organise written, audio, and/or visual information into categories and themes related to the central questions of the study. This approach is especially useful in product analysis and document analysis.	Collating and analysing all newspaper, magazine, television and radio interviews conducted with members of the England cricket team over a one-year period.
Interview	Any technique and associated procedure that involves a conversation between two or more people (the interviewer and the interviewee) where questions are asked by the interviewer to obtain information from the interviewee.	Meeting with recreationally-inactive elderly ladies in order to assess their attitude to exercise.
Focus group	Any technique and associated procedure where a group of people are asked about their attitude towards something. Questions are asked in an interactive group setting where participants are free to talk with other group members.	Meeting and asking a group of exercise professionals about their views on the success of the GP Exercise Referral scheme.

Table 2.2: A broad range of methods are available to the sport researcher and are selected on the basis of what needs to be known from the world and people around us.

nical/non-clinical measurement, questionnaires, observations, literature/content analysis,
..... and focus groups.

Not being able to distinguish between design and method can lead to a poor research strategy and the inability to answer the research problem appropriately. Practically any design can be linked to any collection method, but this is dependent on the research question, so the art and science of research is to be aware as to the relative strengths and weaknesses of each selected method and link it to the most appropriate design. By bringing together an understanding of design and method, the selection of the overall research strategy will emerge.

Research strategy selection

So far in this chapter, research strategies, research designs and research methods have been explored. To consider your research approach as successful, the bringing together of all three of these aspects, underpinned by the associated assumptions linked to each position, must occur. By drawing on a research question already outlined earlier on in the chapter we will see how we can apply Figure 2.9 to help point us in the right direction.

Let us start with a research question already mentioned: "*What is the nature of the coach–junior athlete relationship in the presence and non-presence of parents?*" We can use this as an illustration to show how a suitable research strategy, with associated design and methods, can be selected. One of the first questions asked should really focus on what it is that needs to be known in order to answer the question. That is to say, what knowledge do we need to acquire? In this case, we want to know about *behaviours* exhibited through the relationship dynamics between the coach and junior athlete which may be verbal and/or non-verbal. We would want to identify whether these alter during the two situations: one being when parents are present and the other when they are absent from the coaching situation. Does the parents' presence influence the way the coach, athlete or both act and react to each other? It would seem appropriate (and probably necessary) to conduct this in as natural and real-world setting as possible so not to artifically influence in any way the interactions we are interested in observing.

By reviewing the seven research strategies and by referring to Figure 2.9, it would seem logical in the first instance to consider the experimental approach. This strategy would allow us to manipulate something (i.e. whether parents are present or not) and assess the effect (i.e. the way the coach and junior athlete behaves in each other's company). But as it would be important to set our research within a natural setting and doing this would make it incredibly difficult to control all other factors, establishing causality would be very problematic. By positioning the question within the positivist paradigm may also limit the '*type of knowledge*' we are able to gain when we get round to conducting the research project. We would be bound to collect quantitative data (i.e. numerically based) that, although would allow for some statistical analysis, may not enable us to find out about things that cannot be expressed through numbers, such as descriptions of body langauge, the meaning of hand and facial gestures and expressions or particular emphasis on words and phrases.

By looking at Figure 2.9, we can begin to recognise that some strategies may be better suited than others. By opting for a different approach we can begin to gain knowledge from the participants that would allow us to paint a more detailed picture than others would permit. It may be deemed by some acceptable to approach this research question from an experimental perspective, particularly those who position themselves firmly in the objectivist camp. By applying another approach, however, such as the observational research strategy, we would re-position the research within the constructivist/interpretivist perpective, gaining qualitative rather than quantative data. By opting for the observational research strategy, the researcher would be able to record, unobtrusively, behaviours exhibited by all (i.e. parents, coaches and athletes) in order to determine the social relationships, connections and influences that may exist among all observed. The selection of this approach would lead to a number of different research designs and methods that could be applied in order to build the research plan. This would lead to the selection of instruments, techniques and procedures to collect the data and then undertake data analysis.

So the question must drive the selection of the strategy and the strategy will provide a focus for the design and methods. Overcoming this hurdle in a research project opens up a gateway to effective data collection and project conclusions. The true value of the project can then be realised, enhancing not only the worth of the research to others, but also the researcher's own understanding as to the overall research process.

Learning Activity 2.1

Read the range of research questions below. Using the knowledge gained from Chapter 1 and 2, and by referring to Figure 2.9, allocate a research strategy (design and method(s)) to each. Remember more than one approach may be taken so write down all you feel could be used. Try and consider the strengths and weaknesses of each strategy and rank order them in preference if there are more than two.

- What are the emerging political developments relating to the sport-tourism link in Cumbria?
- What are the ground reaction forces on take-off for a group of high jumpers?
- Why is the introduction of self-administered training plans found on the internet seen as a threat by professional fitness trainers?
- What type of cycling pedal cadence is the most efficient?
- How do the perceptions of emotional climate among injured athletes impact on their personal and social interactions within a sporting team?
- Will the introduction of a new coach lead to higher performance levels throughout the team?
- What are the feelings of older adults (> 65yr) to the introduction of local physical activity road shows?

Research strategy	Ontological position	Epistemological position	Methodological position	Research design	Research method
Systematic literature review	Objectivist/ constructivist	Positivist/ interpretivist	Quantitative and/or qualitative	Cross-sectional or longitudinal	Literature/content analysis
Experimental	Objectivist	Positivist	Quantitative	Experimental (True, quasi-, or natural)	Can include one or more of the following: - Observation - Questionnaire - Clinical/non-clinical measurement
Correlational	Objectivist	Positivist	Quantitative	Cross-sectional	Can include one or more of the following: - Observation - Questionnaire - Clinical/non-clinical measurement
Survey	Objectivist/ constructivist	Positivist/ interpretivist	Quantitative and/or qualitative	Case, cross-sectional, comparative or longitudinal	Can include one or more of the following: - Observational surveys - Questionnaires - Focus groups - Interviews - Clinical/non-clinical measurement
Observational	Constructivist	Interpretivist	Qualitative (but may include aspects of the quantitative approach)	Case, cross-sectional, comparative or longitudinal	Observations
Case study	Constructivist	Interpretivist	Qualitative (but may include aspects of the quantitative approach)	Cross-sectional, comparative or longitudinal	Can include one or more of the following: - Observations - Questionnaires - Focus groups - Interviews - Content analysis
Ethnographic	Constructivist	Interpretivist	Qualitative (but may include aspects of the quantitative approach)	Case, cross-sectional, comparative or longitudinal	Can include one or more of the following: - Observation - Questionnaires - Focus groups - Interviews - Content analysis

Figure 2.9: The selection of a research strategy begins with the question or problem. Each strategy can be linked to a corresponding design and method.

Chapter Review

In this chapter we have considered the importance of research strategy and how each can be linked to different research questions. The choice of strategy and its associated research design(s) and method(s) provide the researcher with a foundation to their investigations. Being able to critically appraise the selected strategy, justifying why it is more suitable than others, and knowing its limitations will provide the researcher with an insight into the very nature of the knowledge, the process of collection and its overall generalisability and value. By using a range of sport-related research examples throughout this chapter you should now be able to:

❏ make the important distinction between a research strategy, a research design and a research method;
❏ explain the differences between the seven main research strategies and be able to list a range of sport-related questions that can be answered using each;
❏ list and describe the range of research designs and be able to link each design to an appropriate strategy;
❏ identify the different research methods that can be used to obtain data.

(Tick when completed)

Further Reading

Vaus de, D (2001) *Research Design in Social Research.* London: Sage Publications. Part One: pages 1–52.
This text offers a further commentary of the differences between design and method, offering the reader a range of illustrations to clarify the point. Easy to access, this additional text supports the chapter.

Burns, R B (2000) *Introduction to Research Methods.* London: Sage Publications. Part One: pages 1–25.
This opening chapter of a popular social science research methods text revisits the debate linked to contrasting perspectives in research. Although more aligned with Chapter 1 of this book, it is worth reviewing your knowledge on research strategy by reading this well-written selection.

Hitchcock, G and Hughes, D (1995) *Research and the Teacher.* 2nd edition. London: Routledge. Part One: pages 3–38 and 77–111.
With an educational bias, *Research and the Teacher* offers the reader a plain talking overview as to designing, planning and evaluating research. Covering the main aspects relating to research design selection, this text should be read by all those wishing to engage in sport research within an educational setting.

Chapter 3
Systematic review research strategy

By linking your understanding of sport in practice to sport-related research examples, this chapter is designed to help you:

- identify the value of a systematic literature review strategy and place into context using a range of sport-related research examples;
- understand how systematic reviews are planned, conducted, and reported;
- recognise the research methods that systematic reviews require.

Introduction

Systematic literature reviews in the field of sport, exercise and health have increasingly replaced traditional narrative reviews and literature commentaries as a way of summarising the growing body of research evidence. The use of such a research strategy among students is typically uncommon primarily due to a lack of familiarity with this research approach, the perceived complexity and the lack of procedural understanding. Undertaking a systematic review, however, can be immensely valuable and allow the researcher to develop a multitude of research and employability skills.

Systematic reviews attempt to bring the same level of rigour to reviewing research evidence as that which was applied in producing such evidence in the first place. The systematic review procedure differs from a traditional literature review as it explicitly focuses on an objective, replicable, systematic and comprehensive search of literature and research evidence, and includes a transparent audit trail of methods and processes. Systematic reviews should be based on a pre-determined protocol so that they can be replicated if necessary.

Key Point 3.1

In the field of sport, exercise and health, the systematic review procedure has been widely used in assessing primary-research evidence. Areas that may be covered include:

- physical activity guidelines;
- health policy;
- exercise take-up and adherence in sport;
- leisure participation and policy;
- injury prevention strategies and models of best practice;
- physical performance assessment methods;
- effectiveness of exercise therapy;
- physical activity programmes for special populations;
- psychological perspectives of sport, health and exercise.

Examples of systematic reviews in the field of sport, health and physical activity are:

- Machotka, Z, Kumar, S, Perraton, LG (2009) A systematic review of the literature on the effectiveness of exercise therapy for groin pain in athletes. *Sports Medicine, Arthroscopy, Rehabilitation, Therapy and Technology*, 1: 5.
- Thacker, SB, Gilchrist, J, Stroup, DF, et al. (2004) The impact of stretching on sports injury risk: A systematic review of the literature. *Medicine and Science in Sports and Exercise*, 36: 371–78.
- Foster, C, Hillsdon, M and Cavill N (2005) *Understanding Participation in Sport: A Systematic Review*. London. Sport England.
- McDermott, BP, Casa, DJ, Ganio, MS, et al. (2009) Acute whole-body cooling for exercise-induced hyperthermia: A systematic review. *Journal of Athletic Training*, 44: 84–93.
- Goodger, K, Gorely, T, Lavallee, D, et al. (2007) Burnout in sport: A systematic review. *The Sport Psychologist*, 21: 127–51.
- Carek, PJ, Mainous III, A (2002) The pre-participation physical examination for athletics: A systematic review of current recommendations. *British Medical Journal*, 2: 661–64.

Systematic literature reviews – what are they?

Systematic reviews are literature-based research studies that can be used to answer a number of questions we may have generated throughout the course of our own studies. In a systematic literature review, primary evidence from scientific studies is first located, then evaluated and finally synthesised using a strict scientific strategy, which must itself be reported in the review. Similar in approach to other research strategies detailed within preceding chapters of this book, the systematic literature review research strategy follows a logical set of principles and procedures. Synthesising information that establishes facts in an unbiased manner ensures that new conclusions can be generalised. The ultimate aim is to provide new information that has value within the field of sport, health or exercise and may be used with confidence for decision-making, guideline creation, recommendation and best practice models, policy development and evaluation.

Research Focus 3.1

In a systematic review conducted by Priest et al. (*Cochrane Database of Systematic Reviews*, 2007, 2: www.cochrane.org) the authors' objectives were to update a review of all controlled studies evaluating interventions implemented through sporting organisations to increase participation. Updating the original 2004 review, they searched a number of related databases (e.g., Sports Discus, MEDLINE, PsycINFO) and a number of freely available online health promotion and sports-related databases between the years 2004–2007.

All controlled studies evaluating any intervention designed to increase active and/or non-active participation in sport by people of all ages were included within the search criteria. Such interventions they included were: mass media campaigns; information or education sessions; management or organisational change strategies; policy changes; changes to traditional or existing programmes; skill improvement programmes and volunteer encouragement programmes.

The authors revealed that despite the thorough review of the published and unpublished literature, no rigorous studies were found that evaluated the effects of interventions organised through sporting organisations to increase participation in sport. Conclusions stated that interventions funded and conducted in this area must be linked to a rigorous evaluation strategy in order to examine overall effectiveness, socio-demographic differentials in participation and cost-effectiveness of these strategies.

Key Point 3.2

Academic literature review   A standardised review that summarises a number of different primary and secondary research studies, theories or ideas and draws conclusions to support, guide and justify the development of a research question or problem.

Systematic literature review   A review of evidence on a clearly formulated question that uses systematic and explicit research methods to identify, select and critically appraise relevant primary studies and to extract and analyse data from the studies that are included in the review.

Meta-analysis   A review of evidence that applies statistical techniques to combine the results of studies addressing the same question in a summary measure.

Why are systematic reviews important?

There are two main practical reasons for the importance of systematic reviews: first, the limitations of the traditional academic literature review that researchers undertake as part of the research project and, second, the added power brought by synthesising the results of a number of smaller studies into one. Traditionally, a literature review is a subjective assessment using a select group of materials to support an (often-predetermined) conclusion. In contrast, the systematic review attempts to be *systematic* in the identification and evaluation of materials, *objective* in its interpretation and *reproducible* in its conclusions. The term systematic in its most basic of definitions describes a system or approach concerned with classifications. Applying this to research, the term provides a basis by which research studies can be reviewed and classified by way of a 'set criteria' linked to the research question(s).

Key Point 3.3

The most important activity during the planning of a systematic review is formulating the research question(s). Here are six types that may be addressed.

- Assessing the effect of an intervention on an outcome.
- Assessing the frequency or rate of a condition.
- Determining the performance of a diagnostic instrument, piece of technique or an assessment protocol.
- Identifying whether a condition or event can be predicted.
- Assessing economic/social value of an intervention, procedure or initiative.
- Identifying cost and/or risk factors.

Smaller primary studies we encounter in peer-reviewed journals (see Reflection 3.1) may appear to have a rigorous research approach and practically significant or insignificant findings. When pooled together, however, with other primary studies of a similar nature, the results from a number of smaller studies may lead to more conclusive generalisations to be made both in confirming a beneficial outcome (e.g. Sodium bicarbonate on short-term high-intensity exercise or the level of physical activity necessary to bring about health benefits) and in eliminating ones of negligible benefit (e.g. the impact of ginseng on endurance performance or the role of stretching on injury prevention). Politically, systematic reviews are also important for larger organisations such as the National Health Service or Sport England (See Key Point 3.1 for reference). For example, the NHS Research and Development Strategy concentrates on the successful utilisation of research findings from systematic reviews rather than the generation of original research which may often be unable to provide definitive answers.

Internationally, the stimulus for systematic reviews has come from the Cochrane Collaboration (www.cochrane.org) a worldwide group of subject and methodological specialists who aim to identify and synthesise primary research studies – normally randomised controlled trials in all aspects of health – but also include aspects of sport, leisure, physical activity and exercise.

Why perform a systematic review?

The key reasons for performing a systematic review include the ability to:

- summarise existing evidence concerning a treatment or technology;
- identify any gaps in current research in order to suggest areas for further investigation;
- provide a framework/background in order to appropriately position new research activities;
- inform policy and decision-making about an organisation and the delivery of a service (e.g., the health care service).

The advantages of the systematic literature review approach over the more academic literature review is that this well-defined research strategy makes it less likely that the results of the literature analysis are biased. This approach can also provide information about the effects of some phenomenon across a wide range of settings and methods. It must be recognised, however, that the systematic review can require considerably more effort than a literature review simply due to the much larger number of primary research studies that need to be evaluated in depth.

Research Focus 3.2

In a systematic review conducted by Thompson et al. (*Cochrane Database of Systematic Reviews*, 2006, 4: www.cochrane.org) the authors' objectives were to determine whether bicycle helmets reduce head, brain and facial injury for bicyclists of all ages involved in a bicycle crash or fall. The methods involved searching a number of comprehensive databases (e.g., MEDLINE, EMBASE, CINAHL, PsycINFO) using a range of selected terms and words. Furthermore, the authors made contact with the International Society for Child and Adolescent Injury Prevention, World Injury Network, CDC-funded Injury Control and Research Centres, and staff in injury research agencies around the world. Controlled studies that evaluated the effect of helmet use in a population of bicyclists who had experienced a crash were included.

Specific inclusion criteria required primary studies to contain details of exact outcomes, accurate exposure measurement, appropriate selection of the comparison group and elimination or control of factors such as selection bias or observation bias.

From extraction and synthesis of data the authors found five well-conducted case-control studies that met the inclusion criteria. Analysis revealed that helmets provide a 63 to 88 per cent reduction in the risk of head, brain and severe brain injury for all ages of bicyclists. Helmets provide equal levels of protection for crashes involving motor vehicles (69 per cent) and crashes from all other causes (68 per cent). Injuries to the upper and mid facial areas are reduced by 65 per cent when wearing a helmet.

Key Point 3.4

According to Mulrow (Rationale for systematic reviews. *British Medical Journal*, 1994, 309: 597–99), systematic reviews meet several associated objectives.

- Reduce quantity of data to a single review.
- Plan research, purchasing and guidelines.
- Make efficient use of existing data.
- Ensure generalisability.
- Check consistency.
- Explain inconsistency.
- Quantify with meta-analysis.
- Improve precision.
- Reduce bias.

Features of systematic literature reviews

Systematic reviews seek to identify all relevant published and unpublished evidence and select studies or reports for inclusion based on an assessment of quality. By synthesising the findings from individual studies in an unbiased way, interpretation of the findings can provide a balanced and impartial summary. Features that distinguish a systematic literature review from a formal literature review include:

- a review 'protocol' that specifies the research question and the methods that will be used to perform the review;
- a defined search strategy that aims to detect as much of the relevant literature as possible;
- documentation of the search strategy (i.e. within a methods section) so that the reader can assess the rigour, completeness and repeatability of the research process;
- an explicit inclusion and exclusion criteria to assess each potential primary study;
- specific information that was obtained from each primary study.

The systematic review process

Guidelines which structure the review process can be placed into clear stages and offer the researcher a framework by which a timeline of activities and milestones can be developed. As with all research strategies, each stage is systematically and logically positioned to follow on from the last and prepare the researcher for the next. The following eight stages act as a starting point, which can be used as a progression monitoring tool.

- Identification of the need for the review.
- Background research and problem specification.
- Requirements of the review protocol.
- Literature searching and study retrieval.
- Assessment of studies for inclusion on basis of relevance and design.
- Assessing the quality of the studies.
- Data extraction and synthesis.
- Report structure and review.

Briefly, as illustrated in Figure 3.1, developing a systematic review requires the logical completion of a number of steps.

1. *Defining a research question.* This requires a clear statement of the objectives of the review, intervention or phenomena of interest, relevant groups and subpopulations (and sometimes the settings where the intervention is administered), the types of evidence or studies that will help answer the question, as well as appropriate outcomes. These details are rigorously used to select studies for inclusion in the review.

2. *Searching the literature.* Published and unpublished literature is carefully searched for the required studies relating to an intervention or activity (on the right groups, reporting the right outcomes, and so on). For an unbiased assessment, this search must seek to cover all the literature, and not be limited to databases, websites or journals merely out of convenience. In reality, a designated number of databases should be searched using a standardised or customised search filter. Furthermore, the grey literature (material that is not formally published, such as institutional or technical reports, working papers, conference proceedings, or other documents not normally subject to editorial control or peer review) is searched using specific databases or websites. Always asking the opinion of your supervisor on where appropriate data may be located is a gateway into a wide range of literature.

3. *Assessing the studies.* Once all possible studies have been identified, they should be assessed in the following ways. Each study needs to be assessed for eligibility against inclusion criteria. At this stage it is typical that all full text papers are retrieved for those that meet the inclusion criteria. Following a full-text selection stage, the remaining studies are assessed for methodological quality using a critical appraisal framework. Poor quality studies are excluded but are usually discussed. Of the remaining studies, reported findings are extracted on to a data extraction form and a list of included studies is then created.

4. *Combining the results.* The findings from the individual studies are combined to produce an overall summary of findings. This combination of findings is called evidence synthesis and the data is usually presented in tabular format.

5. *Placing the findings in context.* The findings from the collation studies need to be discussed to put them into practical context. This will address issues such as the quality and spread of the included studies, the likely impact of bias, as well as the applicability of the findings.

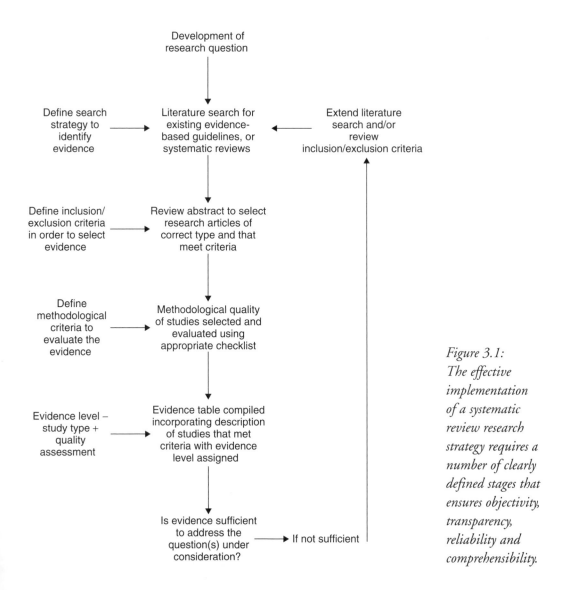

Figure 3.1:
The effective
implementation
of a systematic
review research
strategy requires a
number of clearly
defined stages that
ensures objectivity,
transparency,
reliability and
comprehensibility.

Development of a review protocol

The review protocol is a written document that contains background information, the problem specification and the research strategy of the systematic review. The first stage of any review research is to develop (with tutor approval) the protocol structure. In essence, this is the design and methods of the systematic review. Remember that the value of a systematic literature review from other academic literature reviews is the fact that this approach should be unbiased, so documenting the research strategy ensures transparency and reproducibility. By undertaking this first step, any review should be free of researcher bias therefore providing a more consistent and generalisable piece of research. For example, without a structured review protocol it is possible that the selection of individual studies or the analysis may be driven by research expectations and not a structured unbiased and systematic research method.

Components of a protocol include:

- background – the rationale for the study need;
- review questions – what exactly is to be answered as a consequence of the research;
- search strategy, including search terms and resources to be searched;
- study selection criteria and procedures – which studies will be included, or excluded, from the systematic literature review. It is often wise to pilot the selection criteria on a subset of primary studies before commencing with the main project;
- study quality assessment checklists and procedures – the development of quality checklists will aid in the assessment of individual studies;
- data extraction strategy – this defines how the information required from each primary study will be obtained;
- synthesis of the extracted evidence – the purpose is to clarify whether or not formal statistical techniques could be applied to the data;
- project timetable – this should define and document the entire review schedule.

Generation of a search strategy

It is both necessary and important to the whole systematic review process to determine and follow a search strategy. The development of such strategy is usually an iterative process: one attempt will rarely produce the final strategy. Strategies are built up from a series of preliminary searches, evaluation and discussion with the researcher's supervisor. The benefit of preliminary searches is that the researcher is able to identify previous systematic reviews and assess the volume of potentially relevant studies. Furthermore, undertaking 'trial' searches using various combinations of search terms derived from the research question will allow the researcher to scope out the size of the study base and provide justification for the need for the study.

A list of key terms and words can be created by breaking down the research question. Take for example the studies outlined in Table 3.1, which describes the objectives of the systematic review, the databases used and the search terms and words applied. The researcher may also wish to consider synonyms, abbreviations or alternative spellings (i.e. American spelling) that can be used in the search as well. Some studies limit searches to one language, while others place no restrictions thereby increasing the search field. Once some research studies have been accumulated, the search for references the authors have cited can act as a further method of finding related articles. Once a few connected articles have been located, these will soon link together. This approach will assist the researcher in obtaining a wide and varied range of research for their systematic review.

Author	Study objective	Databases used	Search terms and words used
Brunner et al. (2007)	To determine the effects of aging on Type II muscle fibres in human skeletal muscles.	MEDLINE, PubMed, PEDro Science Citation Index (inception to 2003)	Aging muscle; Aging skeletal muscle; Aging striated muscle; Age changes muscle; Muscles old men; Muscles old women; Fibre aging; Muscle fibre aging; Type II fibres; Type 2 fibres; Type II fibres aging; Type 2 fibres aging.
Machotka et al. (2009)	To evaluate the effectiveness of exercise therapy for groin pain in athletes.	MEDLINE, CINAHL, PubMed, SportDiscus, EMBASE, AMED, Ovid, PEDro, Cochrane Controlled Trials Register; Google Scholar (1990–2009)	Stretching; Flexibility; Injury; Sports injury. Terms used to limit search were: Epidemiology; Injury prevention.
Carek et al. (2002)	To examine the effectiveness of the pre-participation physical examination (PPE) in satisfying the basic requirements for medical screening in athletes.	MEDLINE (1966–2002)	Pre-participation physical examination; Physical examination.
McDermott et al. (2009)	To assess the efficiency of whole-body cooling modalities in the treatment of exertional hyperthermia.	MEDLINE, EMBASE, Scopus, SportDiscus, CINAHL, Cochrane Reviews databases, ProQuest (All dates available)	Cooling; Cryotherapy; Water immersion; Cold-water immersion; Ice-water immersion; Icing; Fanning; Bath; Baths; Cooling modality; Heat illness; Heat illnesses; Exertional heatstroke; Exertional heat stroke; Heat exhaustion; Hyperthermia; Hyperthermic; Hyperpyrexia; Exercise; Exertion; Running; Football; Military; Runners; Marathoner; Physical activity; Marathoning; Soccer; Tennis.

Table 3.1: An example of how the search terms and words should be linked to the research objectives.

Reflection Point 3.1

Relevant research databases where sport science-related articles may be found:

- *Bandolier* (www.medicine.ox.ac.uk/bandolier)
- CINAHL (www.ebscohost.com)
- Google Scholar (www.scholar.google.com)
- MEDLINE (www.ebscohost.com)
- PsycINFO (www.apa.org/psycinfo)
- PubMed (www.ncbi.nlm.nih.gov/pubmed)
- SMARTT (www.smarttjournal.com)
- SportDiscus (www.ebscohost.com)
- The Campbell Collaboration (www.campbellcollaboration.org)
- The Centre for Evidence-Based Medicine (www.cebm.net)
- The Cochrane Library (www.cochrane.org)
- The Joanna Briggs Institute (www.joannabriggs.edu.au/pubs/systematic_reviews.php)
- The NHS Centre for Reviews and Dissemination (www.york.ac.uk/inst/crd)

It is also worth going on to journal websites as they often have access to search facilities through previously published abstracts. Simply type the journal name into a web-based search engine to find a range of freely accessible primary studies. Journals that may be of interest include:

- *Journal of Science and Medicine in Sport;*
- *Journal of Sport Management;*
- *Journal of Electromyography and Kinesiology;*
- *Human Movement Studies;*
- *Journal of Aging and Physical Activity;*
- *Psychology of Sport and Exercise;*
- *Medicine and Science in Sport and Exercise;*
- *Journal of Sports Sciences;*
- *International Journal of Sports Medicine;*
- *Sports Medicine;*
- *Journal of Applied Biomechanics;*
- *International Journal of Sport Physiology and Performance;*
- *Journal of Applied Sport Psychology;*
- *Journal of Strength and Conditioning Research;*
- *Sociology of Sport Journal;*
- *International Journal of Coaching and Sport Science.*

Primary study selection process

The study selection procedure is intended to identify those primary studies that provide direct evidence about the research question and will help the researcher to answer it successfully. In order to reduce the likelihood of bias, the criteria used should be decided upon during the protocol construction, although this may need to be refined after initial trial searches. As the inclusion criteria ultimately determine which studies will be included in the review, it is inevitable that the researcher will have some dilemma as to how broad or narrow to define the criteria. To offer some advice: it is far better to start broad and be liberal, capturing a large range of studies. Following an initial broad review, refinement can then be made to narrow the searches to a more specified focus.

The actual selection of studies should be viewed as a multi-staged process and can be followed by referring to Figure 3.2.

As can be seen from Figure 3.2, the process of study selection should be viewed as multiple parts, interconnected in a logical manner. Thorough consideration of these parts and how they fit together will influence the overall quality of the review. Initially, selection criteria should be interpreted liberally, so that unless a study identified by the electronic and hand searches can be clearly excluded based on title and abstract, a full copy should be obtained. The next step is to apply inclusion/exclusion criteria based on issues such as:

- journals;
- authors;
- settings;
- participants/volunteers;
- research design;
- sampling method;
- date of publication.

As shown in Research Focus 3.3, McDermott and co-workers used a number of inclusion criteria in order to narrow down their initial database searches. By applying their search strategy to locate the primary articles and then implementing an 'inclusion' and 'exclusion' criteria they were able to obtain 7 out of 89 primary studies that fulfilled their study requirements.

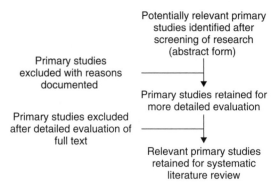

Figure 3.2: Flow diagram of study selection process.

In a systematic review conducted by McDermott et al. (*Journal of Athletic Training*, 2009, 44: 84–93) the authors' objectives were to assess existing original research addressing the efficiency of whole-body cooling methods in the treatment of exertional hyperthermia. The following databases without limits on language were searched: MEDLINE, SportDiscus, CINAHL, the Cochrane Reviews database, and the Physiotherapy Evidence Database. All dates (which varied according to database) were included. Selected key words used for searches were: *cooling; cryotherapy; water immersion; cold-water immersion; ice-water immersion; icing, fanning; bath; cooling modality; heat illness; heat illnesses; exertional heatstroke; exertional heat stroke; heat exhaustion; hyperthermia; and hyperthermic.* This original search revealed a total of 89 possible studies.

Specific inclusion criteria identified before data analysis included: (1) exercise-associated hyperthermia; (2) pre-treatment hyperthermia greater than 38.56C (101.36F); (3) a valid core body temperature measurement to characterize hyperthermia; (4) detailed explanation, sufficient for repeatability of the cooling modality methods; and (5) original research studies with human participants. To ensure quality of assessment two independent reviewers assessed the methodological quality of each selected study. Any discrepancies that existed between the two reviewers were either resolved through discussion or a third reviewer.

From the 89 original studies, 7 met all inclusion criteria. The authors concluded that from the available evidence it would appear that ice-water immersion provides the most efficient cooling. They added that further research comparing whole-body cooling methods is needed to identify other acceptable means. When ice-water immersion is not possible, continual dousing with water combined with fanning the athlete is an alternative method until more advanced cooling means can be used.

Quality assessment checklists

The assessment of 'quality' during the study selection process ensures that the primary research evaluated fulfils a critical level of acceptance into the systematic review. This is important to ensure that studies are of an acceptable scientific standard before proceeding with detailed data extraction. A quality checklist is quite simply a data collection instrument that is derived from a consideration of factors linked directly to the nature of the research question. Checklists provide an objective assessment of the primary research evidence, thereby reducing the amount of researcher bias during the data collection stages. As shown in Key Point 3.4, a checklist is simply a range of questions that allow the researcher the chance to quickly evaluate its general suitability. With a quick search of the internet, the researcher should be able to locate several more that can be adapted to suit the particular requirements of the research project. Each checklist will have some measure of suitability or quality, either expressed simply as 'Yes' or 'No', or providing more depth as expressed on a scale for each item listed. Whatever the nature and structure of the checklist, pilot study evaluations should be conducted to ensure that it evaluates what the researcher intends to evaluate.

Learning Activity 3.1

There are a number of reasons why a 'quality checklist' is important when undertaking a systematic review. Try and consider what these are and why assessment of quality is important. How may it benefit the systematic review process and the applicability of the findings?

It is important that researchers not only define the quality checklist in the study protocol but also explain how the data generated from the checklist will be used. Such data can be used in two different ways, so clarity at this stage is necessary. One way data can be used is to construct detailed inclusion/exclusion criteria. Data collected prior to the main project, such as during a pilot study, can be obtained from a separate checklist to assist the researcher in deciding which primary studies will be included within the main project. The second way is to assist analysis and synthesis. In this case the data are used to identify subsets of the primary study to assess whether differences in the quality of the primary research is associated with the outcomes reported.

It is often the case that primary research studies are very limited in the amount of detail presented. As many journals place word limits on research submissions, the level of detail needed for effective quality assessment may not be reported. This means that it is not always possible to determine 'quality' of a primary research study. It is very tempting to assume aspects of the reported study, such as sample type, design issues and method procedures even though they have not been reported. It is also tempting to assume that because something wasn't reported, it wasn't done. This assumption may be incorrect, so it is the prerogative of the researcher to obtain as much information as possible. Most peer-reviewed articles published in sport-related journals include author contact details. It may be the case that an additional correspondence is required to clarify and obtain further detail. The role of the researcher is to construct and apply a quality checklist that addresses methodological quality and not reporting quality.

Key Point 3.5

This assessment should be completed for each included study and then the assessments should be aggregated in a results section and also discussion/conclusions for each section. Overall review summaries and any discussion of the limitations of the review should also include some summary of the aggregated information as well as transparent discussion of the limitations of this tool. Where studies give no or little information, tick 'unclear'. It is not usually good practice to make assumptions. If this is the case for significant numbers of studies then this will be a major limitation of the review.

Study No. / Title / Authors

No.: _____

Title: _____

Author(s): _____

Source: _____

Relevance assessment

Is the study laboratory based? Y/N/Where? _____

Is the field of the study relevant to the research topic? Y/N/Unclear _____

_____

Name field, i.e. primary/secondary/other (specify) _____

_____

Are the aims of the study relevant to one of questions within the research topic? Y/N/Unclear

_____

Quality appraisal

Is the study reporting a process of structured enquiry? Y/N/Unclear _____

_____

If yes, is it transparent and replicable? Yes/No/Unclear _____

_____

Is the study design appropriate to answering the question? Y/N/Unclear _____

_____

If not structured enquiry tick which applies:

Discussion/opinion piece ❏ Non-systematic secondary review/analysis ❏ Other ❏ Please specify

_____

Ethical issues

Does the study report whether informed consent to participate was obtained from participants? Y/N/Unclear _____

Does the study report whether representatives of the target population were involved in the design /steering of the study? Y/N/Unclear _____

Describe any other ethical problems with the design or conduct of the study. _____

_____

Search documentation (search process)

The process of performing a systematic literature review must be transparent and reliable. This is achieved by understanding the research methods needed in undertaking the review. The researcher must ensure that all primary studies accessed are documented in sufficient detail within the research report so that readers are able to assess the thoroughness of the search. Table 3.2 provides a structured template to follow. In such documentation, the researcher should specify the rationale for the selection of the electronic databases, journals, conference proceedings or other data sources to be searched.

If the researcher wished to use a database for example, a record of the database name, search words used, date of search and years covered by the search (with justification) would need to be clearly documented. For example, if a researcher was interested to find primary research studies focusing on golf fitness, they may use the database SportDiscus, use the terms, 'golf', 'fitness', 'exercise', and 'physical activity', within the search, they may have performed it on 9 August 2009 and the search covered the years 1990–2009. The rationale for covering these years may have been that no golf-related research in fitness existed before 1990. By making it transparent by documenting the process, the reliability of the strategy is increased.

Data source	What needs to be documented?
Electronic database/ digital library	• Name of database • Search strategy for the database (words used, number of articles found) • Date of search • Years covered by search (include rationale for choice)
Journal hand searches	• Name of journal • Year searched • Any issues/volume not searched (reasons provided)
Conference proceedings	• Title of proceedings • Name of conference (if different) • Journal name (if published as part of a journal)
Unpublished research sources	• Research group/researchers contacted (name, contact details) • Research websites searched (date, URL, detail provided)
Other sources	• Date searched/contacted • Website, publication date, location • Any specific conditioning pertaining to the search

Table 3.2: Documenting each search ensures transparency and reliability in the research methods used.

Data extraction from primary studies

The objective of effective data extraction from the included primary studies is to accurately obtain the required information that enables the research question to be answered. This is often a straightforward process once a 'data extraction form' is in place. The data extraction form must be designed in such a way to collect all information needed to address the review questions and the study quality criteria. In most cases, data extraction will define a set of numerical values that should be extracted for each study (e.g. number of participants, research design and methods used, type of intervention, treatment size and effect, etc.) Such numerical data are important for any attempt to summarise the results of a set of primary studies and are a prerequisite for larger meta-analysis studies that apply techniques to statistically evaluate primary studies.

Reflection Point 3.2

Content or literature analysis refers to any technique and associated procedure that seeks to organise written, audio, and/or visual information into categories and themes related to the central questions of the study. The major feature of the content analysis method is objective, systematic and quantifiable analysis of the overt content of documents (i.e. primary research studies). Content analysis attempts to provide a solution to establishing meaning by rigorous specification of the frequency, similarity and differences within text that can be extended to the content of research studies. Further to quantification, content analysis provides the researcher with qualitative synthesis that can establish concepts, themes and frameworks bound within the content of the material analysed.

There is no one correct way of developing a data extraction form. However, most forms are often similar in structure and can be adapted from one review to another, taking due account of the differences in the categories being used. Simply typing in 'extraction form' or 'extraction template' into web-based search engines will reveal a number that can be viewed and adapted to suit the researcher's own needs.

Key Point 3.6

Creating an extraction template within a spreadsheet is one of the simplest ways to ensure all the data is kept together and can be easily reviewed and compared. By assigning rows to the categories you wish to use or information you want to know from the studies, and columns to the actual studies themselves you can begin the process of data extraction fast and effectively.

By keeping all data in one easily referenced sheet, with included and excluded studies documents on different worksheets, the spreadsheet can act as a historical record of decisions occurring during the review process. The added benefit of using spreadsheets is that they can be emailed to supervisors for quick review and comment without having to spend time examining every single form that has been completed. This way both you and your supervisor will save time and increase the productivity.

The data extraction form should be structured logically to help data entry. It is often best with most research method instruments to pilot test it first. This may help identify data that are not needed or missing, and confusion around coding categories can be clarified. This will ensure that extraction and record information from each study is uniformly organised and managed.

Make sure the form also contains some general pieces of information such as the date of extraction, who did it, if it was someone different, the bibliographic details of each study and the source from where the information came from. It is also worthwhile leaving additional space for writing general notes about the study to ensure that notes, questions and reminders during the analysis can be captured in a systematic way.

Synthesis of extracted data

Data synthesis simply involves collating and summarising the results of the included primary studies from the data extraction form(s). Synthesis of the data can be both non-numerical and descriptive (qualitative) and/or numerical (quantitative). The process of carrying out data synthesis should ensure that data is presented in a succinct manner. Presented by way of tables, each should be structured to highlight the similarities and the differences between the included studies. An evidence table, as can be found within the research articles outlined within this chapter, provides a very clear and effective way to present data extracted from a range of primary studies that meet the inclusion criteria. From a critical perspective, it should be possible to assess qualitatively the reasons for differences between studies. The key elements in the approach to data synthesis may include the following characteristics:

- population;
- interventions;
- settings of research;
- environmental, social and cultural factors that may influence compliance;
- nature of outcomes measures used, their relative importance and robustness;
- sample size for each study (may also include intervention group size, control group size, male:female ratio, etc.).

Structuring the contents of a systematic review

Preparation of the systematic review report requires as much care and attention as the rest of the research process. Being able to write the report in a concise manner is an integral part of a systematic review. Clear structure and content will ensure the reader is able to judge the validity of the research and evaluate the scientific rigour of the research methods used.

As documented in Table 3.3, the report structure for a systematic review is really no different to that of any other research study. As would be expected, no lengthy literature review is needed, rather a short account of the background to the research question. The systematic review must contain a section that reports the research strategy, namely the design and methods. It is mainly this aspect that distinguishes it apart from a traditional literature review, so it is vital that the methods are described in sections similar to that found within the review protocol. Detail purporting to the search process and strategies, inclusion and exclusion criteria, assessments of relevance and quality of primary studies, data extraction and synthesis techniques should all be included. The majority of the report will be found rather in the discussion where the principal findings will be discussed, along with their meaning and linked recommendations.

Chapter Review

In this chapter it has been shown that the rigorous and extensive search criteria adopted in the systematic review procedure, alongside the comprehensiveness and quality control ensured by both the researcher and the review process itself, means that it is a highly relevant and appropriate research strategy. Used to objectively and transparently assess the evidence base in relation to the body of research evidence that exists, the systematic review strategy provides a research approach that not only develops important research skills linked to literature searching and evaluation, but also a gateway in the growing body of scientific evidence that now exists with the field of sport. By using a range of sport-related research examples throughout this chapter you should now be able to:

❏ distinguish between a systematic literature review and more traditional literature review;
❏ identify when and why a systematic literature review strategy may be used to answer sport-related research questions;
❏ appreciate the logical set of guidelines that can be applied to plan, conduct and report a systematic review;
❏ understand the value of a review protocol and how its structured framework aids effective data collection;
❏ acknowledge the research methods used within this approach to ensure objectivity, transparency and reliability.

(Tick when completed)

Section	Subsection	Comment
Title		Short, informative and based on the question being asked. It is important to state that the study is a systematic review.
Abstract	• Context • Aims/Objectives • Research strategy • Findings • Conclusions	A structured summary is important in any research project and permits the reader to assess quickly the quality, relevance and generality of the systematic review.
Background		Description as to the problem being investigated with an indication as to why the systematic review is needed.
Review questions		Specific statements that clearly identify each review question.
Review strategy (include design and method)	• Data search strategy • Study selection • Study quality assessment • Data extraction • Data analysis	This should be based on the research protocol and include detail regarding the overall strategy applied. This will include information about the type of design and the methods of data collection.
Included and excluded studies		A clear representation as to the criteria used, the point at which studies were excluded and a detailed coverage as to all those included/excluded should be apparent.
Findings		Numerical results can be presented as tables and graphs (e.g. similarities, differences, frequency of agreement). Non-numerical results can be presented as summaries of each included paper in a tabular form.
Discussion	• Principle findings • Strengths and weaknesses • Meaning of findings • Recommendations	Discuss the evidence considering the bias associated with systematic reviews. Make it clear to what level the findings imply causality by discussing the level of evidence. What are the implications of the review for practitioners/researchers?
Conclusion		Summarise the content referring specifically back to the initial research questions. Were these answered? To what extent? Future directions?

Table 3.3: Understanding the content and structure of a systematic review will help you to identify the differences when compared to a traditional literature review.

Further Reading

Centre for Reviews and Dissemination (2009) *Systematic Reviews: Guidelines for Undertaking Reviews in Healthcare.* York: York Publishing Services. (www.york.ac.uk/inst/crd/systematic_reviews_book.htm)
This free online resource from the University of York is indispensable to any student wishing to undertake a systematic review as part of their studies. Packed full of valuable information, each section logically explains the process in detail. Of particular value to the section about review protocol design.

Petticrew, M and Roberts, H (2005) *Systematic Reviews in the Social Sciences: A Practical Guide.* Chichester: WileyBlackwell.
This book is a worthwhile addition to anyone's library providing a practically orientated explanation as to the systematic review process. Clearly presented and well structured, developing a search strategy will be made easier after reading this.

Glaszious, P, Irwing, L, Bain, C and Colditz, G (2005) *Systematic Reviews in Health Care: A Practical Guide.* Cambridge: Cambridge University Press.
Focused towards those who wish to undertake systematic reviews in health care, this book may not appeal to all. However, opening sections will consolidate your understanding for the importance of systematic reviews and aid you in establishing a structure to your research.

Chapter 4
Experimental research strategy

Learning Objectives

By identifying research situations for which an experimental research strategy would be applied, this chapter is designed to help you:

- grasp the basic concepts that underpin an experimental research strategy and identify the relative merits of this approach;
- identify how an experimental type and design impacts on the validity of research findings;
- link research design with appropriate data collection and analysis techniques.

Introduction

For the researcher interested in sporting behaviour and its causes, an experimental research strategy presents an ideal approach. Through the observation of the sporting world around us, many research ideas emerge that lend themselves to experiments. By applying the scientific method of inquiry, the experimental strategy enables the researcher to discover the effects of presumed causes. What causes an increase in maximal oxygen uptake after training? Or, what is the effect of topspin on a tennis ball? The key feature of experiments is that through the deliberate alteration of something, the researcher is able to see what happens to something else. This is something people do all the time, for example going to the gym to get fitter. The experimental approach, however, differs from this causal relationship, as it makes a deliberate attempt to make observations free from bias.

The purpose of this chapter is to provide clear explanation as to when and how the experimental research strategy should be applied to answer particular research questions. By outlining the key features of the experimental strategy a framework by which the researcher can identify different experimental types and designs will emerge. Through the understanding of experimental research methods, appropriate data collection and analysis techniques can form part of the overall strategy. Although it not the intention of this chapter to explore statistical techniques relevant to experimental research, an overview as to how design and suitable statistical techniques link together will be covered. By the end of the chapter a step-by-step approach to experimental research should be gained.

The importance of experimentation in sport research

Through the study and practice of sport, problems emerge that necessitate an experimental research approach in order to find a solution. As covered in Chapter 1, selecting the most suitable research strategy depends heavily on the nature of the research question. The experimental research strategy is a quantitative approach designed to discover the effect of presumed causes. By the very nature of deductive research, the application of the scientific method of inquiry attempts to test theory by subjecting it to different conditions. Experiments in sport provide the researcher with that very opportunity.

By examining sporting behaviour and attempting to discover the underpinning causes to the effects observed, the researcher's ability to test theories, such as how we fatigue during exercise, or how we experience peak flow during performance can be tested, scrutinised and enhanced. Aside from the theoretical testing that is an inherent part of experimental research, a practical more applied perspective also has an important place within sport-related experiments. By discovering the causes of improved aerobic fitness, increased muscle mass or reduced concentration for example, new training approaches, enhanced performance tools, more specific exercise guidelines or additional assessment strategies may be generated.

Key Point 4.1

Experimental research can be defined as research that attempts to identify cause-and-effect relationships between phenomena.

Establishing causality through experiments

One of the key characteristics of the experimental research strategy is that of cause-and-effect. Quite simply, the overall purpose of any experiment the researcher conducts is to determine with as much confidence as possible what an effect may have been caused by. The effect may be an increase in strength, a lowering of heart rate, a quickening of reaction, or a slowing of pace. Whatever the effect happens to be, the experimental strategy attempts to determine what the cause was by deliberately altering one thing (e.g. training, recovery, caffeine consumption or intensity). By altering only one thing (i.e. variable), while trying to keep all other things (variables) constant, the researcher can begin to gain confidence that if an effect is seen it is more likely to be due to the thing that was altered. In comparison to qualitative research approaches covered in later chapters, tightly controlled experiments are the only means by which cause-and-effect can be established.

It has already been noted that an experimental approach differs from the non-experimental in that the researcher can establish cause-and-effect by deliberately altering or manipulating variables, while trying to keep all other variables constant or controlled. Such cause can be thought of as the independent variable (IV) and the effect the dependent variable (DV). It is therefore the case that experiments require the precise control of all variables except the IV.

Characteristics of the experimental approach

The experimental research strategy has a number of characteristics that distinguish it from other research strategies. In the attempt to discover the causation between phenomena, a number of conditions need to be met. These include, control, randomisation and manipulation.

Experimental control

The concept of control within the experimental approach can take many different forms and have different usages within this methodological approach. Control refers to eliminating the influence of any 'extraneous' factors or variables that could affect observations made on the outcome (the dependent variable). The purpose of control is to enable the experimenter to isolate the one key variable which has been selected in order to observe its effect on some other variable. Control within an experiment, therefore, allows the researcher to conclude that it is the cause and nothing else, which is influencing the effect.

Being able to control external variables apart from the one under investigation (the independent variable) will provide confidence that change to the outcome variable was not down to other variables. For the researcher wishing to conduct experimental studies, control may take the form of:

- being in total control of the events that the participants experience;
- controlling the group so that one does not experience the independent variable;
- controlling the variables so that the consequences of the independent variable can be clearly seen separated from other factors.

Key Point 4.2

'Cause-and-effect' refers to the link between one event (called the cause (A)) and another event (called the effect (B)), which is a direct consequence (the result) of the first (the cause). When determining a cause-and-effect link between two events, probability testing, that is to say statistical tests, allow for a degree of certainty to be attained. This degree of certainty, or probability score (P) provides the researcher with an indication that the effect is a consequence of the cause; so therefore A probabilistically causes B if A's occurrence increases the probability of B.

Randomisation

Randomisation within the experimental research strategy eliminates the influence of extraneous variables acting on one group and not on another. Randomly assigning participants to different groups or treatments provides the researcher with a degree of confidence that each group will be representative of the population from which it was drawn. It therefore has implications for generalising results of the experiment back to the population. Random assignment provides assurance that the extraneous variables are controlled and the bias across groups reduced.

Consider an experiment in which half the participants are in an exercise condition and the other half are in the no exercise condition. Suppose that the participants are also different in a third factor, such as annual income. If the researcher wished to investigate the causal relationship between exercise and anxiety for example, randomly assigning participants into the conditions would eliminate the influence of income differences between the conditions. Not randomly assigning participants to groups means that annual income may have an impact on anxiety, which could mask any causal relationship between exercise and anxiety. Ensuring that participants are assigned to different groups in a random way increases the internal validity of the experiment.

Key Point 4.3

One of the easiest ways to randomly assign participants to groups is by allocating a number to each one, so say 1–20, and then asking a friend to call out a number between 1 and 20. You could either place the first ten numbers called into one group and the next ten numbers to another, or every other number. Although basic, this provides a quick and effective way to randomly assign participants into your groups.

Experimental manipulation

By creating change within a controlled setting and then observing the resulting effect, the researcher may be able to establish what the true cause of the change was. The implication of change in this context therefore is extremely important and distinguishes the experimental approach from other research strategies. This approach deliberately introduces change, which forms the core of the experiment, and such change is termed 'manipulation'. Consider the flight of a football for one moment. The flight of the ball off the boot can make a number of different shapes which are all caused by either single or, more likely, multiple factors. These include the design of the boot, the boot material, the location of impact, the angle of impact and the speed of impact.

From an experimental perspective, the researcher may start by changing or manipulating these in isolation, keeping all other factors constant to see how they alter ball flight. Changing the material, for example, from leather to a rubberised compound, may cause less ball spin off the boot and therefore reduce slice. Alternatively, changing the location of impact on the boot through relocation of the laces, for example, may cause the ball to travel faster for the same impact speed. Through manipulation and control, the researcher can begin to identify what causes alterations and therefore develop new approaches.

If a researcher wished to explore the impact of agility-specific drills on a group of junior hockey players, they could also apply manipulation to their study. The researcher could manipulate for instance the type of practice (e.g. agility versus non-agility), the group (e.g. boys versus girls), or both. If, however, they were interested in how different types of music may alter 5k running performance in elite runners they could manipulate the type of music (e.g. fast versus slow) that the runners listen to. Manipulation in this context therefore refers to the purposeful change or alteration of one variable so that the effect on one or more other variables can be observed. This process allows the researcher the opportunity to begin testing theories and existing models, make improvements and predict future events or occurrences. With research questions wishing to determine whether any meaningful change exists between groups, conditions and/or across periods of time, the manipulation of one factor or variable can provide the researcher with an opportunity to determine the extent of an effect.

Reflection Point 4.1

Validity is an important issue when it comes to applying the experimental approach to research. The two types that probably have the most impact on your research at this stage of your understanding are internal and external validity. Below are explanations and some practical examples that will help your comprehension. These will be mentioned again throughout the chapter so it is important at this stage you understand what they mean and how they can impact on your research findings.

Validity Type	Description	Example
Internal validity	Provides the researcher with a level of confidence that the independent variable caused a change in the dependent variable.	Julie conducted a laboratory experiment to investigate the impact sound had on reaction time. She ensured that as many factors as possible were kept constant for all assessments apart from the one she was interested in; that being sound. In this instance Julie had a *high level of internal validity* as any change in reaction time would be a consequence of the type of sound and no other factor.
External validity	Concerns the degree to which the conclusions in the	Henry conducted a field-based experiment to investigate the impact membership

research study would hold for other persons in other places and at other times.

promotion type had on recruiting new gym goers. He wished to ensure that his study was set in as natural environment as possible so that he was able to generalise his findings. He recognised however that due to the research setting and the *high degree of external validity* he was unable to control for many factors that could lower his confidence in concluding that the promotional type caused change in new gym members.

To seek more information about the meaning and application of validity within the experimental strategy a number of resources can be consulted. The webpage 'Social Research Methods' offers a no-nonsense explanation regarding validity in research and the following link will take you to the 'validity' section (http://www.socialresearchmethods.net/kb/introval.php). Alternatively, for a more thorough grounding Christensen's textbook, *Experimental Methodology* and Crozby's textbook, *Methods in Behavioural Research* listed at the end of this chapter offer a clear overview as to the definition and practical implications of validity when applying the experimental strategy.

Another way to view manipulation within the experimental approach is through the deliberate administration of a treatment on a group in order to observe the response. The word treatment basically refers to something that the researcher imposes on to their participants. For example, the researcher may administer a coordination practice drill to one group and no practice drill to another to see how the drill changes the response, that being the junior players' hockey performance. Or they may administer a training programme, a sport drink, or a different piece of sports equipment to a group. The main aim therefore is to attempt to keep all aspects of the situation constant except one; that being the one thing the researcher wishes to investigate or change (the effect the treatment has on a group of objects or participants). This approach allows the researcher, in a very controlled way, to establish whether a meaningful effect caused by the treatment impacts on those involved in the research.

Learning Activity 4.1

Read through each of the research projects (below) devised by students studying courses relating to sport and exercise science. Try and identify the independent variable (IV) and dependent variable (DV) for each study by highlighting each in a different colour. *Remember, the IV is what you wish to manipulate or change and the DV is what you will be measuring.*

- Two groups (basketball vs. volleyball) completed a standing vertical jump to assess vertical distance (m) jumped.
- Three groups of pistol shooters (novice, intermediate and expert) were assessed for reaction time (ms) during a manual tracking task.
- One group of darts players were assessed for accuracy (mm) before, during and after ingestion of caffeine.
- Four groups of school children (ages 4–6, 7–9, 10–12, 13–15 yrs) completed three tests (trials 1, 2 and 3) to assess peak heart rate ($b \cdot min^{-1}$) recorded during the hop, skip and jump game.
- Two groups of foundation degree students completed seven 1.5-mile runs with RPE recorded immediately before, mid-way and on completion of each run.
- One group of well-trained cyclists completed five indoor 40-km cycling time trials during which power output (W) was recorded at 10-km intervals.
- Six groups of 2nd year sport science students completed four tests during which motivation to work was assessed before and after hypnosis.
- One group of foundation degree students completed three statistics exams with anxiety assessed before, 30 minutes during and 1 hour after each test.

Types of research experiment

For the researcher undertaking experiments, it is a necessary part of the strategy to decide upon an experimental approach that will match the objectives of the research study. This means that some plan needs to be developed that includes the research design type and the data collection and analysis methods. Before discussing the different research designs available to the researcher, it is worth considering the three types of experiments and how they can be linked to sport research. The three are: true, quasi- and natural experiments.

True experiments

So far in this chapter the focus has centred on an experimental type that permits the researcher to control, in principle, all extraneous factors and variables except one; that being the one that is manipulated. Such experimental approach is known as a 'true experiment' and is considered the strongest approach of all experimental types. Providing a high degree of internal validity, the true experiment provides the researcher with the greatest level of confidence that any change observed in the dependent variable is a consequence of the independent variable and nothing else. In order to ensure internal validity, therefore, true experiments tend to occur in artificial settings, such as the sport and exercise science laboratory. The attempt to try and attain a high degree of internal validity will though impact on the external validity of the study. This means that a true experiment may not reflect a real-life situation, with the artificial environment distorting the real-life nature of observations.

The ability to move experiments outside the laboratory (e.g., on to the football pitch or within a school playground) allows for a more natural setting (field experiments). By increasing the external validity of the study, the researcher must recognise that the findings may have more ecological significance, but only by foregoing the ability to control as many extraneous factors as possible. Such approach can still be referred to as a 'true experiment' but may be less ideal. As with a controlled laboratory experiment, the independent variable is still deliberately manipulated. However, it is not possible to have such tight control over all variables. If the researcher wished to conduct a study in a natural setting, therefore, they must be aware of the external factors that, in addition to the independent variable, could change the dependent variable. It would be for the researcher to then decide whether the benefit of increasing the external validity, by setting the research in a more natural environment, outweighs the reduction in the internal validity.

Research Focus 4.1

In a study by Brown et al. (*Journal of Dance Medicine and Science*, 2007, 11, 38–44) a true experimental approach was selected in order to compare the effects of plyometric training and traditional weight training on aesthetic jumping ability, lower-body strength, and power in collegiate dancers. For this study there was one independent variable, namely the training condition and three separate dependent variables (i.e. jumping ability, strength and power).

This study used a non-randomised sample of 18 dancers who undertook a within-group pre-post test design. The dancers were randomly assigned to one of three groups: a plyometric group (n = 6); a traditional weight training group (n = 6); and a self-selected control group (n = 6). The plyometric group performed 3 sets of 8 repetitions of four different lower-body plyometric exercises twice a week. The weight training group performed three sets of six to eight repetitions of four lower-body isotonic exercises twice a week. The control group refrained from all forms of strength training. Each dancer maintained their normal dance classes throughout the six-week intervention. All dancers were tested prior to and following the six-week training period. Tests consisted of assessments of jumping skill and lower-body strength and power. Strength was assessed via three one-repetition maximum tests: leg press; leg curl; and leg extension. Power was assessed with a Wingate anaerobic power test and vertical jump height tests. The results of this study indicate that either plyometric training or traditional lower-body weight training can be useful in improving variables applicable to dance. This study also supports the notion that short-term dance training alone may not be sufficient to elicit improvements in the measured variables.

Quasi-experiments

There are occasions when it is not possible to control, in principle, the influence of all extraneous variables as in the true experiment. Such experimental type is known as a 'quasi-experiment'. As with the true experimental type described above, this approach allows the researcher to examine the impact of an independent variable on a dependent variable, but causal inference is much more difficult. In most research instances, the use of a quasi-experimental approach results from the inability or lack of need to randomly assign the participants into groups. This may be the case for example when the researcher wishes to purposefully compare particular groups (e.g. one school class against another).

Research Focus 4.2

In a study by Bressel et al. (*Journal of Athletic Training,* 2007, 42: 42–46) a quasi-experimental approach was taken to compare static and dynamic balance among collegiate athletes competing or training in soccer, basketball, and gymnastics. This between-group design study used a non-randomised sample of 34 female college athletes who were split into three independent groups: soccer (n=11); basketball (n=11); and gymnastics (n=12). For this approach there were two independent variables. One was group and the other the type of balance. To assess static and dynamic balance, participants performed two different balance tests: a Balance Error Scoring System (BESS) for static balance and a Star Excursion Balance Test (SEBT) for the assessment of dynamic balance. Each completed on both dominant and non-dominant side. Findings revealed that gymnasts and soccer players did not differ in terms of static and dynamic balance. In contrast, basketball players displayed inferior static balance compared with gymnasts and inferior dynamic balance compared with soccer players.

Natural experiments

A third type is known as a 'natural experiment' and involves naturally occurring events rather than naturally occurring groups. This means that the researcher does not manipulate the independent variable like the true experiment, rather a deliberate change is introduced that occurs naturally within the research setting which the researcher does not have responsibility for. Natural experiments, by their very nature, have low internal validity due to the inability of the researcher to control extraneous factors during the study. Because of this, the results of natural experiments are often difficult to generalise back to the population from which the study sample was drawn.

Research Focus 4.3

In a study by Grandjean et al. (*Journal of Sport and Exercise Psychology,* 2002, 24: 320–27) a natural experimental approach was taken to examine an unintended 'experiment' on world-class gymnasts at the 2000 Olympics. During the women's all-around final, the vault apparatus was initially set 5 centimetres too low, potentially undermining the athletes' self-confidence. The 18 gymnasts who vaulted early in the competition became an unknowing experimental group. The remaining 18 vaulted after the error was corrected, becoming a randomized control group. For this between group pre-post test design there was only one independent variable: group. Both groups had pre-test scores (from preliminary rounds) and post-test scores (from the final) on each of the four apparatuses: vault, bars, beam, and floor. From analysis of the data it is clear that the vault error had little if any effect on later performances or on the final standings. The researchers concluded that elite athletes in a closed-skill sport apparently learn to concentrate so well that most can recover from a mishap and refocus successfully for the next effort.

Learning Activity 4.2

In reviewing the previous section you should now be more aware of how each experimental type has both its advantages and disadvantages when it comes to considering the internal and external validity of the research. Now read carefully the studies outlined and attempt to allocate the most appropriate experimental type to each. Remember that there may be more than one answer, so consider how the chosen experimental type and the associated degree of validity may impact on the accuracy and truthfulness of any inferences made as well as the applicability of the findings.

Study One
What does it take to win Olympic Gold in the 100m? An examination of champions' performance times over the last ten events.

Experimental type: _____

Study Two
The effectiveness of bed rest on lower limb anterior cruciate ligament (ACL) recovery time.

Experimental type: _____

Study Three
The impact of foot strapping on medial and lateral heel stability during a walking gait cycle.

Experimental type: _____

Study Four
The effect of multiple-sprints on blood lactate recovery curves.

Experimental type: _____

Designing the experiment

When considering the design of an experiment it is important for the researcher to keep in mind the impact diminished internal validity has on the ability to support the conclusion that the independent and dependent variable were causally linked. If the degree of internal validity within the selected design is threatened, that's to say, it is low, then it is difficult to be confident that the independent variable caused any change in the dependent variable. Based on this premise, the researcher needs to be aware that the selected research design, based on the research question, can have significant impact on the conclusions and inferences made.

Simple quasi-experimental designs

Probably the simplest experimental design is the *one-group post-test design*. This is considered quasi-experimental as it lacks an important element of a true experiment: namely a control or comparison group. For this approach the dependent variable is measured once in a single group (i.e. within-group) following a treatment (Figure 4.1). Consider a single group being given a pharmacological supplement over the course of six weeks and then having their exercise ability assessed. Although producing some valuable scientific data, the omission of a pre-test before the treatment means that it is very difficult to know if the treatment changed their ability or the change was a consequence of other extraneous factors not controlled for. Therefore, without a control group, it would be hard to say whether the same effects would have happened in the absence of the treatment. As a consequence, the internal validity associated with such design is considered very low.

By advancing the first design further, it is sometimes the case that the researcher wishes to evaluate change in a dependent variable within the same group across two occasions (Figure 4.2). By measuring participants before and after the introduction of a treatment a comparison can be obtained. This type of within-group approach is aptly named the *one-group pre-post test design* and can be referred to as a 'repeated measures design'. This approach, although not featuring a control group, is still considered quasi-experimental however, but internal validity is increased as the researcher now has a pre-test comparison to make observations against. Let's suppose the researcher wanted to investigate whether a four-week plyometric strength training programme increased a person's ability to throw a shot-put from their dominant side. After selecting a group of participants and getting them to complete the pre-test throw, they would be given the plyometric training programme to complete. After the four weeks a reassessment of their performance would occur (i.e. post-test).

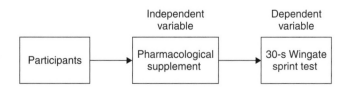

Figure 4.1: A single one-group post-test quasi-experimental design.

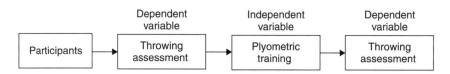

Figure 4.2: An illustration of a within-group pre-post test design.

Unlike the previous two quasi-experimental designs, the non-equivalent control group design employs a separate control group (i.e. between-group or independent group design), but the participants in the two conditions are not equivalent (Figure 4.3). Take the example of a sports nutritionist who wanted to investigate the impact of a dietary programme on weight management. All overweight members of a local health club, as recorded on their personal record sheets, were identified and recruited for the study. Those members who actively volunteered became the experimental group and those that did not, by default, became the control group. Although this approach provided a control group to compare against, because of the selection differences between groups, problems arose because those that volunteered may have differed in some important way from those that did not. This design would therefore make it difficult to know whether any change in the dependent variable was a consequence of the independent variable or not.

To some extent this, the design presented in Figure 4.3, can be extended to incorporate a pre-post test component (Figure 4.4). Although an extremely useful quasi-experimental design, this is still not as robust as a true experiment as the participants have not been randomly assigned, therefore introducing bias. As illustrated in Figure 4.4, although the change in the dependent variable can be assessed across each group, the groups may, by way of selection process, have characteristics that impact on that change (e.g. originate from an office where a high amount of coffee is drunk).

Simple true experimental designs

From the designs presented so far, quasi-experimental designs lack suitable participant randomisation and often appropriate control. With non-randomised allocation and the lack of control or comparative group, the threat to internal validity is increased and inference made

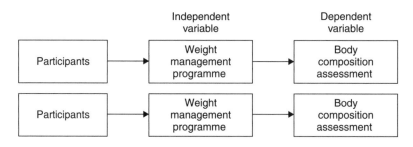

Figure 4.3: A between-group non-equivalent control group design with one independent variable (i.e. weight management programme).

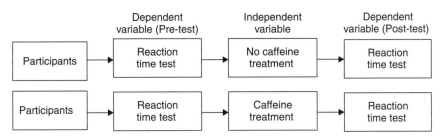

Figure 4.4: A between-group non-equivalent control group pre-post test design with two independent variables (i.e. group and treatment condition).

difficult. Eliminating selection differences through the random assignment of participants to groups as well as the inclusion of a 'between-group' factor provides a control or comparison group, and the researcher can begin to further improve the degree of internal validity and ensure more confidence in the causal relationships between the independent and dependent variables.

Similar to the post-test only design (Figure 4.1), the between-group post-test design involves the random assignment of participants into either an experimental or control/comparative group. Used to eliminate any systematic bias, randomisation of participants in such design will reduce the impact of extraneous variables on the dependent variable. This is also known as an 'unrelated design' because the two groups are not related to each other; they are separate and treated as two distinct groups. In the example illustrated in Figure 4.5, one randomly assigned group wore thermal clothing during 30 minutes of cold water submersion, while the control wore only their swimming costume. After the time was completed each group's core temperature was recorded.

As has already been noted regarding the one-group post-test design, this approach allows the researcher the opportunity to measure the dependent variable only once in each group and neglects any pre-test assessment. This thereby lowers the internal validity of the study. If the researcher had measured core temperature in each group before submersion then a pre-submersion value could be compared with the post-submersion value. If the researcher were therefore to find that both groups' core temperature changed by the same amount as a consequence of the 30-minute submersion, then they would have a high degree of confidence that the thermal clothing had no or little impact on the maintenance of core body temperature.

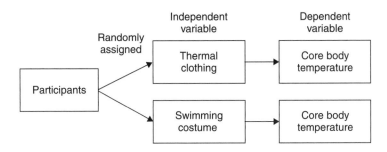

Figure 4.5: An illustration of a between-group post-test design with one independent variable (i.e. clothing condition).

Take another research example. Suppose a researcher wished to investigate the impact of high-intensity fatiguing exercise on muscle activation patterns. By randomly allocating participants to two groups (experimental and control) the researcher firstly recorded all participants' lower-limb electromyographic (EMG) patterns during a flexion and extension movement on an isokinetic dynamometer. Following this, the experimental group completed a 30-s Wingate test and the control group remained static on the ergometer. After the 30-s each once again performed the flexion and extension movement and EMG was recorded (Figure 4.6).

Repeated measures design

Consider an experiment investigating the relationship between hydration status and cognitive functioning in competitive sailors. In independent group designs (i.e. within-group), as outlined and illustrated above, participants would be randomly assigned to one of two groups (i.e. dehydrated state or euhydrated state) and once in this state undertake a cognitive functioning test. In a repeated measures design, the same individuals participate in all the conditions, therefore meaning that participants are repeatedly measured on the dependent variable after being in each condition. The advantages of this approach over others are that fewer research participants are needed and costs can be kept to a minimum. In addition to these more obvious strengths, the repeated measures approach can also be extremely sensitive to finding statistically significant differences between groups.

A major problem with this approach, however, stems from the fact that the order in which the conditions are presented could impact on the dependent variable. Suppose in the example above that all participants experienced the dehydrated condition before the euhydrated condition. Although a change in the dependent variable following the manipulation may be a consequence of the hydration status of the participants, it may also be a result of an order effect. Performance in the cognitive function tests may improve due to learning of test or becoming more familiar with the procedures. There is also the chance of a fatigue effect caused by insufficient time between the two conditions.

There are two approaches to dealing with such problems. To deal with any potential fatigue effect occurring, the researcher can create a procedure in which the time interval between conditions is of sufficient length. The balance between being too short and too long needs careful

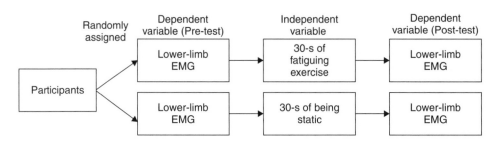

Figure 4.6: A between-group pre-post test design with two independent variables (i.e. group and activity condition).

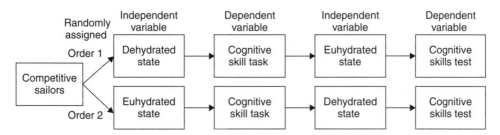

Figure 4.7: A counterbalanced within-group repeated measures design with one independent variable (i.e. dehydration status).

consideration both in terms of impact of the dependent variable, but also participant availability. The second relates to the order effect. In repeated measures design this can be resolved by '*counterbalancing*' the order of conditions. As shown in Figure 4.7, the participants would be randomly allocated to two groups. Each group would undertake both conditions but just in a different order: group one undertakes order 1 with group two undertaking order 2. In essence, all participants are doing exactly the same, just the order has changed. By applying this approach to the repeated measures design it is possible to reduce the impact an order effect may have on the dependent variable.

Key Point 4.4

A counterbalanced approach is a method of controlling for order effects in a repeated measures design by either including all orders of treatment presentation or randomly determining the order for each participant.

By understanding the basic structure of experimental designs, the impact such design has on the threat to internal validity and the link between the research question and the within, between or repeated measures approach, the researcher can use these models as building blocks to create more elaborate approaches to experimental research design. Irrespective of what design is created however, the issues relating to the control of extraneous variables that may impact on the ability to conclude causal links between the independent variable and dependent variable will always be the researcher's challenge.

It is important to remember that each design has its strengths and weaknesses that will impact on the researcher's selection decisions. The choice of a pre-test, a control group and the randomisation of participants will influence the validity of the study and affect the ability to confidently determine causality.

Reflection Point 4.2

The simple experimental designs presented within this chapter act as a starting point for the evolvement of more complex experiments. By understanding the building blocks of basic research design within an experimental research strategy you can be led to more elaborate research questions.

By increasing the number of independent variables, or levels as they are sometimes referred to, the researcher can begin to understand much more information about the cause-and-effect relationships between independent variables and dependent variables. Experimental designs, such as a 2x2 factorial design that combines both within- and between-group models, are not uncommon in undergraduate research. This approach involves two independent variables/levels (e.g. sex and vertical jump score) each consisting of two groups or conditions (e.g. sex (male and female) and vertical jump score (pre-training and post-training)), hence 2x2. In this design the first level (sex) is a between-group factor and the second (jump score) is a within-group factor. By knowing this information about the design you will be able to determine, in advance of data collection, the most suitable statistical test to use (see Figure 4.8).

If you wish to find out more about complex experimental designs, such as the factorial design, then refer to the back of this chapter where a number of texts are recommended.

Learning Activity 4.3

Without looking back through this chapter, try and recall the three key characteristics of the experimental research strategy. Once you have done this and entered them into the grid below, re-read the two research summaries in Research Focus 4.1 and 4.2 and evaluate each against the three characteristics. For each one indicate below whether the characteristics are met or not by placing a tick or cross in the corresponding box.

Characteristic	Brown et al. (2007)	Bressel et al. (2007)
1:		
2:		
3:		

Collection of data in experiments

A further component of the experimental research strategy, and one that comes after the selection of the research design, concerns decisions about the data collection methods – such methods that require the researcher to select appropriate instruments or techniques that are then implemented via a set procedure or protocol to ensure efficient and effective data collection.

Presentation of the independent variable

An important starting point for the researcher is to consider how the independent variable will be presented and the manner in which the dependent variable will be measured. In some studies, the researcher becomes involved in the presentation of the independent variable, requiring their active participation in the administration of that which is to be manipulated. Consider the researcher's involvement in a study that implements a training programme, sandwiched between two 5 REP_{max} tests. In this instance the researcher may be fully involved with the presentation of the independent variable to the participants, monitoring and recording testing and training to ensure accurate accounts are made. This approach has advantages as the researcher is able to ensure familiarity and consistency in the presentation of the independent variable. The limitation, however, is that researcher bias can impact on the presentation. This may have an unwanted effect on the dependent variable.

One way around this is to present the independent variable in such a way that reduces bias. Consider a study that looks to identify the effect of caffeine compared to a placebo on 2000-m rowing performance. In this instance the researcher may choose firstly not to inform the participants as to which solution they are receiving (i.e. single-blind). The value of this approach is that the participants will not be influenced by knowing that one is the caffeine and the other a placebo. To advance this further, the researcher may also wish to remove their own influence by also becoming 'blind' to the solutions each participant is receiving. Known as a 'double-blinded' approach, a third person would organise the solutions, labelling each A and B, devising a testing schedule and then providing it to the researcher. This way, the researcher presenting the independent variable cannot impose their bias on to the procedure or participants in the study.

Measurement of the dependent variable

The selection of instruments and their associated procedures for the measurement of the dependent variable will be dictated by what behaviour the researcher wishes to measure. The researcher in sport has a wide and varied range of clinical and non-clinical measurement tools available to them, spanning broad areas of physiology, biomechanics and psychology. Sport-specific ergometry, video capture systems, cardio-respiratory devices, sport-specific questionnaires, field-based assessment tools, and force-platform technology are among only a few different instruments that when applied in a reliable and accurate manner can produce a sensitive measure of the dependent variable.

The dependent variable in experiments typically falls into three board categories: self-report; behavioural; and physiological. Self-reporting measures are used to quantifiably measure such things as attitudes, emotional states, confidence and motivation levels, or perceived ratings of exertion.

Rating scales (e.g. Likert scales) with assigned descriptions are the most common and allow the researcher to convert rating into numerical responses. Behavioural measures are direct observations of sporting behaviour often by way of video or notational tools and, as one can imagine, are endless in number. These can take the form of verbal and non-verbal and are recorded to produce numerical quantification of behaviours (e.g. time spent in different zones on court). The final measure is physiological in nature and refers to the recording of bodily responses. Indicators from a physiological perspective may include temperature, heart rate, oxygen uptake, blood markers (e.g. lactate), blood pressure, and lung function. From a biomechanical viewpoint, measures may include measures of ground reaction force or movement kinematics.

It is sometimes desirable for the researcher to measure more than one dependent variable in order to build up a more concrete view of the sporting behaviour in question. For example, measuring participants' endurance capacity on a treadmill may require the measurement of velocity, oxygen uptake, heart rate, rating of perceived exertion and blood markers. What this approach does create is the question of importance and order. When more than one dependent variable is measured, recognising the order in which measurements will occur and their associated importance needs to be considered. All dependent variables in the example above may have been of equal value and collected all at the same time period. There may be cases when one measurement leads on to the next and an awareness of impact on each subsequent measure as well as their overall importance to the study needs consideration.

Linking design with an analysis approach

The analysis of numerical data collected from experiments provides the researcher with the opportunity to decipher the meaning behind the numbers. Analysing experimental data by way of statistical analysis methods often incites unnecessary fear among many novice researchers. In reality, once the experimental design is decided upon, the selection of data analysis techniques, whether that be basic descriptive statistics to more complex procedures, is in actual fact relatively straightforward. What is important and one thing most novice researchers do not do well is decide on the analysis method prior to data collection. The point of undertaking statistical analysis on the collected data is that the researcher can determine whether differences across groups or conditions are due to chance or a consequence of a cause. Remember, the whole point of the experimental approach is discovery of cause and effect. Does the independent variable, which is the one that the researcher manipulates, affect the dependent variable? By subjecting the data to statistical analysis reveals to the researcher the likelihood of any effect measured being caused by the independent variable and not just by chance occurrences alone.

What tends to confuse most when it comes to data analysis is not so much the mechanics of statistical analysis but rather the process of matching the research design, which is related to the research question, to the type of analysis that needs to be performed. A wide range of software packages now makes it easy for the researcher to put data in, press a few buttons and get something back. It may not always be the case that this is understood, but the mechanics are simplified.

As illustrated in Figure 4.8 the relationship between research design and statistical analysis tests can been seen. Specific tests are best suited to analysis data collected using specific types of design. Whether a between-group or within-group design, one independent variable or more, or a number of different groups to compare, the decision tree process allows the researcher to consider the type of statistical analysis test whilst designing their study.

To provide some practical examples to illustrate the effectiveness of the decision process, let's consider an earlier quasi-experimental design (Figure 4.5) that was constructed to investigate the effect of clothing on body temperature following 30 minutes' submersion in cold water. In this design, participants were allocated into one of two groups (thermal clothing or swimming costume). With this between-group design there were therefore two groups that did not experience the other condition during the experiment. The independent variable for this study was the type of clothing worn. By applying these three basic design features to our decision tree, that is: i) between-group design; ii) one independent variable; and iii) only two groups, the resultant statistical test will be an independent *t-test*.

Next consider the example illustrated in Figure 4.7. In this study, the researcher wished to examine the impact hydration status had on cognitive functioning. The design was a repeated-measures approach where the same participants took part in all conditions. For this design, this can be considered a within-group design. There was one independent variable, namely the hydration status, which comprised on two conditions (dehydrated and euhydrated). By again applying the basic design features to our decision tree, that is: i) within-group design; and ii) two conditions, the resultant statistical test will be a related *t-test*.

Learning Activity 4.4

Refer back to the three Research Focus boxes (4.1, 4.2, 4.3) earlier on in the chapter. By applying your understanding of experimental research design gained from this chapter and working logically through the decision tree as illustrated in Figure 4.8, attempt to determine which statistical test you would use. It may help to consider the following:

- Is the design within- or between- groups?
- How many independent variables are there?
- How many groups or conditions are being compared?

Research Focus 4.1: Brown et al. 2007
Based on the experimental design, the statistical test would be:

_____

_____

_____

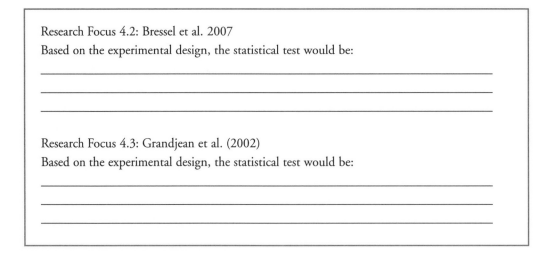

Research Focus 4.2: Bressel et al. 2007
Based on the experimental design, the statistical test would be:

_____

_____

_____

Research Focus 4.3: Grandjean et al. (2002)
Based on the experimental design, the statistical test would be:

_____

_____

_____

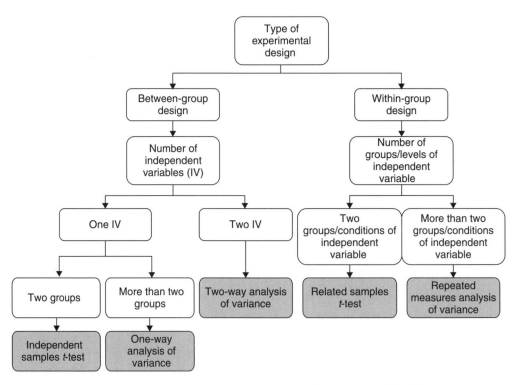

Figure 4.8: Decision tree for selecting appropriate statistical tests based on experimental research design.

Chapter Review

Throughout this chapter we have investigated when and how to apply the experimental research strategy in order to examine a wide range of sporting behaviours. By examining the importance of internal and external validity in experiments, the discovery of cause-and-effect between measured variables can be made more certain. In constructing the experiment, selecting the most appropriate design will allow the researcher to draw accurate and truthful conclusions while allowing for a degree of generalisability. Whether between-, within-, or a combined-group approach is required, being able to make the link to the most suitable statistical technique will guide the researcher to make the right analysis and interpretation. By using a range of sport-related research examples throughout this chapter you should now be able to:

❏ recall a definition for the term 'experiment' and explain why it is different from non-experimental approaches;

❏ list the strengths and weaknesses of this strategy and identify how it can be used to answer specific research problems;

❏ name the three core experimental types and provide sport and exercise science-specific examples for each;

❏ construct a suitable research design based on a range of sport-related research questions.

(Tick when completed)

Further Reading

Crozby, PC (2009*) Methods in Behavioural Research* (10ᵗʰ Ed.). Maidenhead: McGraw Hill
    Higher Education.
This excellent, newly reviewed edition should be on the shelf of everyone wishing to undertake experimental research. By advancing further the key themes outlined within this chapter, complex research designs are clearly examined to help the student understand and apply these approaches to their own research projects.

Keeble, S (1995) *Experimental Research 1: An Introduction to Experimental Design.* The Open
    Learning Foundation, Churchill Livingstone.
This is an extremely practical text with lots of useful learning activities. The book will guide you through a more detailed perspective on the experimental approach with particular reference to experimental design.

Keeble, S (1995) *Experimental Research 2: Conducting and Reporting Experimental Research.* The
    Open Learning Foundation, Churchill Livingstone. Higher Education.
The second edition in the series takes you through the reporting of experimental research, which is particularly useful for when you come to write up your experimental project work.

Christensen, L (2006) *Experimental Methodology* (10th Ed.). London: Pearson.
Advancing on from the basics, this book will offer you a much more thorough grounding within the experimental research approach and design construction. Set out in a clear manner, each chapter ends with internet site recommendations, practical tests and learning activity challenges.

Field, A (2009) *Discovering Statistics using SPSS for Windows*. London: Sage.
Ntoumanis, N (2001) *A Step-by-Step Guide to SPSS for Sport and Exercise Studies*. London: Routledge.
Both of these textbooks provide the reader with a thorough grounding in statistical data analysis. By providing practical illustrations as to how to conduct and interpret the SPSS findings, whether you are a first-time user or are more experienced at using SPSS, you will find these books of particular value.

Chapter 5
Correlational research strategy

Learning Objectives

In developing an understanding of why correlational research is of value, this chapter will explore how a correlational research strategy can be applied to answer sport-related research questions. By identifying research situations for which this strategy may be applied, this chapter is designed to help you:

- explain the basic concept of a correlational research strategy;
- identify the relative merits of this approach and identify how to apply it to sport research;
- describe the pattern and strength of an association by way of scatter plots and analysis techniques.

Introduction

Sport is full of links and connections. Consider the connections between fitness and endurance success, fibre type and strength, motivation and sporting achievement or wealth and sporting opportunities. The list is endless and highlights to us the relationships that exist between phenomena in a sporting context. In wishing to understand more about sporting behaviour and how phenomena relate to each other, the researcher can apply a correlational research strategy that not only enables the degree of relationship to be determined, but also prediction to occur.

Non-experimental approaches to research, such as this strategy, do not attempt to manipulate variables in order to assess the resulting effect, rather observe or make measurement of phenomena in order to study the relationships between them. This is achieved by asking people to describe their behaviour, directly observing behaviour, recording physiological response or, rarely, examining records, such as national census data. It is the very act of determining the degree to which variables associate with each other that provides the researcher with opportunities to discover the intricate interwoven relationships that occur in sport.

The value of association in sport research

We constantly make associations between phenomena encountered through our sporting and academic experiences. It may be assumed, for example, that time spent studying will be associated with better grades, time spent in the gym will be associated with stronger arms, or time spent reading will be associated with more knowledge. We would like to think that all of these are true and time invested would reap some positive reward.

Similarly, we know through our own experiences that if we increase our training load, while considering the correct nutrition and allowing plenty of time for recovery, we should begin to see beneficial developmental changes in our physical status. We also know however that there are many other factors that could also play a contributing role in explaining improved fitness irrespective of our training commitment. The application of the correlational research strategy allows the researcher to investigate whether these relationships or associations between sets of measured characteristics, or variables, exist and to what extent they agree or disagree with each other. The degree to which two or more phenomena vary together can begin to provide the researcher with an indication as to the 'extent' to which such variables are associated or related.

Key Point 5.1

The correlational research strategy, also called known as a non-experimental approach, uses measurements of variables to determine whether variables are related to one another.

Reflection Point 5.1

In a study by Lubans et al. (*Journal of Sports Sciences*, 2009, 27: 591–97) a correlational research strategy was applied to examine the relationship between exercise intensity and pedometer step counts in adolescents. It was hoped that such investigation would provide practitioners with guidelines when implementing pedometers into physical activity programmes. A total number of 106 adolescents completed: i) a Queens College step test in order to estimate maximal oxygen uptake; and ii) a 10-minute treadmill trial while wearing a pedometer and heart rate monitor. During the 10-minute trial all participants were instructed to maintain their heart rate between 65 and 75 per cent of their maximum heart rate while running or walking on a treadmill. At the end of the 10-minute period the total number of steps was recorded and then divided by 10 to determine the number per minute.

Findings revealed there to be a positive significant relationship between the number of steps taken per minute during the 10-minute trial and the estimated maximum oxygen consumption ($r=0.44$; $P < 0.001$). The correlation co-efficient was stronger for boys ($r = 0.55$) than for girls ($r = 0.26$). Based on the results of this study, the researchers indicated that achieving around 130 steps per minute could be used as an initial goal to improve fitness.

Characteristics of correlational research

Throughout the study of sport and exercise, a wide range of phenomena is encountered. Such things as physical attributes recorded during physical activity, scores from questionnaires, movement patterns noted during exercise, or observations during play can help the researcher describe and explain different types of sporting behaviour. Through the process of data collection of such wide-ranging variables, the researcher can begin to develop understanding as to how these may relate to each other. This approach to research can lead to questions about how such associations can be used to predict future sporting behaviour.

The ability to make meaningful associations and predict outcomes inherently infers that the researcher is attempting to generalise to a wider population. Through the choice of this strategy, by its very nature, the researcher is being guided to make inference, or generalisation, to a population from which the study sample was drawn.

Case Study 5.1

Alice, a second-year sports science degree student, undertook a correlational study based around 'aggression in sport'. Being a keen basketball player and having represented the university's 2ⁿᵈ team during their BUCS campaign, Alice wished to find out whether there was a link between the aggressiveness of the player and how successful they were at scoring. Previous research had suggested that the more aggressive an athlete is when performing, the more successful they may become.

Through random recruitment of players, 30 participants took part in this study. Each was asked to complete: i) a self-reporting questionnaire to determine their aggressiveness levels during different situations; and ii) a sequence of basketball shots at pre-set distances around the court. For each participant a questionnaire score and basketball score were determined, which were then placed on to a scatter plot. By visually inspecting the plot and then applying a Pearson's correlation co-efficient statistical test, Alice found there to be a strong positive association between aggression and scoring success (r = 0.80, P < 0.05).

Through effective communication of her findings, Alice was able to state in her results section that: There was a significant positive linear relationship between basketball score and aggressiveness (Pearson's product moment correlation, r = 0.80, n=30, P<0.05).

Can cause-and-effect be claimed?

The purpose of applying the correlational research strategy to sport is to assess whether an association might exist between phenomena of interest. By doing this, the researcher can become informed as to the way selected variables alter when looked at together. What the correlational approach will not allow the researcher to do, however, is suggest a 'cause-and-effect' assumption between measured variables.

Consider the example of a researcher finding that scoring more points during a basketball game increased with the aggressiveness of the player. From this, the researcher could make three conclusions. The first and most straightforward conclusion is that by being more aggressive means the player scores more. The second is that by scoring more points players become more aggressive. The final conclusion could be that something else not measured, a third variable, has caused both the scoring of more points and the development of aggressive personalities. For example, the player's stature (i.e. height) may be associated with aggressiveness by giving them more confidence, but may also be associated with more scoring opportunities and therefore more points. It can be difficult to discern the true cause from the measured effect. What can be concluded is that some relationship has or has not occurred between the measures, but what cannot be assumed is that aggressiveness causes more points, or more points cause aggressiveness.

To further illustrate this, assume another researcher identified that golf handicap seemed to be lower the more time a player spent practising. Again, three conclusions could be drawn from this. Firstly, those players who practise more play better golf and therefore score less. Secondly, scoring less may make the player feel more confident and motivated about their game and therefore they practise more. Or thirdly, an unmeasured variable, such as a reduction of overtime working hours, may impact on both variables. Working less overtime may make the player more relaxed, which impacts positively on their golf score, but also they have more available free time to go and practise their golf game.

Making conclusions based on the associations observed and measured clearly involves the assumption that many unmeasured variables are also likely to impact on the way the findings are evaluated. As the researcher is unable to measure all of these within one single research project, they must therefore accept the fact that there will be certain phenomena that can impact on the associations and that they should not claim that a cause-and-effect relationship exists. What they can determine, however, is the strength of agreement between the two variables they have selected.

Reflection Point 5.2

When collecting data from either a laboratory or real-world setting, it is important to recognise the data fitting into two camps. One is that the data can be in the form of numbers (i.e. quantitative) on the nominal, ordinal, interval or ratio level of measurement. So, for example, the number of football players within teams across different age groups (nominal), the score of an anxiety test scale (ordinal), ground temperature at golf tournaments (interval), or the running speed at lactate threshold (ratio). The other camp sees the data in the form of personal qualities or characteristics that cannot be given a number. Examples come from data collected from patients who provide their opinions on the effectiveness of a physical activity referral scheme or a hockey referee's reasoning for the penalty corner in a match. Because our data may fall into either of these camps, we must make sure the correlational approach can be applied.

The researcher should only apply the correlational research strategy when collecting data that can be expressed as numbers. Although 'quality' or qualitative data may allow for some degree of informal association between phenomena, the researcher cannot apply any numerical method of association between the variables. Choosing to select variables, which may be biological (e.g., physiological characteristics such as age, body mass, stature or resting heart rate) or psychological in nature (e.g., intelligence, personality or attitudes) present the researcher with a range of data that may help to understand the intricate links that exist within sport.

Learning Activity 5.1

Based on your most recent series of practical sessions, recall eight phenomena (i.e. variables) that you encountered – these may be biographical, physiological or psychological variables you either measured or discussed. Next, based on your current understanding suggest a variable that may be related to the phenomena encountered.

Phenomena encountered   **Related phenomena**

For example:

Anxiety levels during competition   *Years of competitive experience*

1. _____   _____

2. _____   _____

3. _____   _____

4. _____   _____

5. _____   _____

6. _____   _____

7. _____   _____

8. _____   _____

Design of a correlational study

Generally speaking, a correlational study is a quantitative method of research in which two or more quantitative variables from the same group of individuals are compared in the attempt to determine if there is a relationship between the two variables (a similarity between them, not a difference between the means). Theoretically, any two quantitative variables can be associated (for example, hair length and 5-km run time) as long as the researcher has scores on these variables from the same individuals. It is important to note, however, that selecting variables to associate must be grounded in previous research and rational logic. Collecting and analysing data when there is little reason to think the two variables would be related to each other is really a waste of time!

Research Focus 5.1

In a study by Nesser et al. (*Journal of Exercise Physiology Online*, 2009, 12: 21–28) a correlational research strategy was selected to examine the relationship between core strength and performance in female soccer players. The researchers' rationale for the study was the fact that since the sport of soccer incorporates the core musculature through running, and kicking, it can be suggested that relationships exist between core strength/stability and performance in this population.

To identify relationships between core stability and various strength and power variables, 16 players completed strength and performance testing prior to off-season conditioning. Each was tested on two strength variables (1RM bench press, and 1RM squat), three performance variables (countermovement vertical jump, 40-yard sprint, and a 10-yard shuttle run), and core strength (back extension, trunk flexion, and left and right bridge).

After determining normal distribution of the test variables, bivariate (i.e. two variables) correlations represented by the Pearson correlation co-efficient were used to identify relationships between test variables. Findings revealed no significant correlations between core strength/stability and the strength and performance measures. The authors concluded that the results suggest core strength is not related to strength and power and that core strength does not contribute significantly to strength and power and should not be the focus of any strength and conditioning program with the intent to improve sport performance.

Selection of participants: More is better than less!

With all quantitative studies, the greater the number of participants the more value the study will have. The reason for this is that the closer the sample size is to the overall population size, the stronger the inference will be. For a correlational study to be of real value the researcher should be aiming to have 30 or more participants as this will increase the validity of the research. However, this is often problematic due to assignment requirements, length of time given to do the project, personal time constraints, cost-associated factors and willing volunteers. This being the case, an attempt to get at least 12 individuals will provide the researcher with a useful set of data that should allow for some meaningful conclusions.

Learning Activity 5.2

Based on Case Study 5.1, Alice was asked to construct both a null and alternative hypothesis. Based on your understanding of these terms note down below what Alice would need to write:

Null hypothesis:

_____

_____

_____

_____

Alternative hypothesis:

_____

_____

_____

_____

Determining associations between variables

Phenomena the researcher evaluates can *relate* in either a positive, negative, curvilinear or neutral way. Considering the type of associations between measured variables provides the researcher with a degree of understanding about how one variable co-varies with another. This ability to collect data from two separate variables using a range of data collection methods, organise them in such a way to unravel a story, and then apply data analysis techniques to interpret the story will ensure the researcher can insightfully report the research findings and make sense of the data.

Positive associations

In a positive relationship, increases in one variable are accompanied with increases in a second variable. Consider the example of a researcher who wished to determine the strength of a relationship between vertical jump height (variable A) and lower leg isokinetic strength (variable B) across an entire cohort of netball players. Based on previous research findings, the researcher assumed that both should increase in association with each other. Following the study they found that as variable A increased so did variable B; so as vertical jump score increased, isokinetic strength also increased.

Further suppose that a researcher wished to discover the relationship between running miles and spend on running shoes. They approached a running club and found out the amount of training and competition miles each member had undertaken in the past 12 months (variable A) and also asked how much money each spent on running shoes over the same period (variable B). It is likely that as the amount of hours spent running goes down, then so should the wear and tear on their shoes, and therefore the amount of money spent replacing them. Findings revealed that this was indeed the case. The runners who were training more spend more money on shoes as they were wearing them out quicker.

Two examples of positive associations are shown in Figure 5.1.

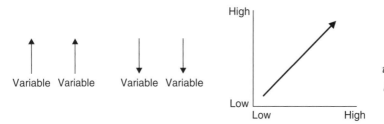

Figure 5.1: Positive associations are found when changes in one variable are accompanied by same direction changes in another variable.

Negative associations

In negative associations, increases in one variable are accompanied by decreases in another variable. Consider the example of a student who was interested in evaluating the association between ball velocity (variable A) and driving accuracy (variable B) in high-handicap golfers. Relating the two variables revealed that as ball velocity increased, the golfer's ability to drive the ball straight deteriorated. By concluding that a 'negative' association existed between the two variables, the student's project supported the notion of a speed-accuracy trade-off in golf driving. Further suppose a researcher wished to determine whether the number of freely accessible open-air playgrounds (variable A) were associated with levels of childhood inactivity (variable B). Through survey and observational data collection processes, findings revealed that as the number of available playgrounds increased, reported childhood inactivity levels decreased.

Two examples of negative associations are shown in Figure 5.2.

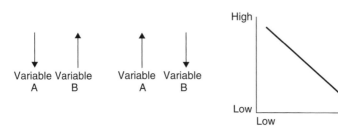

Figure 5.2: Negative associations are found when changes in one variable are accompanied by opposite direction changes in another variable.

Curvilinear associations

In a curvilinear association, increases in the value of one variable are accompanied by both increases and decreases in the values of another variable. In other words, directional changes occur at least once. Some classic curvilinear relationships from a sporting context are the inverted U-theory (Figure 5.3 a), relating to arousal and performance, blood lactate response to incremental exercise intensity (Figure 5.3 b), and the length-tension relationship in muscular force.

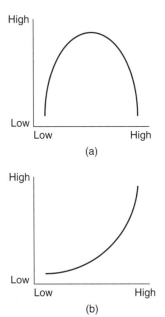

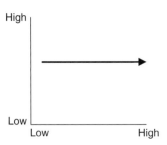

Figure 5.3: Curvilinear relationships are found when increases in one variable are accompanied by both increases and decreases in other variables.

Neutral associations

There are many phenomena that can be measured in sport that simply have no association with each other. For example, peak racket head velocity measured during a tennis serve (variable A) is likely to have little to no association with running velocity at lactate threshold (variable B), or similarly, a basketball player's scoring average over a season should have a neutral association with the length of his shorts!

Figure 5.4: Neutral associations are found when changes in one variable are unaccompanied by changes in another variable.

Reflecting back to previous sections should remind us of the importance of showing how two variables are *related* and the direction of such relationship. Remembering, however, that this does not justify the claim of a causal relationship between the measures does make us consider the full range of conclusions that can be made. There may be a causal relationship, but other explanations usually exist. Remember that the variables may be related because both have a causal relationship with a third variable. So, in the illustration shown in Figure 5.4, if you find that A is associated (i.e. correlated) with B, any of the following may explain the *cause* underlying that relationship:

Learning Activity 5.3

Consider each of the following studies described below. Indicated are whether a positive or negative association was found and the range of explanations to support findings.

Study One
A study of hockey players showed that the longer they had been playing together as a team, the more similar their opinions on social and political issues were.

Positive or negative? Positive

Explanation A:
Players that have been in teams longer could become more similar *or* being more similar may lead to more longevity in the team.

Explanation B:
Having had similar life experiences may have made them develop similar beliefs *and* made them more likely to stay together.

Study Two
An intelligence test was given to all the children in a gymnastics group. The results showed that the longer children had been in the group, the lower their IQ scores.

Positive or negative? Negative

Explanation A:
The gymnastic environment has an adverse effect on cognitive development.

Explanation B:
More intelligent children did not regularly attend the gymnastic group.

Study Three

In a study of British cities, a relationship was found between the number of elite swimmers and the number of swimming pools.

Positive or negative? Positive

Explanation A:
The availability of pools stimulates a greater interest in swimming, which will lead to an increased number of elite performers.

Explanation B:
Both the number of swimming pools and elite swimmers is related to the size of the cities.

Study Four

A football coach found that the more training sessions players miss, the lower their performance level during matches seems to be.

Positive or negative? Negative

Explanation A:
Absent players miss training opportunities to develop.

Explanation B
Players with multiple responsibilities (jobs, family obligations) find it difficult making it to training and also have trouble finding time to train.

The importance of scatter plots

It is often easier to interpret the meaning of collected data when it can be viewed visually. When determining the relationship between two measured variables, the use of a *scatter plot* is the typical way to evaluate the nature of such association. The name scatter plot simply means a way to show scattering of pairs on a graph made up of a Y-axis that goes up the side and an X-axis that goes along the bottom.

Consider Case Study 5.1. The purpose was to investigate the association between basketball score and aggressiveness. The researcher wished to evaluate whether aggressiveness (variable A) was dependent upon score (variable B) and sampled a total of 30 players across a range of teams. With the Y-axis representing one variable (aggressiveness scores) and the X-axis the other (basketball scores), the construction of a scatter plot can represent each participant's points in a visually clear way. As illustrated in Figure 5.5, each point provides a co-ordinate that locates each participant's

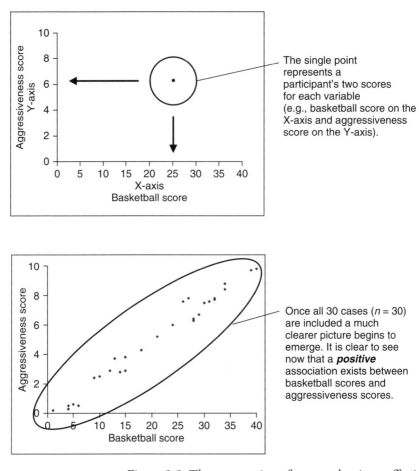

Figure 5.5: The construction of scatter plots is an effective visual way to assess the nature of the association between measured variables.

position. Once all of the data, that is to say, all of the 30 participants' scores are plotted the researcher can begin to identify the nature of the association.

Through the use of a scatter plot, the researcher is able to visually identify the type of relationship between the two measured variables. By applying the descriptions from above, they can conclude at this stage that a positive relationship exists and three conclusions can be made.

1. As aggression increases players score more points.
2. Scoring more points makes players more aggressive.
3. A variable not measured may have caused both the scoring of more points and the development of aggressiveness to increase.

Through the creation of a simple scatter plot using software packages such as Microsoft Excel, Minitab or SPSS for Windows, the ability to visually assess the nature of the association begins to offer even more insight into the way variables may or may not be associated.

Learning Activity 5.4

From what you have learnt so far in this chapter, read each study description and draw an arrow on the graph to reflect the direction of the relationship. It may help to label the axes first.

Study One

Observing a professional football game, Charlie found that as the noise level of the crowd increased (X-axis) the concentration (Y-axis) of the players decreased.

He concluded that the direction was?

Based on Charlie's study, what three conclusions can be made?

1. _____

2. _____

3. _____

Study Two

Collecting data across a series of break-times, Emily found that the more sports equipment provided to the children (X-axis), the more time they spent running around (Y-axis).

She concluded that the direction was?

Based on Emily's study, what three conclusions can be made?

1. _____

2. _____

3. _____

Assessment of association strength

The determination of association direction begins to inform the researcher as to the nature of the relationship, but doesn't tell them all they need to know about relative strength between the measured variables. The importance of determining the relative strength between the two provides them with a degree of confidence as to how one variable may impact on the other. So by being able to evaluate how well the variables relate to each other indicates the degree of association between measured variables.

When the measured variables that are to be correlated are classified as continuous data (i.e. interval or ratio levels of measurement) it is common to select a data analysis technique known as a *Pearson's product moment correlation co-efficient*. When data is regarded as discrete (i.e. ordinal level of measurement), the *Spearman rank order correlation co-efficient* is applied. There are occasions when this is not always the case, for example when the interval or ratio data from one or both of the variables does not possess a normal distribution. When this occurs, it is common to put the data into rank order (i.e. convert it to ordinal level data) and perform as Spearman correlation co-efficient. For more details on why this is done and how to achieve this refer to the further readings at the end of the chapter.

The correlation is a useful approach that will provide the researcher with a co-efficient value (or more often known as an r value). This value will always range from -1 to +1 and reflects the strength of association between our variables. At either end of the extremes, -1 and +1 means that there is a perfect negative or positive relationship between our measures, that is to say, all of the points fit perfectly in a straight diagonal line. As illustrated below in Figure 5.6 it can be seen that for a perfect relationship to exist (i.e. Pearson's r value of -1 or + 1) all the points on a scatter plot will form a line.

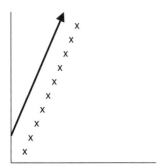 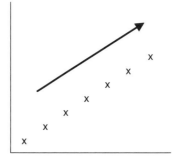

Figure 5.6: As can be seen from these two scatter plots, all of the points form a perfect diagonal line, but are at different angles. Both of these would result in a correlation co-efficient value of + 1 as they are both positive.

The use of these scatter plots is simply to illustrate what the plots will look like in order to obtain a perfect correlation. In the real world, however, it is exceptionality rare to find such a perfect relationship and more common to see positive or negative trends in our scatter plots that provide a correlation value of somewhere above -1 and below + 1.

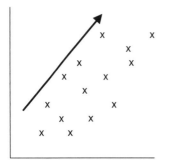 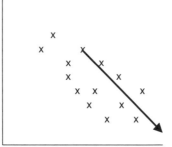

Figure 5.7: Both of these scatter plots show directional trends, whether that is a positive or negative trend. What we see differently here is that all of the points do not form a perfect diagonal line.

Typically, as the points start to spread out, the strength of the association gets closer to 0.0. This indicates that the two variables are becoming more weakly associated. There are exceptions, however, as illustrated in the bottom right diagram in Figure 5.8. Here all of the points are on the same line, however they all share the same value on the Y-axis. This therefore means that although one variable is increasing (X-axis), the other variable is not. This therefore will result in a neutral or no relationship between the measures.

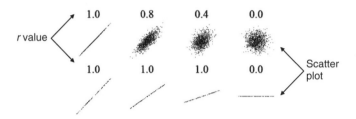

Figure 5.8: Visual inspection of a scatter plot can begin to reveal the approximate strength of a relationship.

Through the use of statistical packages to determine the *r* value for the relationship, it is also common to be presented with a significance value (known as the 'probability' or '*P*' value for short). Such value provides the researcher with a means of accepting or rejecting our null hypothesis. Based on criteria, often set at a 95 per cent level of confidence, the *P* value will indicate to the degree of significance in the association. Without over-complicating the issue here, if the *P* value is less than our critical value (usually 0.05, that is to say 95 per cent divided by 100 per cent) then the researcher can conclude that there is a significant correlation between the variables. So if *P* is less than (<) 0.05 the null statement can be rejected, therefore accepting the alternative hypothesis. Alternatively, if the *P* value was found to be more than (>) 0.05 the null hypothesis is retained. (If you wish to know more about the theory behind this, consult the further reading at the end of the chapter.)

Presentation of correlational findings

The ability to present coherent and accurate findings is fundamental to a successful project. It is often the case that a lot of hard work and time is devoted to organising, planning and conducting the correlational project for it to fall down at the last hurdle by inadequate or inappropriate communication of findings. By reflecting back through the chapter so far, aspects covered that relate to the design, analysis and interpretation should end up in the research strategy and findings section of your work. For the researcher wishing to ensure a comprehensive account is included the following points should be considered.

- The type of association – was it positive or negative? And what was the strength of the relationship? The correlation co-efficient value should be included, which is the *r* value, to support the results statement.

- A clear scatter plot to depict visually the association between the measured variables. Make sure that both axes are labelled and the correct units of measure are included. Think about how the reader will view this so ensure it is well presented – this can make a big difference!
- If significance has been found, make sure to include this. More importantly though, make sure this is linked into the meaningfulness of the significance. Is it of practical value to the reader?
- A statement within the discussion that simply and effectively explains whether the null hypothesis has been accepted or rejected. This will indicate to the reader the researcher's key conclusions based on their findings.

Chapter Review

Throughout this chapter we have investigated when and how to apply the correlational research strategy. By measuring phenomena without the need for manipulation the relationships between variables can be discovered. Although the researcher cannot be certain of cause-and-effect, the degree of agreement in the form of a correlation co-efficient can be determined. The application of the correlational research approach to solving sport-related problems offers the researcher opportunities to uncover relationships about behaviour that may impact on future performance and achievement. By applying a range of sport-related research examples throughout this chapter you should now be able to:

❏ describe the basic concept of the correlational research strategy and provide a range of examples with the field of sport;
❏ list the strengths and weaknesses of this non-experimental strategy, justifying when and when not to use it;
❏ describe the four types of relationships that can exist between variables and link these to appropriate means of determining significance in the association.

(Tick when completed)

Further Reading

William, C and Wragg, C (2006) *Data Analysis and Research for Sport and Exercise Science: A Student Guide*. London: Routledge.
A 'how to' approach to relationships within the field of sport and exercise studies that will help you to understand some of the more complex aspects of the correlational strategy.

Field, A (2009) *Discovering Statistics using SPSS*. London: Sage Publications.
This text will provide the interested reader with detailed explanation as to the statistical importance of the correlational approach. By providing practical illustrations as to how to conduct and interpret the SPSS findings, more developed users of SPSS will find this chapter particularly useful.

Ntoumanis, N (2001) *A Step-by-Step Guide to SPSS for Sport and Exercise Studies.* London: Routledge.

This book provides a valuable description as to how to conduct a correlation in the SPSS package within a sport and exercise science context.

Chapter 6
Survey research strategy

Learning Objectives

It is the process of surveying what is around us that allows us to begin to make sense of our physical and social world and how we operate within it. Through the recording of beliefs, feelings, motives, preferences, occurrences, thoughts or opinions we can start to understand more about sport within this context. By identifying research situations for which a survey research strategy would be applied, this chapter is designed to help you:

- describe the characteristics of a survey research strategy;
- define and explain the linked stages of survey research;
- explain the importance of survey design and sampling techniques to improve this research approach;
- identify the range of data collection method(s) that can be applied to the survey strategy.

Introduction

When we think about the word survey, several thoughts often spring to mind. We've all at some point taken part in a survey or surveyed something in order to gain a better insight or view. We may have in the past been stopped by a researcher wanting us to complete a survey about something or had to survey the surroundings so that we could locate someone or something. We've maybe questioned our tutor in order to gain some feedback about our biomechanics assignment, quizzed a friend about the football result from the weekend, or asked for our lecturer's opinion on our exercise psychology research idea. Whatever the instance, we have used or been asked to use a range of techniques to gather information from people or things in order to find out something of interest.

The value of survey research in sport

Imagine you've been stopped outside a sports stadium following a game by a researcher who wants to know about your match day experiences. She shows you a short typed-out questionnaire pinned to a clipboard and asks you to read the top and complete the nine questions. Offered a pen, you survey the questions, read the instructions and complete the tick-box questionnaire. Passing the clipboard back, you leave the researcher with some insight into opinions and feelings about your day's experience. Take another example: you are out on the golf course with a tricky second shot to a closely guarded green. You survey the landscape around the green to see where the best place would be to hit your next shot. You want to avoid the deep bunker on the left, the tree on the right and the water past the green. Your ability to gain an overall view of the layout in front of you will help you make the correct decision. Through the completion of your survey, you execute the shot with it landing safely on the green.

Key Point 6.1

Survey is defined as a systematic gathering of information from a sample of individuals for the purposes of describing the attributes of the larger population of which the individuals are members.

These two examples, the first viewed as collecting a range of opinions from someone, and the second, taking in an overall view of something, begin to unravel the term survey. In the context of this chapter the term survey is defined as a systematic gathering of information from a sample of individuals for the purposes of describing the attributes of the larger population of which the individuals are members. Being quite a wordy definition it's worth reading it again. In essence, the researcher wants to get the views, opinions, motives, plans or feelings of a group who represent a bigger group; this might be in the form of numbers or words. And systematic because they are following a research process that has clear logical steps. By collecting a range of attributes, the researcher attempts to describe basic characteristics or experiences of the group (sample) that then makes generalisations back to the larger population from which the sample has been drawn.

Case Study 6.1

Harry, a second year BA (Hons) Sport Studies student was undertaking a six-week work placement in a local secondary school. Having observed many PE sessions, Harry became aware that around 50 per cent of pupils were not wearing the 'official' school sports uniform for their PE sessions. Following one session, Harry asked the teacher as to why this was the case, but he did not provide a conclusive explanation. Knowing that wearing of sport kit was compulsory, and with the Head of PE's permission, Harry decided to conduct a small-scale study entitled 'Reasons for official sport clothing non-conformity in Secondary Education PE Lessons'.

Harry selected a survey research strategy as he wanted to collect attitudes about the uniform and its purpose and felt that this approach would enable him to most suitably answer his research question. Through probability sampling, he randomly selected 30 students from the school register (sampling frame) who all received a self-completion closed questionnaire. This occurred once, that being on a Wednesday when all children had their PE sessions. Having successfully collected all 30, Harry analysed the data.

Findings revealed that the key reasons for non-conformity were due to the kit's poor design and quality of material. He recommended that a new PE kit be designed and that a different distributor be selected. Following a presentation to the school teachers, Harry was assigned the task. Harry was pleased to return twelve months later to find that non-conformity had dropped to 5 per cent.

Why conduct surveys?

Phenomena such as age, gender, marital status, previous education or sporting interests, as well as behaviours, individual preferences, beliefs, and opinions offer insight into who people are and what they may be thinking or feeling to a given issue or situation. Intended to probe the individual's point of view, the survey allows the researcher to describe people and what they experience. Although there are many research strategies to choose from, it is often the case that survey research is really the only strategy for asking questions the researcher wants answering from individuals.

Learning Activity 6.1

Survey research offers the opportunity for the researcher to find out about individuals' attributes, behaviours, beliefs, preferences and/or opinions on something or someone. Depending on the nature of the research question they may be interested to find out about quantities or qualities. This activity is intended to start you thinking about how you may construct simple questions in order to find out more about the individual and whether individuals share the same opinions – therefore qualitative. Being able to gain information from the sample is at the heart of survey research and will enable you to achieve your objectives.

Select one topic that you have recently covered in a unit or module. It may be *'performance profiling an athlete'*, *'the use of open questions when coaching'* or *'video analysis and player performance development'*, for example. Having chosen your topic area, imagine you're going to ask a fellow student a series of questions about the topic. Using the headings below construct two questions for each that will seek to find out more about the student's thoughts and opinions. Base one question from a qualitative perspective and the other from a quantitative perspective.

Belief   Preference   Feeling

So, for example, if we had selected *'performance profiling an athlete'* as our topic area, we may well ask the student from a qualitative perspective the following questions:

- How do you *believe* performance profiling impacts on athlete improvement?
- Why may you *prefer* to work with the coach and athlete together rather in separation?
- How do you *feel* your answer to the last question impacts on the performance profiling process?

From a quantitative perspective, we may ask the following:

Do you *believe* performance profiling impacts on athlete improvement?

Strongly disagree   Disagree   Neutral   Agree   Strongly agree

Indicate your *preference* as to the number of athletes you would be comfortable working with during a single session?

1   2   3   4   > 4

How do you *feel* your answer to the last question impacts on the performance profiling process?

Don't know   No impact   Low impact   Medium impact   High impact

Listen to their responses and see how each answer informs you as to the respondent's thoughts and understanding. Think about how the use of such questions can open up to you a wide range of possibilities when wanting to find out about individuals. Which questions do you consider to be open and closed? What impact do these have on the depth of response?

Based on your standardised questions you could now go and ask more students in your group and begin comparing responses. Are they all the same or do they differ? Which student/questions differ and why may that be the case? Which individuals in particular seem to offer similar answers? Is there a reason for this? Do you think their views reflect the general consensus of the class? What about the whole year group?

Measurement concepts

Survey research, like other approaches, involves setting clearly defined objectives for data collection, constructing a suitable research design, preparing a reliable and valid collection method, administering and scoring the instrument, analysing the data and reporting the findings. Similar to other research strategies covered in the book, survey research allows for the collection of both qualitative and quantitative data. The generation of numerical data can mean causal links between measures may be established, offering the opportunity to make statistically supported generalisations to larger populations.

Dependent on the data collection methods used however, collection of qualitative data may provide a more enriched perspective of individual qualities and characteristics. Constructing appropriate data collection instruments, therefore, allows the researcher the opportunity to collect relevant data to answer the key research question. With an appreciation for relative merits of both, survey research, therefore, offers a non-experimental quantitative and qualitative approach that certainly suits the multi-disciplinary nature of sport.

Although survey research can be applied to simply describe a population, such as the number of football clubs with chartered status, the particular support needs of elite athletes, or the motives for exercise adherence, we may also be interested in making planned comparisons between groups or occasions, so, for example, the motives for exercise adherence in two separate locations. We may wish to look at changes over time, so surveying a sports team before and after a series of coaching sessions to gauge their opinions on its success. It maybe that we wish to know the effects of some behaviour – for example, those who take protein supplements to increase muscle mass compared to those who do not.

Research Focus 6.1

In a study by Creswell et al. (*The Sport Psychologist*, 2007, 21: 1–20) a survey research strategy was applied to examine rugby players about their experiences to better understand their beliefs about central factors (influences, antecedents, symptoms, and consequences), processes, and changes within the burnout syndrome.

In-depth interviews were held with nine male professional New Zealand rugby union players a minimum of three times during the season to build an account of their experiences at different points. Interviews were conducted pre-season, mid-season (11–14 weeks after pre-season), and at the end of the season (35–43 weeks after pre-season). A standardised interview guide was used to ensure that participants were all given the opportunity to respond to the same open-ended questions. Interview data relating to a specific context or time periods were content-analysed separately. These analyses were then grouped to form a logical chronological order of events so progression and change could be observed. Both inductive and deductive processes were employed analytically to identify core themes in the data. The use of deductive and inductive processes in tandem ensured that the analysis was guided by both existing theory and the data.

Findings revealed that at some time during the season, reports of players were consistent with descriptions of burnout in previous literature. The researchers commented that these players' reports of reduced accomplishment, physical and emotional exhaustion, and sport devaluation were similar to those described as burnout in earlier interviews with rugby players.

Comparisons, therefore, can play an important role within survey research and we must ask ourselves for every question that needs answering whether a comparison of some sort will be involved and whether the comparison will be possible from the data we intend to collect. If we intend to collect numerical data for instance, knowing whether a comparison is to be made will help us decide on a statistical strategy to make sense of the data in light of the research question.

Characteristics of survey research

Survey research is uniquely placed among the broad array of strategies because of the useful ability to describe the characteristics of a large population from either a quantitative, qualitative or mixed-research approach. With the additional benefit of being able to conduct relatively inexpensive surveys, especially self-administered ones, accessing locations via the internet, email or telephone and the standardisation of the method, survey research is a popular approach to the study of sport. The ability to obtain large sample sizes that improve generalisability as well as the flexibility in deciding how the survey will be administered opens up a wide range of sport-related research questions.

The survey approach can have immense value if it is the researcher's intention to record the prevalence of attitudes, beliefs and behaviours in people. When considered how people display these characteristics through their involvement in sport, the researcher can begin to see how the survey strategy can be used to capture a wide range of perspectives within and between different populations of people. Whether through evaluation of a change over time, differences between groups, or causal links between characteristics, the survey strategy provides an opportunity to delve deep into the perceptions and realities of the world within a sporting context.

Approaches to survey research

Survey research can be approached in a number of ways. From a natural scientist's perspective, prescribing to an objectivist ontological position, the purpose would be to survey people in order to quantify numerical aspects of their physical dimensions, such as age, mass or stature, or social dimensions, such as motivation levels, self-esteem or anxiety. Ascribing to such ontology that views knowledge generation through the collection of universal, observable facts not impacted upon by social factors, the natural scientist would survey and record, providing an opportunity to deductively test a theory through the creation of set hypotheses.

From a social scientist's perspective, prescribing to a constructivist ontological position, social dimensions would not be objectified in such a way. Rather, social phenomena would be considered accessible only through the interpretations of the individuals involved. Clearly, such a survey approach taken by the natural scientist that considers the collection of numerical data to describe social dimensions would be viewed as illegitimate by the social scientist. Instead, a survey approach that allows the researcher to interpret the meaning, significance and value of things, events and people, would provide a more culturally determined set of social phenomena.

The distinctions raised above are important as they have an impact on the approach to survey research. Although the researcher does not necessarily need to prescribe to one or the other, acknowledging their impact on the research question and selected methodology is important. As the nature of the collected survey data may or may not be numerical, depending on the type of instrument used and the way the questions are constructed, the choice to some extent should be carefully considered in relation to the way in which the researcher views reality and the way in which they gain knowledge from it.

Causality and survey research

It is important to remember that with any research strategy, the survey approach does have a number of considerations that may impact on the validity and reliability of the findings. The first key point relates to the assumption of causality, previously discussed in Chapter 4. As mentioned, a survey can be used to collect quantitative data (i.e. numerical data from a questionnaire) and therefore can been treated by statistical analysis to test a theory.

Suppose a theory states that the longer we socialise with others, the closer our values become. Taking an objectivist approach, we decide to test this within a sporting context. We set up our survey research to assess whether the length of time hockey players spend together as a team relates to their values on teamwork. We choose to sample a large range of hockey teams and get players in each to complete a survey, in the form of a questionnaire. This would be specifically designed to find out about their time spent together as a team and their views on working in a team. Having obtained numerical data from the survey, we subject it to some analysis that reveals a negative association between the amount of time spent together as a team and values on teamwork.

By applying the three types of explanation when interpreting associations, we arrive at the following conclusions: i) Because of our different values on teamwork we spend more time together as a team; ii) Because we spend more time together as a team we develop different values on teamwork, or; iii) Another factor not measured altered time spent together and values independent of each other. From our survey findings we can conclude that the theory was not supported. Although we can make this claim we are unable to be conclusive as to the reasons from the association; the answer could be i, ii or iii! By selecting this survey approach that investigates causality between attributes we must therefore tread cautiously when interpreting our findings (refer back to Chapter 5 for more details).

Taking a constructivist approach here, we may have opted for a different survey approach, such as an interview or focus group, which allowed us to obtain more meaning about the players' experiences, how their cultural background impacted on the team and why conflicts may have arisen. These views of reality from the players who experienced it, recorded through instruments that capture subjective interpretation of the social world they function in, is in contrast to the objectivist approach of a natural scientist who would view reality as universal, objective and quantifiable.

Such strength of the survey approach, however, can actually be a disadvantage. With such rigidity in method and design, the lack of flexibility could hinder exploration of deeper social issues that a social scientist may wish to investigate. Thinking carefully as to your overall research question and the type of data you want to obtain when examining your chosen sporting topic can help you to select particular research methods that offer a little more flexibility in approach.

Learning Activity 6.2

The art to undertaking successful survey research is the ability to set out a very clear plan before starting data collection. By establishing a plan, the researcher will be able to align their research question with the most suitable design, population and sampling strategy, research method(s) and data collection tool(s).

By developing a framework early on in the research process the opportunity to develop ideas and adjust the plan in accordance with the researcher's work brief and academic expectations can occur.

When reading through the stages of survey research try and create a plan in the form of a table or list. Use the questions outlined below, as well as aspects from other chapters in the book to help. Chapter 8 that examines the 'Case Study' research strategy, for example, outlines guidance in creating a 'case study protocol', which may be very useful to this process.

1. What will the survey goals be (how do these link to the research question)?
2. What survey design will be used – how will the choice be justified?
3. Who will be selected to take part in the research? What sampling technique will be applied?
4. What data collection method(s) will be used – how will this be constructed? What type of data will be collected (i.e. quantitative, qualitative, or both)?
5. How will the selected instruments be administered?
6. How will the data be analysed? How will the research be presented? Poster, scientific report, presentation, video/web blog, audio recording, newspaper article, summary sheets, etc.?

A step approach to survey research

When undertaking any research study, the process of breaking down the whole into parts will make survey research more achievable. Remember, research involves undertaking a systematic, logical process of inquiry. As with all other research strategies covered in this book, conducting survey research requires just as much diligence in planning. Through developing a structured survey research plan before commencing practical data collection, the researcher will be in a much better position to continuously evaluate the research process. This will aid in foreseeing and resolving any problems well in advance. The knock-on effect will be an improved ability to communicate the chosen design and data collection methods with clarity.

Establishment of the survey goals

Guided by the research question, the decision to select the survey research strategy will be governed by a series of underpinning requirements from the researcher. These will focus on the need to use a methodology that asks people about themselves with the hope to generalise from the study sample to the wider population. The first stage to conducting the survey research based on the research question will be to develop survey goals. This early stage is an important one and ensures the vital connection between goals and a more refined and specific research question. Equally important is that it will allow the researcher to reflect, making sure that undertaking this approach is really the correct choice, or whether a different strategy would be better suited to the research question.

The process of defining the survey goals will draw attention to what knowledge the researcher wants to gain from people and should lead to the development of more specific and meaningful questions and propositions. There are several important questions that need to be asked, which begin the process of survey research formation.

The first question relates to 'who' is going to be surveyed? At this point, having a vague idea as to who the sample will be and their likely characteristics and attributes gives the researcher the chance to plan access to the participants and allows for a sampling strategy to be considered (both of these topics are explored in more detail later on in this chapter). The researcher may want to find out athletes' perceptions and attitudes towards physiological sport science support services offered at a university, the level of weekend members' satisfaction of provision at a local 'premier' fitness centre, parents' opinions of a new basketball kit for the Under 9's team, non-active people's motives for watching sport on television, or school teachers' opinions about the government's drive to increase PE within the National Curriculum. Irrespective of the general question, having an idea about 'who' is to be surveyed (e.g. athletes, gym members, parents, non-active people or teachers) leads to what knowledge is to be collected.

The next question the researcher can ask themselves relates to what characteristics do they wish the sample to have? Is their age important for the study? What about gender? Do they have to have a certain amount of experience, or come from particular local areas or schools? Does their occupation matter? Considering 'who' at this stage will really help the researcher to plan their approach and create the design and sampling strategy.

The third question relates to what knowledge needs to be obtained from the participants. Based on the overall study question the researcher should be able to narrow this down into more purposeful objectives. There may be an interest in exploring opinions, beliefs, motives and/or attitudes towards some aspect of sport, establishing the frequency of events/occurrences at particular locations or determining associations between habit and prevalence, such as the link between smoking and in-activity. Knowing this, a more structured and meaningful plan can emerge.

Consider the researcher who wished to explore athletes' perceptions and attitudes towards physiological support. Having decided who exactly they were targeting, they begin to establish more specifically what knowledge they wanted to obtain. For this study they focused in on athletes between the ages of 18–35 who had a minimum of two years' experience working within a support system. They were interested in topics relating to the support process, the personnel providing the support, the quality and value of the feedback, the relevance of the assessments, and external support networks. By being clear about the sample and the knowledge that was required, the researcher was led to the design stage.

Research Focus 6.2

In a study by Dale (*The Sport Psychologist,* 2000, 14: 17–41) a survey research strategy was applied to describe the experience of elite decathlon participants during their most memorable performance. Seven elite male athletes were purposively sampled for the study. After a level of rapport had been gained with the participants, the researcher began each interview with an open question. This was 'Would you please take a few minutes to think about your most memorable decathlon competition and describe your experiences during that competition'. Following response, the researcher then facilitated the interview with a range of follow-up themes.

Through transcription, content analysis and subsequent construction of connected topics and themes, the researcher concluded that the thematic structures and dialogues revealed similarities among athletes. Of significance was the reoccurring theme relating to distraction during the most memorable performance. It was thought that due to specific coping strategies and the ability to focus on the task at hand, the elite athletes were able to achieve excellence by being well practised at overcoming distractions during competition.

Selecting a survey design

By articulating the survey goals clearly and concisely, a more structured start to survey research will occur: if the researcher begins with muddled goals and is unable to develop meaningful questions, any findings collected and interpreted will also be muddled. The goals will inevitably link to the survey design and data collection methods, so being thoughtful at this stage will ensure the research process is a success.

Establishing goals in accordance with the overall research question starts opening the envelope of research design. When choosing the correct design for the research, the main questions that need to be asked relate to when and how often the survey will be given and to how many groups (irrespective of how the groups were selected or the size – see later when we discuss sampling).

Consider the five studies below. Read them carefully and think about the two questions above: when and how often will the survey be given and to how many groups?

(1) A community-based health centre wished to develop a series of 'Exercise for Life' workshops for dwellers in the local area. In 2005, a student on work experience conducted a survey on a random sample of people to find out and describe what they would like to see covered in a series of six workshops.

(2) A student working on a placement for the local health authority wanted to know how much knowledge people had acquired from the series of 'Exercise for Life' workshops that had now been running for over four years. Surveys were conducted with random selections of attendees from workshops offered in 2006, 2007, 2008 and 2009, and the findings were compared.

(3) The health centre has continually updated its workshop content in line with the changing attitudes of the local community. In 1990, a similar programme existed, called 'Get Fit 4 Life'. Over the course of the year over 1000 people attended. Every five years since, the health centre has been monitoring attitudes by surveying a different random sample of people from the 1990 delivery. This approach means that some people may be surveyed more than once and others not at all.

(4) Wanting to understand how knowledge and attitudes of those participants attending the very first series of workshops had changed, a researcher surveyed a random sample of attendees from the 2006 series and has continued to survey them at the same time of year ever since.

(5) For the last four-month period in 2009, a series of 'Active Living' workshops has also been running at the same time in a neighbouring health centre. A survey comparing participants' knowledge and attitudes towards exercise and diet will be conducted at the workshop's completion from a random sample attending each class.

By reviewing the examples, a difference should be seen in the way each has been constructed. Each requires a survey research strategy, but the design is not the same for all. In fact, each one, as illustrated in Table 6.1 requires a different design type. By working through the table below and re-reading the five studies again, it is clear to see why asking the questions 'when' and 'how often' will the sample be surveyed provides an indicator a to survey design.

A cross-sectional survey design offers a real insight into people's beliefs, opinions and/or preferences at a given point in time. A survey to find out which seats offer the best view at Wembley Arena or people's thoughts on government expenditure in hosting the next Olympic Games, are examples that both use a cross-sectional approach. If the researcher wanted to find out about change, then longitudinal designs can be used. That could be a trend design, where they may survey a group of coaches in summer, another in autumn and another in winter; a cohort design, where they select a sample of children, for example, from a Key Stage 3 class in 2009 and the following year when they have moved to Key Stage 4 take another sample from the same group; or a panel design, where they may select a sample of hockey players and survey them at the beginning, middle and end of the season.

If the researcher wanted to compare groups, so for example, those who only used static machines in the gym compared to those who only used free weights, they could select a comparison design. It is important to be aware that making contrasts between groups can also fall under the banner of the 'experimental' research strategy and such design may take on similar characteristics to that found in Chapter 4.

What was the survey finding out?	When was the survey given?	How often was the survey given?	How many groups was the survey given to?	What were the results?	Design type
Preferences for workshop content	2005: a year before the start of the workshop series	Once	One: a random sample from the local area	Description of preferences	*Cross-sectional* (data are collected at a single point in time)
Knowledge acquired from workshop attendance	Same time of year in 2006, 2007, 2008 and 2009	Four times	Four random samples of participants from different workshops	Estimate of changes in knowledge	*Longitudinal: Trend* (surveying a particular group over time)
Attitude to health and well-being	Started in 1990 and every 5 years after that (1995, 2000, 2005, 2010)	Five times	Five random samples of attendees from the 1990 programme	Estimate of changes in attitude	*Longitudinal: Cohort* (surveying a particular group over time, but the people in the group may vary)
Attitude and knowledge towards diet and exercise	Same time of year in 2006, 2007, 2008 and 2009	Four times	One: the same sample	Estimate of changes in attitudes and knowledge	*Longitudinal: Panel* (surveying the same group over time)
The merits of the two workshop series	Once in 2009; after the completion of the workshops	Once	Two groups: 1) the 'Healthy Lifestyle' attendees and 2) the 'Active Living' attendees	Comparison of attitudes and knowledge	*Comparative* (contrasting one group against another: see experimental research strategy)

Table 6.1: By linking the design to the research question, the research plan for the survey approach can be determined (extracts from Fink, 2008).

Sample importance to survey research

Selecting the sample for a research study is often the one aspect the researcher spends least time considering but is probably the most important part of the design. This aspect tends to be taken for granted, not given the due attention it deserves. A thoughtful and well-planned sampling approach can have a significant impact on the quality of the overall study. Also, by understanding the importance of sampling and the varying techniques that can be used, the researcher can begin to articulate both the strengths and weaknesses of the selected approach. Being able to discuss these issues within the research report will demonstrate to others a critical awareness as to the impact of the research design and, in particular, sampling, on the overall survey's findings.

A sample refers to a part of something that shows the quality or character of the whole. In the context of this text, the sample is a representation of the target population the researcher wishes to investigate. A clear explanation as to the target population allows for purposeful generalisations to be made. For generalisations to be made, the beliefs, behaviours, opinions and preferences of the selected sample should reflect those of the population from which they have been drawn.

Sampling from a target population

The first stage in selecting an appropriate sample is to have a clear picture of the target population. Suppose the researcher is interested in examining experienced football referees, elite runners, active elderly women, PE teaching-assistants or pre-adolescent inactive children? Being able to define the target population will allow them to begin the process of selecting an appropriate sample from the population. Take the first example: they want to survey experienced football referees to establish their views on the use of pitch-side technology during matches. They want to identify whether referees feel that such technological assistance would help or hinder them in their capacity to fairly officiate a match.

To start this process, the researcher would need to begin by considering what their operational definition for the target population would be. If their particular focus was on experienced referees, then a starting point may be how they are defining the term 'experienced'. Should an 'experienced' official have refereed a certain number of games across a wide range of playing standards? If so, how many games and to what standard? Should they possess particular refereeing awards and badges? Or should they have a certain number of years' experience at refereeing? It may be that all these are important and the researcher needs to take all into account when defining the target population. It is through having a clear picture of the target population, that they can start to establish the type of sampling technique they may wish to use.

Once a target population has been selected based on an operational definition it then becomes possible to consider the sample. It may well be the case that the population is so small that all members can be sampled. The researcher may be interested in surveying all 11 employees of a small sports clothing company and therefore it's relatively easy. It is often the case, however, that the target population is made up of many more members and therefore attempting to sample all would be unrealistic both in terms of time and resources. Consideration therefore has to be given to how a sample can be extracted from the target population.

Learning Activity 6.3

Identify *three* different specific populations you may encounter during your daily sporting activities and that may relate to your broader research topic area. These may be coaches, referees, parents, PE teachers, sport officers, tutors, students, performers or assistants. Consider their gender, age, physical and mental ability level and experiences. So for example, you may have encountered senior secondary school PE teachers or junior tennis players.

Now try and describe with as much detail as possible the three. Think about what characteristics people in your chosen population share. What specific skills may they have or need? What environments do they regularly encounter? What activities do they participate in? What physical attributes do they have in common? Do they share social and cultural experiences that group them together? Are you able to describe these?

Make sure to compare your *three* populations and take the time to reflect on how they may or may not be different. What features, qualities and/or characteristics are you using to differentiate between the populations? How may an understanding of your target population(s) impact on your research? And how easy will it be to obtain a sample from your selected population?

Development of a survey sampling frame

How well a sample represents the target population is dependent on the sampling frame, the specific technique used to select the sample and the sample size. Once the population of interest has been defined, the next stage is to determine the 'sampling frame' – which refers to the list of units within the target population from which the sample will be drawn. These units could be people, places (e.g. schools, sports fields, leisure centres) or things (e.g. coaching records, attendance logs, equipment use). Ideally, the sampling frame will be identical to the target population. So, if a researcher wanted to sample leisure centres they would ensure that their list contains all possible leisure centres that fit within their target population operational definition. The importance of this is that each unit in the sampling frame has an equal chance of being included within the sample.

Often, however, this is not the case. For example, a researcher may wish to survey local opinion on the recent closure of a swimming pool by taking a sample of the community (the target population of interest), but doing so by only surveying people who were on the swimming pool's membership register (the sampling frame). In such a scenario, the sampling frame may not represent the population as the register will be biased, based only on those who used the facilities.

The goal, therefore, is to locate or construct a list that includes all members of the target population. This, however, can be extremely problematic, particularly within the scope of an undergraduate research project. Consider a student who wished to target students across a local network of sport colleges. In this instance, they may be able to obtain registers for all those who attend classes, thus are able to generate a representative sampling frame. It may be the case, however, that another student wanted to target their local sports centre. Although they could obtain a list of all memberships, there may be many others that use the facilities and are not registered.

Sampling techniques

This nicely links to sampling techniques. Remember that the process of sample selection should reflect the characteristics and qualities of the selected target population. By selecting appropriate sampling techniques, the researcher can ensure that the sample is indeed representative and therefore corresponds as closely as possible to the population. To maximise this, all members of the target population should have an equal chance of being selected for the sample. Because the ability to generalise from a sample is limited by the sample frame, it is important that within any research report, the process undertaken to determine the sampling frame is detailed, indicating the likely chance each unit has of being included within the sample.

Sampling techniques are typically divided into two clear types. The first type of sampling is referred to as non-probability sampling. In this approach the samples are selected based on a judgement regarding the characteristics of the target population and the needs of the research question. With these techniques, outlined in Table 6.2, the researcher is less confident that the chosen sample will reflect the target population. This will impact on the precision of estimate, that is, our ability to make estimations about the population based on the study sample. By adopting a non-probability sampling technique some members of the target population could have a greater or lesser chance of being selected than others. By opting for this approach, the researcher is increasing the likelihood that the chosen sample will not represent the population. This being the case, the survey's findings may not be applicable to the target population at all.

The second is known as probability sampling and provides a statistical basis for saying that a sample is representative of the target population. In this approach each member of the population should have a known probability of being included within the sample, implying a random chance of being selected, therefore ensuring objectivity in choosing a sample. As outlined in Table 6.2, a range of probability sampling techniques can be deployed, depending on both the research question and the nature of the target population. If the researcher wants to increase the likelihood of the sample reflecting the selected target population then this approach should be selected. What this means in plain talk is that although the researcher cannot be completely confident that the sample represents the target population exactly, they can determine the amount of error associated with an estimate of the population.

Consider a sample of 30 physical training officer recruits from the 200 trainees at the RAF Physical Training Centre. They may well show very similar qualities and characteristics compared to the overall target population. By deploying a random sampling approach each member of the population has an equal chance of being selected and, therefore, the sample should resemble the population. Ideally, the use of all 200 trainees would offer the best solution in eliminating error, but this is often unachievable. Instead, we have to accept the fact that there will always be some degree of discrepancy between the two.

The researcher cannot be completely confident that the sample which they have drawn truly reflects the overall opinions and behaviours of the entire group and, depending on the sampling techniques, may actually increase the differences between the two. So, the greater the sampling error associated with the selected sample, the lower the precision of estimation back to the population. Trying to make generalisations from a sample of 30 back to the overall group of 200 can become extremely problematic and it is easy to make incorrect assumptions and aspersions about the target population based on the survey's findings.

No matter how the sample is drawn from the larger population, therefore, the sample will always misrepresent the population to some extent. It is possible to determine this amount of misrepresentation, known as sampling error. By calculating such error, the researcher can begin to estimate the degree to which the sample and the target population differ. By calculating the sampling error one can become more confident in the predictions and generalisations made as a result of the survey findings. Located on the internet, a wide rage of resources can help establish the sampling error within a research study. Additionally, listed at the end of this chapter, further readings direct you to texts that guide you through this process.

Unless the researcher is able to sample the entire population, sampling error cannot be avoided. It can be reduced, however, by obtaining a sample of sufficient size. This brings us on to the final factor that will determine how well the sample reflects the target population: sample size. The sample size simply refers to the number of units that need to be surveyed for the study. The most appropriate way to establish the correct sample size is to apply statistical calculations that can easily be found by typing in 'sample size' into any popular internet search engine. Heavily dependent on resources and time, increasing the size will certainly increase the accuracy of the sample. However, for every unit added to a sample comes the additional resource drain on time and money.

The researcher must, therefore, decide whether such sampling techniques and the implications of the findings match what they are actually attempting to solve through the research. For many projects, the opportunity to have a large sample population may not be practical or realistic. Nevertheless, understanding the sampling technique deployed and its consequential effect of sampling error will assist the researcher in drawing conclusions about the survey data.

Learning Activity 6.4

How you select the sample from the target population can have a significant impact on the nature of your conclusions and scope of the recommendations. Applying the knowledge you have gained so far in this chapter and referring back to Table 6.1, consider how each sampling technique would impact to the research scenario below.

You want to explore why the fitness suite satisfaction level is low among 'weekend' gym members compared to those who attend during 'mid-week'. The centre has already conducted a questionnaire on all members (target population) and recently purchased new equipment for the fitness suite. For your research study you will undertake interviews and conduct a number of focus groups to find out more as to the reasons for the initial questionnaire findings.

Insert within the questions below the different probability and non-probability sampling techniques covered. Replace the blank space with 'haphazard', or 'random', for example. Try and answer the questions in relation to the research scenario above first, then once you have done this try and apply these to your own research question.

- If I chose a '_____sampling technique' how would I select my sample?
- Will gym members be willing to participate if I chose the '_____ sampling technique'?
- If I chose a '_____ sampling technique' would I be able to generalise my findings?
- What are the limitations/advantages of choosing the '_____ sampling technique'?

Selecting a data collection method

The most important question that now must be asked is what will be the most appropriate data collection method(s) for the research study? This decision will be directly related to the research problem that is attempting to be solved, but also influenced by the sample that has been selected, physical resources, time availability, facilities and cost. The research method, comprising of the collection technique and procedure, allows the researcher an opportunity to record data needed to answer the research question. As the choice of methods can have a large impact on overall survey findings, the ability to think smart will maximise the quality of the data.

Standardisation is the key characteristic of survey research methods that provides a degree of consistency in the instruments used. Consistency here refers to assessment across participants to ensure comparability in findings from everyone involved. It doesn't mean that everyone has to provide the same answer to the questions. Rather, the instrument used and the procedure undertaken to administer the questions should be the same for everyone. Whether that be a

Sample type	Description	Advantages	Disadvantages
Non-probability			
Purposive sample	Selecting units purposely based on specific qualities or characteristics that relate to your research question.	• Inexpensive • Using best available information	• No estimates of accuracy • May miss important elements
Volunteer sample	Actively asking members of the target population to take part in the survey. This involves constructing your sample based only on those willing to volunteer for your study.	• Co-operative respondents • Easy to access	• Not representative of population • May have biased opinions
Haphazard sample	Selecting units due to their ease of contact and availability.	• Available sample • Reduces time and cost	• No necessary relation to population • Sample may not suit study needs
Snowball sample	Previously identified members identify other members of the population.	• Can lead to a large study sample quickly • Can all have similar qualities and characteristics	• All members of the sample may be very similar, distorting generalisability
Convenient sample	The use of a group of individuals or units who are readily available.	• Easy to acquire a study sample • Can be useful as a pilot study sample	• Not representative of population • May introduce unwanted bias
Quota sample	Selected based on the proportions of subgroups needed to represent the proportion in the population.	• Willing respondents • Allows for a quick process	• May only represent the population based on superficial characteristics

Table 6.2: The advantages and disadvantages of sampling techniques.
Continued overleaf

Sample type	Description	Advantages	Disadvantages
Probability			
Simple random sample	Every unit in the population has an equal chance of being selected using a random table of numbers.	• Sample should accurately reflect population • Sampling error can be calculated	• Potentially expensive • Sampling frame required
Stratified random sample	The target population is grouped according to meaningful characteristics or strata.	• Ensures random representation of contrasting groups based on their qualities/characteristics	• Often requires large sample sizes to produce statistically meaningful results
Systematic sample	Every X[th] unit on a complete list of eligible units is selected. Selecting every even, odd, 5th, 10th unit from your sampling frame list.	• No need to assign numbers to participants' names and then look them up (as in random sampling)	• If inherent ordering is apparent may bias sample
Cluster sample	Natural groups or clusters are sampled, with members of each group sub-sampled afterwards.	• Allows for more concentration of sample by first grouping unit together (clustering)	• Labour and time intensive • Requires a large initial population

Table 6.2: Continued

questionnaire, a series of interview questions or the running of a focus group, without such standardisation, analysing trends and patterns of data within or between samples would be meaningless. Without uniformity of approach any differences observed within a sample may be, for example, down to the procedures and tools used rather than underlying population differences.

Suppose a researcher was interested in children's physical activity levels and the identified problem focused on why many young people seem to reduce their physical activity levels once they finish compulsory schooling. Through a process of narrowing the problem down, the researcher would form a specific question; say the impact of local amenities and events on continued activity involvement in this target population. They have been able to get access to a local sample of 30 post-16 school leavers aged 17–19 who have all volunteered to take part in the research study. They opted for a cross-sectional design and applied a volunteer sampling strategy. At first, they obtained details about all that was locally available to the school leavers so that they could begin creating some specific questions to ask them.

At this point, the researcher decided on both the technique and procedure that would best capture the school leavers' thoughts on this matter. They knew that there were a number of instruments and techniques that could be used, namely questionnaires, interviews or focus groups, and a range of ways these could be administered to the group, that being face-to-face interviews, individually or in groups (focus group); telephone interviews; self-completion questionnaires on printed paper or questionnaires administered electronically via the internet or email. They wanted to make sure they got as much quality information from all by allowing them the opportunity to explore openly all of their thoughts on the issues. They were aware, however, that they had a very short timescale and would be collecting and analysing all the data alone.

If you were in this situation what choice would you make? How would your choice impact on the quality of your data? Is one instrument or technique better than any others on this occasion? Would you be able to use more than one? And, if so, how would you organise this? How best could you administer or conduct this to ensure quality in your responses? Is one approach quicker than any others considering the time constraints? Is one instrument or technique easier to evaluate than the others? How may this impact on the findings in relation to your initial research question? These are all important questions to think about when considering which research method to opt for.

Data collection instruments

As has been experienced before, the way in which we gain information from people via the questions we ask them can have a significant impact on the quality of their responses. Just think back to the last time you filled out a self-completion questionnaire for example. It may have been an end of year sport biomechanics unit evaluation or part of someone else's final year dissertation. In either case, the data collection instrument used may have required you to provide an answer to a pre-determined question, probably by ticking a box or maybe writing in response in a few lines.

Based on your own experiences consider the following questions: How easy was it to fill out? Were you able to understand all of the questions? Was anyone available to help you if you didn't understand? What did you do if the answer you wanted to give did not fit the answers provided? Was there space for you to add extra comments? Were all the questions closed?

How about an interview? You may have had one in order to get onto your sports course, or as part of a 'careers in sport' module. This may have been individually or in a larger group. To be successful here requires a clear understanding of the questions asked so effective communication of an answer can be given. By being asked either general or more specific open style questions allows you to give more subjective answers. The interview gives you and the interviewer much more freedom and flexibility in the way it unfolds.

Think about the last time you had an interview and consider these questions: How did the questions link? Did they allow you to evolve your answers throughout? How were you supported if you didn't understand a question? Were the questions more open than closed? Did you feel you had more freedom to express your thoughts and opinions? Did you have more opportunity to elaborate on the interviewer's questions? What feedback, in the form of verbal and non-verbal, did you receive during the interview? How did this make you feel? If there was more than one of you, were you able to put your point of view across? Did the interviewer engage all in the process? Were some members more dominant than others? Were your views shared by others?

Reflecting on our own experiences is an important process and will help us in our decisions. What is important, however, is that ultimately the decisions made should ensure the researcher is able to maximise data in order to answer the research question. The questions the researcher wants to ask the participants through the instruments used can influence the type of responses obtained. Whether a questionnaire, interview or both are chosen and how these are administered will dictate the nature of the participant's responses. Add into this the style of questions asked, so 'open' or 'closed' (open allowing the respondent to reply however they wish, while closed offering a set of fixed answers), and instruments can be selected in order provide the researcher with a large degree of response variation.

Table 6.3 opposite illustrates the range of data collection techniques that can be used in order to collect data. In addition, the type of procedure that is applied to administer the instruments will also impact on the nature and scope of responses received from participants.

Responses to questions

An important point to consider having selected a data collection approach is whether the type of instrument selected matches the type of response required. Consider a researcher who was interested in establishing adults' attitudes on the impact of aggressive behaviour in football, shown on television, has on children who watch and play it. In order to collect the data, they decided to choose a self-completion questionnaire that required the adults to answer a series of closed questions and rate their responses on a scale of 1 to 5 (i.e. Likert scale). They administered the questionnaire and following data collection presented the findings numerically. Because they opted for closed questions using a number scale to record attitudes, they found it difficult to fully explore the reasons lults felt the way they did.

wing a quantitative approach, the researcher may have inadvertently missed the y to identify the subjective deeper experiences of the adults. If they had taken a

Data collection procedure	Data collection technique	Advantages	Disadvantages
Face-to-face (individual/group)	Questionnaire, interview, focus group	• Personal contact allows for checking in understanding • Allows for elaboration if not clear • Flexibility of questions • Rapport building	• Time associated with administration and analysis • Interviewer bias can impact on responses • Cost of travel, printing, etc.
Self-completion web-based/ electronic/email	Questionnaire	• Cost-saving • Ease of editing/data mining • Fast delivery time to respondents • Potentially quicker response times • Novelty through use of images, colour, fonts on web-pages	• Samples could be linked (access) • Confidentiality • Layout/presentation issues • Need for very clear instructions • Obtaining email addresses • Respondents need computer access • Emails easy to delete
Self-completion paper-based/mail	Questionnaire	• Allows respondents to answer at their leisure • No researcher bias involved	• Time associated with delivery to and from • Level of understanding • Detailed instruction required • Response rate
Telephone	Questionnaire and interview	• People can be contacted fast over the phone • Can lead to a better response rate than mail surveys	• Lengthy calls can cost • Lacks familiar personal approach • Responses can be misinterpreted • Difficult to record responses' accuracy – introduces bias

Table 6.3: Typical data collection methods used during survey research.

qualitative approach, they may have gained greater meaning behind their numerical responses. In this instance, numerical representation of attitudes failed to reveal all. Because of the way the questions had been constructed, the adults were unable to fully communicate their attitudes and opinions to the researcher. Although some nice data was collected through the use of the self-completion questionnaire, the way in which the instrument had been set up (i.e. closed questions) did not really allow the researcher to fully answer their research question.

A better approach then may have been to include several open-ended questions, allowing the adults the opportunity to expand and explain their answers. Time, resources, and the researcher's ability permitting, they could have constructed individual face-to-face or focus group interviews providing a more enriched account of the adults' true feelings and beliefs. Words that express their own subjective thoughts could have provided a better picture than numbers. The type of data analysis that then would have taken place would not have been descriptive or statistical in nature, but qualitative, exploring narrative and content. By recording the interviews, for example, and then transcribing, coding and interpreting the data would have offered a different insight. So the extra time and effort spent on this could have provided a much clearer picture as to the attitudes of the adults and led to more meaningful conclusions being drawn.

Learning Activity 6.5

Take time when constructing the data collection approach. You may be lucky and be able to use questionnaires already constructed, such as those commonly used in sport and exercise psychology or physical activity. If this is the case just make sure you know how it functions, what data it will produce and how you will analyse and interpret this. Which ontological view does this approach fit into and does it link to what you want from your research?

If you have to construct your own instrument or develop a focus group of interview questions don't be put off as this is a straightforward process. Refer to the end of chapter readings for a range of texts to support you in this. Your most important ally is your tutor, so make sure you seek support soon in the research process. By indicating on your research plan at the beginning whether an instrument needs developing, you will give yourself plenty of time to construct, pilot and amend your instrument and technique ahead of the main research study.

To help you in this process you may want to ask yourself the following questions:

- Are questions easily understood by the respondent? How will you check this?
- How long will the instrument or process take? How many questions?
- Do respondents know how to indicate a response? Will this be explicitly indicated?
- Will respondents understand what they have to do? Will there be clear standardised explanation?
- Will privacy be respected and protected? How will you ensure this?
- How will information be recorded and collected? What technique will enhance accuracy?

Conducting the survey

The administration of the survey, whether it is a postal questionnaire, face-to-face interview or focus group must be carefully considered before commencement. As is typical with survey research, a pilot study should have already been undertaken to enhance the instrument and increase familiarity in techniques such as question asking, note-taking and recapping. It is at this point that the researcher must recognise their own skill set and knowledge base and be realistic as to their level of experience in conducting surveys. Seeking and receiving additional training and advice from a tutor may therefore be paramount.

As will probably be found when administering the survey, there is often a reluctance to take part. This can be for a number for reasons. These may range from scepticism, competitiveness or survey fatigue to dislike of form-filling, assumed lack of time and/or privacy. How and where the survey is conducted can therefore have an important impact on the number of responses and involvement with the research. Asking people in the High Street on a busy Saturday afternoon about their views on a local swimming pool development may not provide the findings hoped for. Similarly, trying to explore a golf coach's thoughts on the coach–player relationship in his golf shop may be a little awkward for him and his members. The setting, therefore, will impact on the quality of input from the respondent.

The manner and style of the interviewer when approaching people will also dictate the nature of their responses. How they communicate both verbally and non-verbally throughout the data collection process may alter the respondent's own perceptions, thoughts and opinions. The researcher must ensure neutrality throughout, not attempting to direct responses or force their own opinions on to respondents. Interviewer appearance is also important; would you feel more comfortable openly talking to a smartly dressed professional student or a scruffy sports-kit wearing student? Think about how others would perceive you and the impression you give. How may this impact on the successfulness of data collection? What impact will this have on the respondent's willingness to support your research?

If administering a questionnaire, the way in which this is sent could impact on the success rate. The issue of 'response rate' and 'non-responders' is of particular importance when using questionnaires and therefore implementing strategies can help increase the rate of return. Response rate is simply calculated by dividing the total number of returned questionnaires by the total number administered then timing the answer by 100. So, if a researcher sent out 50 questionnaires to a local junior football club and received 29 back then they would have a response rate of (29 ÷ 50) x 100 = 58 per cent. In an ideal situation we would have a response rate of 100 per cent but practically this very rarely happens, particularly as a sample size goes up.

Structuring the survey report

Irrespective of the way survey research is presented, whether it is a poster, scientific report, presentation, video/web blog, audio recording or newspaper article, the structure should follow a similar pattern and include the key aspects of the selected research strategy. With a clear expression of objectives linked to the research question, the project must justify the reasons why a survey approach was applied above all others. The researcher must make reference to the target population providing an appropriate operational definition. The sampling frame, sampling technique and likely sampling error should also be included. The selection of research design (e.g. cross-sectional, longitudinal) needs to be expressed and justified, as well as the data collection instruments and the procedures that relate to their administration. This should include the total number in the sample, attrition rate (if applies) and the process of survey collection. Finally, detail should be included that conveys the data analysis techniques likely to be used. These may be descriptive or statistical in nature.

Chapter Review

Throughout this chapter the wide-ranging survey research strategy has been encountered and dissected. This non-experimental research approach, which employs questionnaires and interviews, attempts to understand more about people's sporting attitudes, beliefs, opinions and demographics. Through the implementation of selective sampling techniques, instrument design and administration, the researcher is able to establish relationships between factors and determine how attitudes change over time. By covering both social and natural sciences, the survey research approach offers flexibility in design and method while maintaining a logical systematic structure throughout. It is this very reason that makes the survey strategy incredibly valuable to the researcher interested in sporting behaviours and their meanings. By using a range of sport-related research examples throughout this chapter you should now be able to:

❏ explain the key characteristics of the survey research strategy;
❏ define and explain the linked stages of survey research;
❏ understand the importance of survey design and sampling techniques to improve this research approach;
❏ identify the range of data collection method(s) that can be applied to the survey strategy.

(Tick when completed)

Further Reading

Bryman, A (2008) *Social Research Methods*. 3rd edition. Oxford: Oxford University Press.
This is a particularly useful research methods textbook that complements this chapter well. Packed full of practical activities, clear diagrams and comprehensive explanations, aspects relating to data analysis and survey instrument construction are of value to the reader palling on undertaking a survey strategy.

Vaus de, D (2008) *Surveys in Social Research*. London: Routledge.
A comprehensive book that takes the reader through the complete survey research process. Although lacking in relevant sport-related examples and illustrations, looking beyond this, *Surveys in Social Research* will offer all that is needed for anyone undertaking survey research.

Chapter 7
Observational research strategy

Learning Objectives

By identifying research situations for which an observational research strategy would be applied, this chapter is designed to help you:

- review the characteristics of an observational method;
- appreciate which observational strategies suit which kinds of research questions;
- be able to select an appropriate observational strategy based on your specific research question;
- identify the varying roles the researcher may play in observational research and their implications to research outcomes;
- understand how observational study reports may be organised to help communicate research findings in a clear and coherent way.

Introduction

We collect all our data through observing the facts that we can see. Strictly speaking then, all research can be classified as observational in nature. What separates this approach from others covered within this book are the series of primary assumptions that govern how it is conducted and the generalisations developed as a consequence. Solely involving the researcher making observations, the use of this strategy in sport is extremely valuable. Through the systematic inquiry into the nature and qualities of observable group behaviours the researcher can learn what it means to be a member of a group and how those being observed interact with others to form social connections.

The value of observational research to sport

Directly observing is a fundamental part of learning and is an important part of the discovery process for us as researchers. By observing sport performers before, during and after competition, coaches delivering individual or group sessions, sport-related practitioners in their own workplace, gym-users during their workouts, children during formal PE sessions or participants in a biomechanics research study, we are able to establish meaning to the way people behave in a range of situations. Providing us with unique insights into complex social structures and interconnected behaviours, the application of the observational research approach to sport can offer the researcher a Pandora's box of opportunities. Understanding groups in their natural sporting or workplace environments, away from control and manipulation, provides the researcher with an extremely valuable opportunity to play a number of roles within the research setting and use a range of research methods to collect data.

Reflection Point 7.1

Observational research refers to a non-experimental approach, which involves the direct observation and measurement of behaviour that may occur in a range of settings. Data collection methods can be broadly categorised as primarily quantitative or qualitative based on the nature of the research question. Qualitative observation research emphasises collecting in-depth information on a small number of individuals or within a very limited setting; quantitative observation research emphasises data collection on specific behaviours within larger groups that can be easily quantified.

Although the observational strategy may appear very simple, a great deal of thought is required to ensure the researcher is able to make accurate and meaningful observations. We can all stand on the sidelines of a pitch and make a few notes about the way players respond to the referee's decision or watch a runner and comment on her technique as she changes pace. To fully explore the behaviour we are observing however, whether that be the social interactions, identities and interconnected relationships on that pitch or movement sequencing, timing and rhythm during the run, we must approach this in a much more systematic way. The reason for conducting observational research may range from a desire to learn about behaviour to a research attempt to test a specific proposition drawn from a theory of human behaviour.

Learning Activity 7.1

Observing behaviour and recording it accurately is a key goal when applying this approach. The purpose, therefore, of this activity is to help you become more aware of the different observational skills required when looking at someone's behaviour. It should also allow you to recognise the systematic and selective nature of observation and how your own feelings and knowledge may influence what you notice.

Observe a person who is sat in front of you for three minutes and write down ten statements that describe the person and his or her behaviour. Once finished, answer the following:

1. Which statements describe the observed as a person (physical characteristics, etc.)?
2. Which statements describe the person's behaviour?

Now observe a sport performer in action for three minutes (the internet may provide you with a good video clip) and again write down ten statements that describe the performer and his or her behaviour. Once finished, answer the following:

1. Which statements describe the sport performer as a person (physical characteristics, etc.)?
2. Which statements describe the sport performer's behaviour?

Now you've had the chance to observe a range of people from very passive to very active, try to compare and see what observational skills were required for each. The following questions may help you:

• Which observation was easiest to do? Why?
• Which observation provided the most raw materials for description? Why?
• Consider the order of your statements for both observations. What does this tell you about what is most important or apparent to you?
• Try to compare your observations with those of another student. What differences or similarities do you notice? How do you explain these? How can you use this information to assist you with your own observational project?

As with other research approaches that occur in natural settings (e.g. case study and ethnographic), away from controlled conditions, the observational research strategy attempts to gain a holistic or whole perspective of the study group. Conducting the research in a natural environment attempts to ensure that freely occurring behaviour is maximised and not contrived or artificial. For example, observing the behaviours of sports centre staff to a sudden influx of members may provide a valuable insight into management processes, staff capabilities and physical resource provision. By artificially constructing this situation by asking a group to suddenly appear all at once and then observing the staff's response removes unanticipated behaviours the researcher may really be there to observe and record. Observing over a period of time allows for a more natural take on the staff, their interactions with members and each other, and their collective behaviours during busy times. Through freely occurring behaviour across a less manipulated approach, the researcher can then begin to offer solutions to problems that really exist.

Unlike the experimental research strategy, the observational approach is not concerned with having straightforward, right or wrong answers. Furthermore, changing the study direction is quite common because there may be more than one question and new ones may appear as progression is made through the research process. For this very reason, such naturalistic approaches to research are often avoided by students and their tutors alike. The very thought that the research direction and question are unknown, means for many that this is not a viable and valid research approach.

Such a conclusion is drawn more because of a lack of insight than the robustness of the approach and accepting that with all dynamic systems change is inevitable, the observational strategy is fundamental if we are to know more about sporting behaviours.

Case Study 7.1

Erin, a third year Sport and Development Coaching student found university sport-team trials at the beginning of term intimidating occasions. Put under pressure with a lot riding on selection, her experiences, as well as that of others, had not been positive. Hoping to help coaches make the 'trials' experience more positive for new players, Erin decided to conduct her final year research study in this area. By observing behaviours exhibited during these trials, Erin aimed to identify what could be the cause of these perceived feelings. She hoped, as a result of her research, that a framework could be developed that offered an inclusive and supportive set of guidelines that could be applied during sporting trials.

Erin selected a systematic approach to her qualitative observation research, whereby she attended all trials across a range of sports and observed behaviours at critical points throughout. Each trial ran for 90 minutes, so players, coaches and assistants were observed for selected time periods (i.e. 15 minutes each) at the start, mid, and end points of each trial. By applying this event sampling design, she took an observer-as-participant role, which allowed some slight involvement with the group while recording their behaviours. On data collection templates she had previously piloted Erin noted down all linguistic, extra-linguistic, non-verbal and spatial behaviour throughout each time period.

After each trial, Erin collated all the observation templates and made detailed notes of her findings. Once all the trials had been completed, Erin was able to identify several common themes that related to player status, confidence levels, experience and a lack of personal acknowledgement by coaches. As a consequence of Erin's research, she was able to present her Athletic Union with a series of recommendations that could be implemented when conducting sporting trials.

Characteristics of observation research

The observational approach in many ways is unique to other strategies encountered within this book. Although we have already discussed that all research uses observation in one way or another, the nature of this particular research approach provides the researcher with unique challenges that are not always encountered when other approaches are applied. The very nature of observational research requires the researcher to take on a specific role with the intention of observing and then capturing social behaviour as accurately as possible. In considering their involvement with any selected participant(s), therefore, they must consider how the degree of personal contact and insight into the participant's 'world' may influence the validity of the findings; that is to say, how they interact with the participant(s) and how their involvement may alter their behaviour.

Take the example of a researcher, who wishing to understand players' behaviour when being issued with a red card, wanted to offer more advice to officials in order to assist them in diffusing aggressive behaviour. If the researcher, as participant in the football game, knowingly intimidated and provoked other players, thereby creating an unnatural response, the observable behaviour would not necessarily represent that normally displayed when issuing for an offence. If another player, however, not knowing about the ongoing research (i.e. unobtrusive), had instigated provocation then any response would represent behaviour within a more naturally set social context.

It is important, therefore, that the researcher understands the role they play in the research and how this can impact on the research setting. They must ensure their role is 'empathically neutral' and that they do not cast their own beliefs, views, goals, experiences, values or research biases on to the research participants. They have a moral and ethical responsibility as the researcher and must, therefore, consider their important position and how it can impact on the research and the generalisability of findings. Be aware that altering the naturalistic behaviours and social interactions observed through the researcher's presence impacts on the very purpose of why they are there in the first place.

Research Focus 7.1

In a study by Mesquita et al. (*International Journal of Applied Sports Science*, 2008, 20: 37–58) an observational research strategy was applied to examine the coaching behaviours of youth amateur volleyball coaches within the practice environment. In order to describe and categorise the information transmitted by the coach, the researchers systematically observed coaching behaviour within the teaching/coaching settings. By using an Arizona State University Observation Instrument (ASUOI) comprised of 14 categories, seven of which were directly related to the instructional process (i.e. pre-instruction, concurrent instruction, post-instruction, questioning, physical assistance, positive modelling, negative modelling), the researchers observed 11 coaching sessions; one per coach. The procedure used for data collection in the study was event recording, which refers to a cumulative record of the number of discrete events that took place within the coaching sessions within a specified time.

A total of 6401 recorded behaviours were observed from the 11 training sessions. The results showed a predominance of instructional behaviours such as pre-instruction, concurrent instruction and post instruction (35.94 per cent). However, the researchers reported that the amateur coaches in the present study showed a lower use of instructional and praise behaviours compared with that of top-level professional coaches as verified in earlier studies. The results highlighted the contextual and specific nature of the coaching process, which emphasised the need for a deeper analysis concerning the coaching behaviours in relation to the substantive content demonstrated by the coach as in relation to the type of practice.

A further factor to consider when applying this strategy to answer a particular research question relates to the focus of approach. Observations can, broadly speaking, be split into two categories: macro and micro. Macro refers to the observational activity that encompasses a broad focus, viewing the group 'as a whole' and observing all activity; for example observing a cricket team during their entire innings, or a swimming squad throughout a training session. Focus at a micro level, on the other hand, uses small and highly specific behaviours as the unit of observation. The researcher may wish to observe the cricket team only when they're in a huddle after a wicket or the swimming squad between exercise drills. It is important to recognise, however, that these two broad categories are not mutually exclusive. For example, the researcher may use the macro approach at the start of a project and change to the micro as their familiarity of this approach increases, and an understanding of the participants and their environment grows.

One of the unique factors of observation is the length of time the researcher spends in the field. Typically, the amount of time depends very much on the research question and the role assumed by the researcher, as some roles (covered later on in the chapter) require the researcher gaining a degree of rapport with people within a given situation and setting. What will also dictate the time allocated to this is the defined period the researcher has been allotted to complete a project. When considering how long is needed with the selected participants, the time taken to plan needs to be factored in. By being realistic as to what can and cannot be achieved in that time will prevent unnecessary decisions being made. Prolonged time in the research setting needs very careful planning and therefore careful consideration when designing a study is essential.

What is often neglected in the planning, and is the distinguishing characteristic of this approach, is the process of entering and leaving the field of study. Again, it is very likely that the research question will dictate this and it will be a relatively straightforward process. There may be projects, however, that require a much more calculated entrance and exit strategy, particularly if the researcher has created strong bonds with the group being researched.

Types of sporting behaviour

One of the most important questions that should be asked during an observational study concerns the behaviours that should be observed. The very nature of this question lies at the heart of any research project and knowing the type of behaviours that are desired will allow for, not only focus within the research question, but also selection of the most appropriate research methods. The spin-off to this is that the researcher will be more productive during data collection and be able to articulate their findings more accurately.

If we think for a moment about a sporting event we recently watched or took part in, we could probably outline a long list of the behaviours we observed. Before you move on, just stop for 60 seconds and consider all the behaviours you witnessed at that event. Make a mental note of them all now. Once you've done that try and group them based on similar characteristics: e.g. were the behaviours observed through speech or were they displayed through physical form?

Behaviours we observe with our senses provide us with a window into the complex world of how people function, feel and interact when playing or engaging in sport and exercise. Remember the social world is multi-dimensional and as a researcher our primary goal is to be aware of others – watching, listening, and waiting to record what we observe. Hopefully, during the brief exercise above, you would have noticed that behaviours can easily be categorised based on key characteristics. These will range from emotional constructs such as sadness, surprise, anger or fear to more physical manifestations such as pushing, pulling, kicking, hitting or throwing. What you may not have recalled were behaviours linked to linguistic or verbal communication. The type of speech, such as the words used to express thoughts and feelings, the loudness or quietness of voices, the pace of speech and possibly the emphasis placed on certain words or phrases can tell us a great deal about behaviour. The way the father angrily speaks to his son after the football match, the softness of voice used to console a performer who just lost out on a medal, or the emphasis or intonation on positive affirmations used by the coach during a half-time talk can all provide us with a real insight as to what the participants may have been thinking, based on the outward behaviour they were exhibiting.

Having a clear idea as to the type of behaviours that may need to be observed when in the field, allows for the construction of appropriate operational definitions ahead of data collection. As illustrated in Figure 7.1, four main behavioural types exist, each likely to be encountered during observational research. Recognising each and knowing how participants may exhibit these is vital to effective data collection.

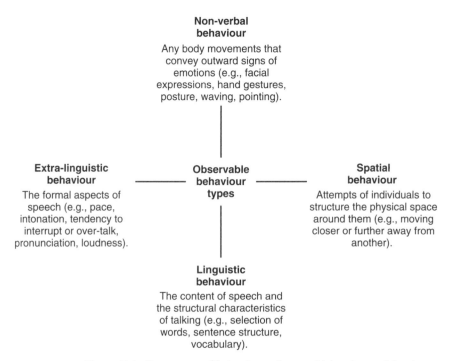

Non-verbal behaviour
Any body movements that convey outward signs of emotions (e.g., facial expressions, hand gestures, posture, waving, pointing).

Extra-linguistic behaviour
The formal aspects of speech (e.g., pace, intonation, tendency to interrupt or over-talk, pronunciation, loudness).

Observable behaviour types

Spatial behaviour
Attempts of individuals to structure the physical space around them (e.g., moving closer or further away from another).

Linguistic behaviour
The content of speech and the structural characteristics of talking (e.g., selection of words, sentence structure, vocabulary).

Figure 7.1: Four types of behaviour that could be observed by the researcher.

Reflection Point 7.2

The next time you tune into the sports report on television, try and watch out for these four types of behaviour exhibited by the newsreader. Is there one that is more predominate than the others? How many behaviours have you noticed and how often do these occur? Do you find one type of behaviour harder to recognise then the others? What techniques could you use to improve this? Does the newsreader have particular idiosyncrasies, that is to say specific behaviours that may be unique to them? Do the behaviours tend to follow a pattern; a scratch of the arm after a pause in speech, for example? If so, what meanings could we make of this?

Having had a go at this, now construct yourself a data collection form. Think about all the information you want to collect while observing the newsreader and try to build that into your form. Leave plenty of space so you can write comments and timings. Now repeat the exercise and see whether you are able to capture more of the behaviours exhibited. Has this approach made a difference? What differences have you noticed? How could you adapt such an approach for your project? Can you identify the limitations of this approach? What solutions could you develop to resolve any difficulties?

Naturalistic versus systematic observation

The first decision for the researcher will be to select the type of observational strategy they wish to implement. Broadly speaking, these fall into two main categories. The first is known as a naturalistic observation that views the observation as an uncontrolled process, whereby the researcher does not structure the observation in any way, rather approaches the observation in an unstructured manner, recording behaviour as it happens in a natural setting – whatever that may be! For example, Researcher A may wish to observe referee behaviour throughout a game. They start the observation at the beginning and record right up until the final whistle. They do not stop for breaks, pauses in play, or periods of inactivity, they simply record everything that they observe with their senses.

The other category is more of a controlled approach and is known as systematic observation. These are more careful observations, being more specific and less global than the naturalistic approach. The systematic observation is structured with more purpose; whether that is specific events, incidents, types of behaviour, or specific time periods. Researcher B may choose to observe the referee only when in a particular area of the pitch, at specific time intervals throughout the game, during times when they are booking a player, during specific pauses in play or when giving instruction/feedback to the players. This way, Researcher B is not observing continuously, rather basing their observations on critical or pre-defined periods or events.

Observation research design

By considering the broad difference presented above, there will be an impact on the data collected and the resultant findings generated. The selection of the most suitable approach, therefore, provides a key starting point in the development of the research design. By working through the decision chart (Figure 7.2) the researcher will be able to determine which design structure will be best suited to the type of research question they may wish to answer.

Consider the three research scenarios listed below. Each one will require reflection back through the chapter and reference to the decision chart in order to find the most appropriate research design. Note that there may be more than one approach that could be deployed in order to answer these research questions. The important point, therefore, is the ability to justify why a particular design has been selected over another and what are its implications to the research scenarios.

Try and answer this question as you go along: Why do you consider your selected design better than the other approaches?

1. As organiser of an annual football tournament, held in a local park, you were aware last year that an increased amount of litter was left behind following the event. Hoping to reduce the amount this year, you place litterbins and notices around the area. You want to find out if people use the bins, where in the park the largest amount of littering occurs, and what exactly is being littered? Which observational strategy could you use to evaluate the successfulness of your 'reduce the litter' campaign?

2. You've just designed a brand new innovative running shoe and want to gauge people's initial thoughts and behaviours when they see it for the first time. Will they be surprised, excited, curious, critical or nonchalant? And what will their body language suggest? Will they be engaged or not really that bothered? Because of its uniqueness, you are very confident that no one would have seen anything like this before, so capturing their initial responses will be really important. Having organised a focus group and fully briefed all volunteers beforehand, you intend to record people's verbal responses and an associate will observe people's behaviour. Based on this approach, which observational strategy would your associate use to establish the non-verbal behaviours of the group?

3. As a basketball coach, you have noticed that irrespective of the player, when in a specific position on the court, aggressive behaviour is displayed. Not wanting to alter the players' behaviour, you ask a friend to secretly make observations each time the undesired behaviour occurs. You want to know what situations occur just prior to the incidences and what form of aggressive behaviour the player exhibits. Exactly where on the court do these incidences occur, and are other players also involved? Which observational strategy could you use to establish what could be the cause of the behaviour?

Now that the three scenarios have been read you should now be able to recognise which design matches each problem. Let us start by reviewing research scenario 1. The most appropriate approach would be to conduct a behaviour trace design and observe the evidence either periodically

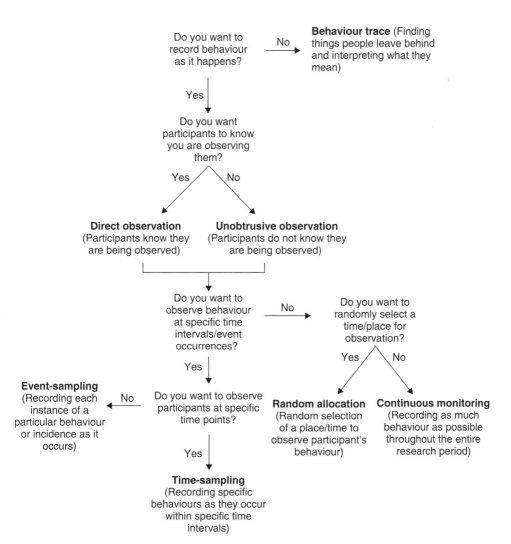

Figure 7.2: Observation research design decision chart.

throughout the event or when the event had finished. You are not so interested in observing the act of throwing litter away, rather where the litter has ended up. You'll need to know where litter is being placed so tracing evidence throughout the event may allow you to change the locations of the bins and notices. Subsequent observations (i.e. longitudinal design) would then provide you with confirmation as to the successfulness of your bin and notice placement. From these findings you can evaluate the successfulness of your campaign and make recommendations to other organisers.

Research scenario 2 would require the use of an unobtrusive event sampling design. Selecting an unobtrusive observational approach eliminates any worry that the players will react differently by knowing that they are being observed. Known as the Hawthorne Effect, participants can react to the attention they receive from an observer and in turn behave differently. Not informing the participants, however, that data is collected may be considered unethical so consideration must be given to protect the participants' rights.

Finally, the research associate in scenario 3 opted for a direct continuous monitoring design that allowed for observation of behavioural responses to the new running shoe throughout the entire focus group session. Selecting this approach would ensure that behaviour could be monitored throughout and not at specified time intervals or as a result of events or incidences. Such an approach does require the researcher's full attention and a varied range of data capture tools would need to be used. With large data generation this strategy can provide a really valuable insight into the behaviours exhibited by the group, but careful pre-observation planning is essential.

Learning Activity 7.2

The purpose of this activity is to help you focus on the first steps of planning a 'direct time-sampling' observational strategy, defining terms and determining whether or not the selected behaviours occur frequently enough to be measured by this approach.

Try and find a coaching session you could go along to where you could observe two players. These may be fellow students during a formal practical lesson, a university or college coaching session or a local team's weekly training meet. Start by choosing six behaviours you expect to see throughout the course of the session. Ahead of your observation your first task is to write down the six and operationally define these. Remember the purpose is to clearly define your terms so others can 'operate' from the same basis of understanding.

Behaviour 1

_____

_____

Behaviour 2

_____

_____

Behaviour 3

_____

_____

Behaviour 4

_____

_____

Behaviour 5

_____

_____

Behaviour 6

_____

_____

Now on a separate sheet create a grid for each player as shown below. Making sure the boxes are large enough to scribe sufficient detail into, write the headings along the first row. Next, in the first column, write in your selected time intervals. If you are observing a 30-minute session for example, you could break down the time into 5-minute blocks.

Example grid for one player based on 7 x 7matrix:

Time (min)	Behav 1	Behav 2	Behav 3	Behav 4	Behav 5	Behav 6
0–5						
5–10						
10–15						
15–20						
20–25						
25–30						

Having planned out your observation sheet, you can go and observe the two players in action. You are trying to observe firstly whether the players are exhibiting the selected behaviours and secondly the frequency of their occurrence. By using a tally mark system you can quickly know how many times these occur within the given time interval (i.e. if a player shows aggressive behaviour three times in five minutes mark it with /// tally marks in the time interval). If possible, try and note down the events/incidence/activities linked to the behaviour.

After doing the data collection firstly re-examine your operational definitions. Identify any changes you feel would make the tally task easier and more precise. Next, consider what the data is revealing. Are there patterns in behaviour? Are the players showing certain behaviours at particular times? Are there any similarities or differences? What could have influenced these behaviours? Are they linked to types of events/activities within the session or other incidences you've noticed?

Also consider how you could make this activity more advanced. What was the exact duration of the behaviour? And was there an observable effect as a consequence? Comparing behaviours exhibited by different teams, sports or age groups may also provide interesting findings. What about observing behaviours on- and off-tasks (e.g.when the player has the football and when they do not)? Are there differences and what could contribute to these? Do these happen at different times? What could the cause of this be?

Role of the researcher

Determining the researcher's role during observational research data collection is an important aspect and must be selected on the basis of a number of key considerations. Remember, the very purpose of the observation is to provide a narrative that informs as to a group's complex social structures and interconnected behaviours. Recording what is observed allows the researcher to tag meanings to recorded behaviours and make sense of social interactions. The way the researcher may, or may not, interact with the participants can therefore have significant implications as to the value of the data and project conclusions. To understand the importance of role the researcher must consider the problem they wish to solve, the participants' willingness to be studied, their prior knowledge of or involvement in the participants' environment, and finally their selected observational strategy.

Putting these points into a realistic context let us consider the following scenario:

While watching a school teacher deliver PE lessons to a particular class, we notice the children's behaviour seems to alter dependent on the session activities. When indoor gym sessions are conducted the group tends to be more apathetic and disengaged, while when quick cricket is selected more engagement and enjoyment is noticed.

To understand this problem further and attempt to establish the reasons why this may be the case, a student researcher decided to apply an observational approach. They selected a continuous monitoring approach observing the class throughout their two sessions in order to collect as much data as possible. They also observed a second class in the same year group doing the same sessions with the same teacher, as this way they would be able to determine whether it is the session activity that causes the behaviour change or some other factor. Unlike the first class, the second class were unfamiliar to the student researcher and they had to consider that the children's behaviour may change in their presence. They therefore selected to observe both classes without their knowledge. Unobtrusively, they positioned themselves in an upper gallery of the sports hall out of sight of the children. Based on their research approach therefore, their role in the project was as a 'non-participant' observer.

Based on the research question, the selected strategy, the group the researcher intends to observe, the environment in which the observation will take place and the influence the researcher's presence may have on the group's behaviour, a role that best suits our research approach must be selected. It is important to recognise, however, that the researcher's role is not set in stone during the research process. Because of the dynamic nature of this research strategy, the role of the researcher throughout the data collection period may change. What is important is that the researcher, as investigator, is able to recognise when this happens, why this happens and how it may impact on the outcome of their research; that is to say, will they still be able to answer their research question? The role needs to be fluid throughout this process and being adaptable will aid in collecting meaningful observations.

Table 7.1 below provides a clear description as to the range of roles the researcher could take during the data collection period. Each role the researcher may take will have an impact on the observed behaviours so it is important to build role involvement into the research plan.

Role	Description	Benefits/drawbacks	Sporting example
Non-participation	There is no level of involvement with participants and the researcher is either not present at the scene of data collection or out of sight of the group.	✓ No influence on participants. ✗ May miss observations due to detachment.	Watching football fans at a match via a closed circuit camera system from a location several miles away from the football stadium.
Complete observer	There is still no level of involvement, but the researcher is present at the scene. There is no level of interaction or participation with the group.	✓ No/limited influence on participants. ✗ May miss observations due to detachment.	Observing a hockey match while stood on the sidelines.
Observer-as-participant	Mostly involved with observing the participants with only slight involvement with the group.	✓ Participants more willing to talk and 'open-up'. ✗ Brief involvement may lead to misinterpretation and bias.	Observing a coaching session, with occasional conversation and physical involvement with the group.
Moderate/ peripheral member	Balance is maintained between researcher and participants, between participation and observation.	✓ Able to view participants from both researcher and participant perspective. ✗ Involvement with participants may be difficult to manage.	Acting as a classroom assistant, supporting PE delivery by taking aspects of the session, while observing the group.

Table 7.1: The role of the researcher in observational studies.
Continued overleaf

Role	Description	Benefits/drawbacks	Sporting example
Participant-as-observer	Researcher becomes more involved with the participants' central activities, but does not commit to the group's values or goals.	✓ Strong bonds can be achieved that unravel deeper behaviours. ✗ Involvement may impact on objectivity of research.	Observing a field-sport first-hand while on a hunt, but not sharing the same values about animal hunting.
Complete participation	The researcher goes native and studies the group in which she/he is already a member. The investigator is seen very much as a member and not a researcher so they do not unnaturally alter the flow on interaction.	✓ The flow of interaction between researcher and participant allows for a true insider's perspective. ✗ Researcher may jeopardise role through over-involvement.	Embracing all the rituals of cyclists, that is to say, shaving legs and using specific jargon in order to find out how they interact and behave as a sporting sub-culture.
Complete membership	In this ultimate role the researcher and participant relate to each other equally in respect to their shared experiences, feelings and goals. In this role, researchers may never return from the field.	✓ Shared experiences allow for full data-gathering opportunities through a sharing of information. ✗ Researcher can be 'contaminated' by the insider's status, beliefs and values, which can bias objectivity.	Living with a tribal group in order to observe the role exercise plays in their day-to-day functioning. The need to share experiences and values is required in order to get acceptance and access to group members. Does not return from the group.

Table 7.1: Continued

Observation research setting

It is important to remember that when observing behaviour, the setting in which behaviours are framed can have an influential effect on the group and on how the researcher perceives them. A child dancing in a hall may change their behaviour depending on their familiarity with the surroundings, those that are present and the type of activities others are doing. A sport performer's behaviour may alter if they are playing home or away, or a crowd's behaviour may be different if they are standing or sitting in football terraces. The skill of describing the setting, prior to observation, will help the researcher make more sense of the actual behaviours. It will also have an important impact on the type of data collection techniques that may be selected as well as the role the researcher may play within the field. By defining this during the planning stage, the researcher's awareness of its potential influence on behaviours can be realised.

Learning Activity 7.3

Try and observe the two environments outlined below.

Description of a sports hall   *Description of a physiology laboratory*

If you are unable to observe directly, remember the last time you were in these spaces. List for each environmental cues that provide you with clues as to the kind of behaviour you might expect or is permitted within each space. Your description should include the physical boundaries of the setting and the arrangement of objects within the setting, i.e. map of setting, layout of equipment, signs, space. You may also wish to consider temperature, other nearby environments that could influence behaviour, the time of day the observations took place, duration of the observation and the date.

   Once you have made two detailed lists consider the following points:

i)   What features of each environment give the strongest cues as to what kind of behaviour is expected and allowed?
ii)   Think about those cues that have certain meanings based on social expectations and those that are purely physical.
iii) Place an asterisk (*) in front of each statement listed that is an environmental cue linked with specific social expectations.
iv)   What are the expected social expectations linked to these?
v)   What does it tell you about how behaviour in settings is defined?
vi)   How does the setting influence behaviour? And how may the setting be rearranged to alter behaviour?

Development of data collection techniques

The purpose of the observation is to describe, not judge, and therefore the data collection process and the associated techniques of data recording must ensure the reporting of accurate descriptions that are factual and thorough. As the researcher observes, their own experiences and biases can easily impact on their interpretations and therefore they must develop sound techniques that allow for objective recording. By recording the setting that was observed, the activities that took place in that setting and the people who participated in those activities, the researcher should be able to generate an accurate account of the behaviours exhibited within the field of study. In attempting to achieve this, they must make sure that the approach taken to record behaviours is directly linked to the research question and the selected strategy.

How data is recorded can take many forms. The most common in observation research is the use of a diary, journal or reporting template that can act as a 'scribble pad' and/or 'prompt' capturing what the researcher is witnessing. As events, incidences or critical moments occur in the field, the researcher must attentively respond to these, accurately reporting without bias or evaluation. The need for clear written articulation cannot be underestimated if behaviours are to be truly captured.

Through the use of diaries and journals, recording occurrences as and when they happen provides an unstructured approach that requires a high level of experience and ability to articulate observations clearly and accurately. Not bound within a tight framework of pre-determined questions or prompts, rather set within a looser collection of themes, the use of a diary or journal can be extremely valuable as it offers more flexibility. Remember though, that this research strategy is dynamic, in that the approach and role may change while in the field. Having the ability to adapt quickly and record the unexpected will offer a more vivid and vibrant description as to the interconnectedness of the participants within their natural setting.

Research Focus 7.2

In a study by Pate et al. *(Journal of School Health,* 2008, 78: 438–44*)* an observational research strategy was applied to describe the physical activity levels in children attending preschools. With millions of young children attending preschools and other structured child development programmes, the researchers' reasons for the study were that little is known about children's physical activity levels while in those settings.

By applying a systematic approach, a quantitative observational rating scale (1 to 5) was used to record physical activity levels in 493 3–5-year-old children in 24 preschools. The observational system assessed physical activity level and activity type (e.g. running, sitting, walking and riding), social environment (e.g. initiator of activity, group composition), and non-social environment (e.g. child location and activity contexts). A minimum of 600 30-second observation intervals were recorded for each child by a group of researchers who took on a 'complete observer' role.

The key results indicated that children engaged in moderate-to-vigorous physical activity during less than 3 per cent of the observation intervals and were sedentary during more than 80 per cent of the observation intervals. Boys were more likely than girls to engage in moderate-to-vigorous physical activity, and 3-year-old boys were more active than 4- and 5-year-old boys.

The researchers concluded that based on analysis of over 2000 child hours of systematic, direct observation, children attending preschools were engaged in moderate-to-vigorous physical activity during only 2.6 per cent of observation intervals. During over 85 per cent of intervals, children were engaged in either very light activity or sedentary behaviours.

The development of observation templates before entering the field allows for pre-defined operational definitions to be embedded in the recording instrument. These will act as reminders, set questions as prompts, timing periods as guidelines and procedural checks as observation progresses. Developing such templates based again on the research question and strategy selection allows for the opportunity to think ahead and plan the time in the field wisely. Maximising data collection is paramount, particularly during short-term undergraduate project work, so thinking about what needs to be collected during the observation will create focus and attentiveness.

It may help by answering the following questions:

- Am I interested in knowing at what time particular occurrences happened?
- Do I want to report the number of times a particular behaviour occurred?
- Do I wish to write more detailed accounts as and when incidences occur?
- Do I want to draw pictures that indicate where events took place within the space?

Whether it is one or all of these, the creation of a data recording template or diary during the planning stage will ensure comprehensive capture of data, without missing or misinterpreting the behaviour observed. Take at look at the observation template (Table 7.2). In this example a very structured approach was taken to ensure the researcher reported behaviour in a clear framework. Created to record coach behaviour throughout a group session, the outcomes detailed down the left-hand column provide the researcher with very clear statements that focus the observation during the set period. Prompting, guiding and reminding the researcher ensures that important aspects are not missed during the session.

As mentioned earlier, the selection of the data recording technique is dictated in many ways by the specific nature of the research question and the observational strategy selected. To illustrate this, let's assume a researcher is applying the observation approach to solve the problem of why during a high-handicap player's golf swing, her right leg straightens causing her to lose rotational torque in the backswing. At this point, the researcher could go to the observational strategy decision chart (Figure 7.2) and work their way through until they reach an approach that would best suit the problem. Based on a decision and the technique they intend to use, they would be unwise to select a time-sampling approach if they were observing the action in real time. With the speed of the movement, it would be extremely likely that they would be unable to see all aspects of her movement and determine the reasons for the unwanted movement. If they were able to use a camera, however, to video the movement and then slow it right down to 100 hertz a second, they

Outcome	Evidence	Notes
Preparation – *Did the coach:* • Welcome players, outline objectives for the activity and communicate ground rules for acceptable behaviour? • Check players' equipment, ability and readiness to participate?		
Safety, organisation and group management – *Did the coach:* • Identify potential risks within the coaching area? • Set up the coaching area and equipment required for the coaching activity safely, reporting any problems to a responsible person? • Identify health, safety and emergency issues and procedures related to the coaching environment? • Conduct the activity in a safe manner? • Ensure the practice area and equipment is suitable for future use?		
Coaching delivery – *Did the coach:* • Motivate, encourage and reward players, using effective communication methods to do so? • Use language and terminology appropriate for the age and skill level of the group?		

Table 7.2: Sample observational template used to evaluate coaching performance during group delivery.

Outcome	Evidence	Notes
• Adapt the activity to the needs of the individual and the group?		
• Use questions to check for players' understanding of the coaching activity?		
• Use a range of coaching styles to promote learning?		
• Deliver the activities in an appropriate sequence and allow enough time for them to be attempted?		
• Provide clear and accurate explanations and demonstrations that support the appropriate technical model?		
• Observe and correct basic faults?		
• Reinforce the key coaching points at appropriate times?		
• Ensure that all players are actively involved in appropriate activities to develop their performance?		
• Provide and encourage opportunities for appropriate feedback?		
• Conclude the activity summarising players' strengths, achievements and progress?		

Evidence – Session plan (P), Observation (O), Questioning (Q), Other (O)

Table 7.2: Continued

then could apply the time-sampling strategy by selecting designated time periods throughout the movement. By opting for a video capture technique here, they are able to select an approach to best assess the player and resolve their problem.

Research Focus 7.3

The internet is a great place to find a variety of observational templates from a range of research disciplines. Spend some time reviewing the different approaches researchers have taken in order to report what they observe. To get you started, have a look at this template developed to record observations made on PE teachers:

http://www.ncpe4me.com/pdf_files/Principals_Assessment_PE_Teacher.pdf

Having selected a few templates, think about how they compare and what differences you may notice. Try and determine what type of behaviours they are focused towards, and begin to consider how you may report such findings if you were to use similar templates during your research project.

Consider another research example that illustrates how the research question and related strategy have a very important impact on the choice of recording technique(s). A student researcher wished to observe movement patterns throughout an entire 60-minute PE session in the hope of determining how much hall space is actually utilised by the children. They opted for a 'naturalistic' continuous monitoring approach, and next had to decide which recording technique(s) could be used. Their first thought was a video camera. With lots happening during the session, the ability to record the mass of activity onto videotape and then watch it back later initially seemed appealing. In this instance, however, the use of a camera may be inappropriate, as firstly there may be ethical implications, and secondly the student may be unable to obtain coverage of the entire space all of the time. They therefore concluded that this approach may lead to missing data. Likewise, being a lone observer may not allow them to watch all of the class all of the time and again they may miss times when the children occupy areas out of their view. Instead, the student came up with an alternative plan that allowed them to have eyes on every member of the class while watching all spaces in the area.

To achieve this, additional support was needed. By developing an observational template that divided the larger space up into smaller zones, they allocated one zone to each observer. Remembering to provide each with a very clear brief outlining the procedures to ensure consistency, they were able to monitor all the area all the time. Having six zones and six observers meant that each were able to not only record the amount of time spent in each zone, but also the children who were more/less active, and the number of children going into each zone at any one time, and the type of activity that took place in each zone.

Collection and presentation of observations

Whichever data collection approach is selected, the ability to accurately note down observations, either during or after field engagement, will impact on the quality of the conclusions. Taking field notes is a skill that needs development and any pilot study preparation conducted should include some element of note taking. A useful exercise is to team up with someone more experienced and independently observe the same activity for a short space of time. Immediately afterwards compare notes and discuss each other's observations. Consider how they may be different and why that might be the case. Think about the way each has described what was observed and try and develop a wider repertoire of verbs to help describe behaviours more accurately.

Merely reporting that '*the player looked bored*' firstly demonstrates a judgement made and secondly offers very little insight into the player's actual behaviour. Reporting instead that '*the player was looking down at the ground, head tilted to one side, with her hands on her hips and a stooped posture*' reflects what can actually been seen and known. Making an assumption during the observation only prevents the researcher from recording what they really see. Describing behaviour through the use of words requires practise so do not over-estimate the time needed to develop these skills.

If camera or audio recording techniques are being applied during the observation, the opportunity to review the footage later does allow for more time to go through the tapes. Do not leave this too long after being in the field though, as the more time that passes the harder it becomes to recollect information. Evidently, making notes during the observation, supported by recorded data does provide the best solution when and where possible. However, clear articulation through written work is still paramount for effective communication of findings.

An important aspect of observation research is the ability to cut up field notes so that they are able to unravel the themes that have emerged. Sticking them back together can then provide the narrative and meaning behind the observations. Either before, or during the initial stages of data collection, the researcher should have established categories of behaviour linked into their research question. These categories, based on the characteristics of the people being observed and events that occur, allow for conclusions to be drawn based on the initial research question.

Consider Case Study 7.1. Erin, in her project, categorised participants into coaches, experienced players and newcomers, as well as a further category that classified verbal instruction into positive, negative and neutral. As her field research developed she then was able to refine these further. The verbal instruction category, for example, was further classified by the volume of instruction: high, medium and low. After each refinement, the reviewing of the field notes allowed her to develop some tentative themes and narratives.

Once finished in the field, the researcher must begin to unpick or cut up the notes and link in observations into themes that have emerged. The researcher can begin to identify certain regularities or patterns in the data by asking: what type of behaviour was it? How frequently did it occur? What were its causes or antecedents? What were its consequences? Who did it impact upon? What were their responses? By attempting to categorise all of the data collected into some formal account so that such patterns, trends, similarities or differences can be identified, the researcher will then be able to start the task of explaining the meaning behind the observations.

The final written report will be a culmination of the observational approach taken. This will begin with an opening literature-supported rationale for the problem and a clear statement of the research question. Followed by a thorough account of the selected strategy, this section will include an overview as to the nature of the participants studied, the field setting(s) used, the role(s) the researcher played, the observation type and design selected, and the data collection methods deployed. By providing a detailed analysis and interpretation of the data, the researcher will then conclude their report by exploring what the findings mean in terms of further analysis and contextual relevance.

Reflection Point 7.3

By deploying the observational research strategy within your project, you will be developing key employability skills that will have direct relevance to work-based employment situations. Try and reflect on this chapter and your own practical experiences when using this approach and make a list of all the employability skills you are able to demonstrate.

Once you have made a list, try and link these skills to particular aspects of your project work. So for example, if you feel you have developed an 'awareness of cultural differences' throughout your project work, then signpost when and where during your project this happened; so maybe during your field-based observation period where you observed junior sports performers from a range of cultural backgrounds. Following this, attempt to link forward into a range of potential employment situations; choose a career or job you are particularly interested in and think about the role and responsibilities involved. When may you need to deploy these skills and in what situations could this occur? Showing you are able to recognise which employability skills you are developing and being able to apply these to a variety of employment scenarios illustrates an applied vocational awareness.

Chapter Review

Throughout this chapter we have explored a non-experimental approach to research. When and how to apply the observational research strategy will depend on the nature of the research question, and is bound by the desire to understand more about our sporting behaviours and how they impact on our social interactions. By selecting an approach that allows the researcher an opportunity to get closer to the sample, observation research can be extremely valuable in understanding more about sport and exercise in a social context. By recognising the differences between quantitative and qualitative positions, naturalistic and systematic approaches, and the impact the researcher's role may play on data collection, you should now be able to:

❑ describe the basic concept of observation research and know how this approach is different from other research strategies;
❑ describe a naturalistic observation approach to research and discuss how this differs from systematic observations;

❏ list and define the four types of observable behaviours and link to appropriate research methods;
❏ appreciate how the observational strategy decision chart can be applied to help select the most appropriate research design.

(Tick when completed)

Further Reading

Finding additional reading in the area of observation research in sport is difficult and only a few texts make any reference to the observational approach. Listed below are several sources outside the area of sport that may be of value to those wishing to advance their knowledge in this area. The only true way to understand this approach, however, is to have a go and experience it for yourself!

Frankfort-Nachmias, C and Nachmias, D (1996) *Research Methods in the Social Sciences.* 5th edition. Chapter 12. London: Arnold Publications.
A general research methods text for social science studies. Chapter 12 provides a gentle opening into the realms of observational research methods, although no reference is made to sport. The rest of the textbook offers a sound grounding in qualitative research and if this is a field you wish to pursue then well worth the read.

Lee, RM (2000) *Unobtrusive Methods in Social Research.* London: Open University Press.
An excellent text for those wishing to conduct unobtrusive research. Logically set out with clear definitions, useful examples and recommended reading following each chapter. The glossary is particularly useful in clarifying understanding of key terms frequently used.

Lofland, J, Snow, DA, Anderson, L and Lofland, LH (2006) *Analysing Social Setting: A Guide to Qualitative Observation and Analysis.* 4th edition. Andover: Wadsworth Cengage Learning.
Packed full of practical examples, this text will help you with gathering, focusing and analysing your observational data. Set out in a step-by-step fashion, the contents can be easily applied to the study of sport and exercise.

Chapter 8
Case study research strategy

By identifying research situations for which a case study research strategy would be applied, this chapter is designed to help you:

- review the characteristics of a case study research strategy;
- identify the key phases of the case study approach;
- understand how case study protocols may be prepared;
- appreciate how case study reports may be organised to communicate research findings in a clear and coherent way.

Introduction

Studying single or multiple cases in depth provides the researcher with an enriched perspective of an individual, group, programme, organisation or community. By exploring how a case study approach to research can be applied effectively to sport, this chapter provides a guide through the characteristics of the case study strategy. Examining the various types of approach that may be taken, by the end of this chapter you should be able to comprehend the concept of a case study approach to research, identify which approach would be best suited to your specific research question and know when and how to conduct this method to holistically capture your case.

As outlined in Chapter 1, the study of sport has traditionally had a strong emphasis on the quantitative perspective, stressing generalisability, probability, prediction and falsifiability. Several chapters have already explored some of these more traditional research strategies that are deductive in nature. Integral within our study of sport, however, are inductive approaches with a strong emphasis on qualitative elements. Allowing us to ask the 'why' and 'how' questions provides us with a much deeper level of understanding about our case that would otherwise be unachievable through more strictly controlled research strategies.

The value of case study research in sport

In some respect, all research can be considered 'case study' in nature as there is always some case or unit under enquiry. Whether attempting to identify the coach-athlete relationship in swimming, the impact of funding on a local sports club, imagery strategies used by a junior golfer or the force generation patterns throughout a sprint-start sequence, the researcher collects some evidence from a 'research case'. The term 'case study', however, is usually employed to denote a specific form of research enquiry. What really distinguishes a 'case study' from other research strategies is the amount of detailed information or evidence obtained from a case and the way the researcher goes about generalising their findings.

Key Point 8.1

Case study research is a strategic approach that involves the detailed and intensive analysis of a single case. The term can be extended to include multiple-case research, whereby two or more cases are compared.

The case's perspective is central to the research process and therefore the researcher must apply systemically a strategy that allows for the description and explanation of phenomena in its natural setting (i.e. naturalistic). By searching for evidence in a natural context, the researcher is able to look at specific meanings, both of processes that may have led to particular outcomes, and/or changes that may have occurred over time or between aspects within the case. By investigating a case away from precise manipulation and control, seen as a characteristic of the experimental strategy, the researcher is able to see how a selected case operates and ways in which behaviours, events and incidences are shaped.

Case Study 8.1

Shane, a third year student on a BA (Hons) Sport Studies course has been asked as part of a research module to explore the impact of the PE, School Sport and Club Links strategy (PESSCL) on a local school's development. Reviewing the different research strategies on offer, Shane decided that in order to gain an in-depth picture of the school, its members, the way it functions, the policies and the curriculum he would opt for a case study research strategy.

He understood that any findings made as a result of his case study may be difficult to generalise to other schools and he would have to be cautious in his conclusions. While recognising these limitations of this research approach, Shane accepted that in order to gain a level of evidence that would allow him to fully paint a picture of the school he would have to put up with this.

Prior to the commencement of data collection, Shane identified the scope and boundaries of the case. He decided to include only academic and support staff and not involve any external agents allied to the school. He also decided to focus his study on formal school time only and not include any extra-curricular involvement. Having created his case study protocol and a series of case questions to focus on, Shane decided he would spend a total of five days within the school in order to collect as much relevant evidence as possible.

> *While at the school, Shane was able to collect sufficient data to draw several flow diagrams that showed how the PESSCL scheme was being integrated into the school sport delivery. In addition, by reviewing archival records and selected documents he was able to create a list of all the personnel connected within the school (i.e. sport co-ordinators, teachers, teaching assistants and administrators) who were involved with the implementation and delivery of the strategy. Based on this list, he was then able to arrange individual interviews with all the personnel and collect interview data about the effectiveness of the strategy at the school. Finally, Shane was allowed to observe several PE lessons and undertake a focus group with some of the school children and their parents in order to get their view of the scheme and how they felt it impacted on their own personal development.*
>
> *Through his case study research, Shane gathered a varied range of evidence that highlighted the effective delivery of the PESSCL strategy. He was able to make several key recommendations to the school, thereby enhancing the impact. He also created a valuable resource pack that was disseminated to other schools via the local school-sports partnership officer.*

Generalisability of case study research

Attempting to generalise or transfer findings of human behaviour or occurrences observed from natural settings to others has lead to contentious debate among researchers. Questions have arisen centred on the true value of the case study approach in enabling generalisability and whether the results are widely applicable. Unlike experiments, where a high degree of confidence in a causal relationship between phenomena can be achieved, it may be extremely problematic to draw conclusions from a case study and assume all similar cases will behave in the same way. Because of the subjective, naturalistic nature of the case study approach, generalisability of findings should be viewed as a way of approximating future expectations, rather than predicting occurrences and behaviours. The strength of the case study strategy is its ability to create a harmonious relationship between the reader's own personal experiences and the case study itself, facilitating a greater understanding of the phenomenon within its context. This way, any generalisations can be viewed as naturalistic and not predictive. Without such precision and control within this research strategy, how the researcher generalises the findings from a research case to other people, groups, or institutions requires a sharpened ability to communicate findings in as vivid and vibrant manner as possible. Therefore, it will only be through accurate interpretation and clear presentation of results that any generalisation from case study research be possible.

Research Focus 8.1

In a study by Dorgo (*International Journal of Sports Science and Coaching,* 2009, 4: 17–30) a case study research strategy was applied to reveal the content of practical knowledge of an expert strength and conditioning coach. Through such examination, the researcher hoped to enhance the current knowledge base for effective coaching and improve education programmes.

By applying a qualitative case research design, the case (i.e. the participating coach) was selected based on a list of criteria typically associated with expert coaches. Multi-method data collection included observations, interviews, and document analyses. Collected documents included various forms of training plans, such as periodised season plans, and single training-session plans. In addition, handouts and educational booklets provided to athletes were collected. Once data from various sources were separated and organised into chronological order, data from interview transcripts, observation notes and collected documents were all coded. After the initial coding the researcher refined the codes and, for interview and observation data, typed those into the text. Following this, the coded, typed, and printed data chunks were organised into main themes.

Following the data analysis, ten major knowledge categories emerged, which were separated into the Foundational Practical Knowledge and Applied Practical Knowledge clusters. The findings revealed that the participant's set of practical knowledge was structured in several layers and was only partially built on the Foundational Disciplinary Knowledge originating from formal education. Analysis suggested that most aspects of the participant's practical knowledge were developed through field experience, real-life practices, and other professionals. The researcher concluded that coach education programmes should be expanded and modified to reflect all aspects of knowledge used in practice.

Characteristics of case study research

Case study research is somewhat unique and distinguishes itself from other strategies discussed in this book. As already eluded to so far, this approach brings with it a range of specific characteristics that can open up opportunities for the researcher to investigate naturally occurring social situations within a sporting context.

By investigating the holistic and meaningful characteristics of real-life cases, such as an individual, managerial processes, organisations, maturation of systems/policies, a class, a family, a school, a club, a team, a town or even a profession, the research itself is integrated into the practical 'natural' experiences and activities of the selected case. Four key applications of the case study approach that attempt to establish the importance of this research strategy have been previously documented by Yin (2008: see end of chapter reading). These are:

1. the explanation of complex links in real-life settings;
2. the description of real-life contexts in which events occur;
3. the description of events themselves;
4. the exploration of situations in which events create no clear outcomes or consequences.

Through the application of case study findings the researcher is able to seek out patterns and themes 'within' the case. This can then lead to further analysis through 'cross' comparison with other cases.

Case study framework

The characteristics of this approach can be broken down into three key phases that form a framework for case study research. As shown in Table 8.1, a case study framework can be broken down into discrete phases. It is important to recognise that this framework is flexible and should be moulded to

Phase	Stage	Activity	Purpose
Phase One	Getting started	– Define and refine the research question(s) – Begin construction of the case study protocol	– Focuses efforts – Creates guidelines and procedures for the course of the project
	Selecting the case(s)	– Specify population/organisation and set boundaries of case – List what you are specifically looking for in your case	– Sharpens external validity of study – Allows for flexible theoretical development
	Crafting instruments and protocols	– Decide on the data collection methods – Quantitative and/or qualitative	– Strengthens a triangulated approach – Maximises evidence capture
Phase Two	Entering the field	– Data collection and analysis – Flexible opportunistic data collection	– Speeds analysis – Facilitates emergent themes
	Analysing the data	– Within case description – Multiple case comparison	– Gains familiarity with data and preliminary theory generation
	Shaping propositions/ hypothesis	– Tabulation of data for each theme – Search for causes (why) behind relationships	– Confirms, extends and sharpens theories – Builds internal validity
Phase Three	Enfolding the literature	– Comparison with literature (conflicting and similar) – Build discussion around collected evidence and emergent themes	– Builds internal validity, raises theoretical level and sharpens definitions
	Reaching a conclusion	– Summary through 'naturalistic generalisation/approximated future expectations'	– Ends project with final recommendations, reflection and tentative generalisations

Table 8.1: A case study framework (adapted from Eisenhardt, 1989).

suit the specific requirements of a research study. Applied in the correct order the application of such a framework can be an indispensable tool to the researcher. Each phase follows a logical order of planning, doing and reviewing. Phase one enables the researcher to effectively chart out their case study approach, defining the population, case, and data collection procedures. Phase two prepares the researcher for field-entry and describes the stages necessary to conduct successful data recording and analysis. The final phase details the interpretation and implementation of findings.

Designing a case study

The design of the case study provides the blueprint or plan by which the research will be conducted. By setting up a series of guidelines that the researcher follows ensures the implementation of the research methods does not lose momentum and develop into a collection of unrelated components that do not allow for the completion of data collection. Case study research design can be comparative (i.e. compare two or more cases), cross-sectional (i.e. assess one case at a single point in time) or longitudinal (i.e. assess the same case multiple times) and therefore the researcher must consider which approach would most suitably link to the research objectives (refer back to Chapter 2).

If a comparative research design is to be selected, the researcher must decide whether their previous experience and skills, and specific research timeframe, would permit successful completion of the research. When time is a factor, which is often the case with undergraduate research, the single case cross-sectional research design is the best option. This will provide a purposeful amount of evidence that will allow a thorough understanding of the case, expose behaviours, events and/or incidences, and attempt to explain their occurrences. In contrast, a multiple case approach (i.e. comparative design) does allow for comparisons across cases and may allow the researcher to uncover much deeper meaning about the relationship between each case, their similarities, differences and the impact these may have. Similarly, a longitudinal design that may cover a time span of two to five years may not be achievable given the timescale and financial resources of most research projects.

By investigating a case more than once or by increasing the number of cases within any one study the complexity of the research both in research design and evaluation and interpretation of the evidence will increase. It is, therefore, recommended that comparative and/or longitudinal case designs are for those who not only have access to sufficient resources and time, but who have also completed a small-scale single case project and/or appropriate exploratory pilot study work.

Key Point 8.2

When developing the research design for a case study project, it is important to be familiar with the different types that may be selected.

- Cross-sectional case design: a single case is studied at a single point in time.
- Comparative case design: more than one case is studied at a single point in time.
- Longitudinal case design: a single case is studied two or more times across a period.

Preparing the case study protocol

What really makes an effective case study is the preparatory work ahead of the actual evidence collection part. To be successful requires the development of a 'case study protocol' that allows continued reminders about the study purpose, any anticipated problems, mechanisms by which the findings will be collected and interpreted and explanations as to how the case study will be formatted and presented.

To start with, the case study protocol should include an overview of the project. This should contain the project aims and objectives and any relevant case study issues. Factors such as case study boundaries that define the extent of the case need to be included. Breaking down key players, situations and evidence streams, helps the researcher to ensure they focus 'inside' the case and concentrate the research question appropriately. It will also help to describe 'critical incidences' within a tighter framework, that otherwise may be difficult to interpret.

Reflection Point 8.1

When planning the case study protocol remember to consider the following:

- The aims and objectives of the study: what is the project purpose and what exactly will be done to achieve this?
- Case study boundaries: try to consider the edges of the case. How far will they go? If a school is the case, will the boundaries go as far as parents? Governors? Education Authorities? Or just those working within the school (e.g. teachers, pupils, and support staff)?
- What will be included and excluded? Consider all sources of information, from people to documents.
- The key players: who are the participants in the case that need to be accessed? These may be 'gatekeepers' that open access to others (e.g. a coach of a team).

Background information relating to the case can further help shape the case study protocol and help to shape more focused research objectives. Such information may assist in developing a rationale for site/case selection, propositions or hypotheses that can be tested, and maybe the broader theoretical or policy relevance to the enquiry. This again provides the researcher with a continued point of reference during the data collection phase and detracts from the researcher 'losing their way' while collecting the evidence.

By its very nature the case study approach is a field procedure, so obtaining permission of access to the case and study site is vital. The researcher may need to produce documents in advance of any formal entry into the case, so making sure these are prepared is important. It would be likely that the researcher has to present at the very least an outline of the case study protocol, along with ethical approval documents. Further material may be required in the form of a Supervisor notification letter, exact data collection templates and possible informed consent forms.

Having sufficient resources in place ahead of any data collection in the field is paramount. Access to personal computers that can be portable, writing instruments, paper, dictaphones, video recorders and quiet places to write private notes at the site, are all important considerations for effective evidence capture and need to be mentioned in the protocol. Remember, incidences and opportunities may arise sporadically throughout the researcher's time with the case, so being prepared could make a real difference in the quality and quantity of evidence. Where and when possible, making a clear schedule of the data collection activities that are expected to be completed within specified periods of time can help plan ahead and organise both physical time and resources wisely. The case study protocol, therefore, is an indispensable item that all researchers must construct.

Reflection Point 8.2

The case study protocol is a set of guidelines that can be used to structure and govern case study research. It therefore outlines the procedures and rules before, during and after the case research project. Case study protocols also ensure uniformity in research projects where data collection is performed in multiple locations and/or if more than one researcher is involved in the data collection process. By using the section heading and contents below, the researcher can construct a protocol that provides a suitable project framework. By compiling more detail at an early planning stage of the project, the researcher can ensure their preparedness ahead of field entry.

Section	Contents	Purpose
Preamble	Confidentiality issues Documentation layout Presentation/formatting style Layout of protocol	Contains information about the purpose of the protocol, guidelines for data and document storage and final document layout and presentation.
General	Overview of research project Description as to the characteristics of the case study method	Provides brief overview of the research project and the method employed.
Procedures	Initial approach to case(s) – Selection of case(s)	Detailed description of the procedures for conducting each case. These procedures

Continued overleaf

	– Number of cases – Establishing contact Scheduling of visits/ contacts Lengths of sessions Equipment and stationery	should be utilised to ensure uniformity in the data collection process and allow for 'within' and 'between' case comparisons if required.
Research instruments(s)	Qualitative – interview guides/question templates (open and closed questions)/ recording sheets Quantitative – survey questionnaires/data recording collection sheets	To ensure appropriate consideration and instrument structure to facilitate uniformity of data collection.
Data analysis guidelines	Overview of data analysis processes – How data processing will occur Description of 'within' case analysis process (descriptive/ explanatory/ individual case report) Description of any 'cross' ase analysis process Data schema (i.e. themes/ topics) Summary of primary types, sources and purpose Summary of secondary types, sources and purpose Description of data display types that will be used in analysis and reporting	Detailed outline as to the procedures of analysis prior to data collection allows for more focused analytical processes and meaningful data interpretation.
Appendix	Participation request letter University/college ethics approval form Overview of study to non-academic community	Template letter sent to potential participants inviting them to participate. Adherence to institutional ethical regulations.

Preparation of questions for the case

When developing the case study protocol, it can be extremely valuable if the researcher is able to, in advance of field entry, construct a series of case questions that act to remind them of particular points or incidences they wish to explore. By linking each question with a list of probable sources of evidence ahead of engaging with the case, the potential locations of evidence in advance of actual data collection can be identified. By reducing unnecessary disruption to the case and ensuring the researcher retains the study focus, any evidence collected should be more purposefully linked to the research questions.

Take for example a student researcher who was interested in evaluating the efficacy of a county 'Gifted and Talented Junior Sport Development' programme. Say they wanted to find out how the programme was organised and how it was delivered. Who was employed by it, when and how decisions are made, and who makes them? Who are the end users and what are their perceptions? By linking these desired research questions with particular sources of evidence, such as the programme director, the director's immediate supervisor, assistants, organisational charts/frameworks/processes, job descriptions, participants and parents/volunteers and/or coaches, the researcher can begin to create a series of case questions and possible sources of evidence ahead of case engagement. By constructing a table or list that specifies the questions and the potential evidence streams the researcher can be prepared. This will have a knock-on effect as they will have time to reflect on their actions, discuss potential problems with their supervisor and, if required, develop alternative plans ahead of data collection.

Learning Activity 8.1

Imagine that a researcher is planning to undertake case study research to explore the performance-related experiences (i.e. during training and competition) of the GB Track cycling team. In advance of their entry into the field, which will involve a 3-week period at the Velodrome and a 4-week period abroad at competitions, list down all the different sources of evidence that may be available to the researcher. Attempt to identify where these may come from. What data collection techniques may need to be used to obtain this evidence?

Sources of case study evidence

As part of the case study protocol framework, a series of case questions would have already been constructed. Linked into this, possible locations of evidence would also have been established. Consider there to be five main sources of evidence that the researcher is likely to obtain during this data collection phase. These are:

- documents and archival records (e.g. plans, policies, data records, minutes of meetings, contracts);
- surveys (e.g. structured/semi-structured interviews, self-completion questionnaires, focus groups);
- observations (e.g. linguistic, non-verbal, spatial behaviours);
- physical artefacts (e.g. pictures, prints, trophies, awards, memorabilia);
- clinical/non-clinical physical measurement (e.g. cardio-respiratory measures, physical activity levels, etc.).

Dependent on the selected case in question, that is to say, whether it is a single individual or a much larger organisation, the amount and source of evidence is likely to be different. In addition to these five sources of evidence, the researcher could also be collecting important data by capturing video footage, watching films, taking and reviewing photographs, collecting and reading life histories and/or undertaking psychological assessments on participants. In accessing the varied range of evidence streams, the researcher will require a wide range of practical skills necessary to access, collect and process the data.

Entering the case

The researcher's role is to find and evidence as much data about the case as possible. This doesn't mean however that they need to go steamrolling in without any plan. Data collection has to be calculated when and where possible to avoid upsetting the very people who hold the key to the data that is required!

What is important to recognise throughout this stage is that data collection procedures may not always be systematic, as in other research strategies such as experiment or survey approaches. These research strategies are more prescriptive in their logical order or events in collecting data. For the case study approach, the process of collection is much more demanding due to the inherent real-world nature of the case. The need to take advantage of any unexpected opportunities is therefore extremely important in order to capture enriched data about the case. It is during these moments that the researcher is very likely to witness the exact issues they wish to investigate or expose incidences that they seek to understand.

Throughout the collection of data, there are a number of important points that need considering. The researcher will be confronted with newly encountered situations that should be seen as opportunities for data collection. By continually having a firm grasp of the issues that they wish to study allows all encounters to be viewed as possible sources of evidence. Such a grasp focuses the relevant events and information to be arranged into manageable proportions. Reflecting on these events in a personal diary or log will ensure that during the evidence-processing stage, the researcher is able to recall these moments with clarity.

It is often difficult for a new researcher to remain unbiased during the research process. We all have our own values and beliefs that shape us. Encountering new people in a variety of new situations, as in case study research, can lead to such beliefs influencing the way the case is viewed. Such a biased approach affects the researcher's outlook on the case and can have an unwanted impact on the data collection methods they opt for. Furthermore, the researcher may allow such biases to cloud their judgement when they come to interpret and report the findings. Having an unbiased view away from any preconceived notions or ideas will allow for a more open-minded, non-judgemental, sensitive and responsive approach to people and situations as and when they're encountered.

Research Focus 8.2

In a study by Hare et al. (*The Sport Psychologist, 2008*, 22: 405–422) a case study research strategy was applied to explore the perceived affect of personal and situational variables, perception of pain, and imagery ability on the function and outcome of an Olympic athlete. The study adopted a longitudinal case design to examine in-depth an Olympic athlete's use of imagery during rehabilitation from injury, and on return to competitive sport.

By way of a purposive sampling approach, the participant selected was a recent Olympic and World Championship medallist from an aquatic background. To gain an in-depth understanding of these factors, data collection was in the form of semi-structured interviews and questionnaires across three phases of injury rehabilitation, and return to competition. After the transcription and verification of data analysis a number of key themes and categories relating to experiences were revealed.

Findings highlighted that the usage of imagery throughout the rehabilitation period altered and was perceived by the athlete to affect outcome (i.e. personal and situational variables, perception of pain). The researchers in conclusion supported the view that an athlete may use different types of imagery to achieve different types of outcomes during rehabilitation and leading back into competition.

Presentation of case study research

Bringing together all of the evidence collected during case fieldwork is a formidable but rewarding component of the whole case study project. It is here where the researcher can really begin to unravel the narrative of the case and develop the emerging stories about the experiences recorded. Writing up a case study project is often demanding due to the wide range of evidence collected. Developing a structure, therefore, as one would when writing up a more deductive study, isn't so straightforward. It is important that when planning the discussion and analysis, guidance is sought from a supervisor who has constructed the marking criteria. They will be able to provide a detailed picture as to where the emphasis should be placed and particular aspects they may be looking for.

Typically, the discussion will be made up of a chronology. By outlining the order in which things happened during the field exposure a framework is provided. This in turns allows for events to unfold more naturally in the text, with critical incidences linked in as they happened. This approach also offers the researcher an opportunity to make links between incidences and past/future events.

A further aspect that will bring strength to the report will be the logical coherence of the discussion. A chronological account on its own may not highlight all the emerging themes and issues, so the need to emphasise key aspects through cross-referencing will be vital.

Reiterating the research aim and objectives of the project will also allow for a more coherent structure. An attempt should be made to address these and answer emerging questions that developed from the case. Can any kind of generalisations be made or are the findings merely exploratory? Try and think how the end-user, whether a hockey team, yoga club, individual athlete, swimming coach or local authority may benefit from the findings. The application of the project is what will give it real value. Finally, can any potential theories be inductively generated from the study? And could this be applied to other similar cases or tested through future deductive research?

By thinking about the outline, format and audience for the case study report, effective delivery of the findings can be achieved. Remember that the research will lead to large amounts of documentary evidence, in the form of published reports, publications, memos, and other documents collected from the case, so make sure the report is well planned in advance.

Reflection Point 8.3

What to do during case study research	What not to do during case study research
Begin by setting a structure: Always begin by setting out your protocol. Without this you will get lost in the process.	*Misunderstand your question or answer the wrong question:* This needs focus at the very beginning so you understand what you are attempting to do.
Stay organised: When exploring a specific issue, remember what it is and where it fits into the overall problem. Setting out initial questions will help you stay on track.	*Proceed in a haphazard fashion:* For example, not identifying the major issues that need to be examined or jumping from one issue to another without outlining your overall approach.
Step back periodically: Summarise what you have learnt at key times throughout the project and what the implications appear to be. Use a diary to log your progress: it will be invaluable later on in the project.	*Ask for a barrage of evidence without explaining to the participants why you need the information:* Remember, clear explanation will ensure you receive the data that you really need.
Ask for additional information when you need it: But make sure that the participants in the case know why you need the information.	*Fail to synthesise a point of view:* Even if you don't have time to explore all the key issues, be sure to synthesise the point based on where you ended up.

Relax and enjoy the process: Think of the project as both an exploration, journey and problem-solving process. Always focus on actionable recommendations, even though sometimes they may not be the most elegant solution to the problem.

Not asking for help: Whether it is a misunderstanding related to the overall problem, or whether you are struggling with a specific analysis, be sure to ask for help when you need it.

Learning Activity 8.2

By undertaking case study research a wide range of employability skills can be developed and enhanced. Attempt to list the skills you think are needed in order to successfully complete a case study project. Once you have done this explain where these skills are needed in the following employment roles:

- Postgraduate researcher.
- Secondary school PE teacher.
- County sports development officer.
- Personal trainer.
- Physical training officer in the RAF.
- Elite athlete.
- Exercise referral officer.

Chapter Review

Throughout this chapter we have investigated the value and application of case study research to the sporting world. When studying sport the researcher is confronted with a wide range of instances that require a more detailed, enriched account of an individual or group of cases. Not wishing to establish a causal link between variables in a controlled manner, the researcher can select this strategy to capture a case in operation, recording real-world events and incidences. By formulating a well-defined and pre-planned case study protocol, building a range of case designs, and utilising varied data collection methods, this approach can lead the investigator down many exciting avenues within sports research. By using a range of sport-related research examples you should now be able to:

❑ describe the basic concept of this approach and identify how case study research differs from other research strategies;

❏ create a logically structured case study research plan that identifies and defines three clear phases of development;

❏ appreciate how the construction of an effective case study protocol can help guide you through the research design process;

❏ consider the skills required to undertake case study research and how these can be applied to a range of employment roles.

(Tick when completed)

Further Reading

Gearing, J (2006) *Case Study Research: Principles and Practice.* Cambridge: Cambridge University Press.

An extremely useful textbook that has a strong emphasis on collecting evidence from the case. Be aware though that there are not many working examples so you will have to apply the information found within to your own area of interest.

Sport England (1999) *Best Value Through Sport: Case Studies.* London: Sport England. (www.sportengland.org)

A valuable resource for students and lecturers alike. Packed full of sport-related case studies, this document can be used very effectively as a basis for seminar-based learning activities on the case study method.

Yin, RK (2008) *Case Study Research.* 4th edition. London: Sage Publications.

One of the bestselling books when it comes to the case study method. More suited to those wishing to further their understanding of this research strategy, full of examples, but not from a sporting context. Thorough in content and explanation, a must-read if your final year independent project is a case study!

Chapter 9
Ethnographic research strategy

Learning Objectives

By demystifying ethnographic research and demonstrating its accessibility to students, this chapter is designed to help you:

- understand the nature of ethnography and identify the key characteristics of this research strategy;
- describe the ethnographic research process and establish the researcher's role in ethnographic fieldwork;
- apply an understanding of ethnography to sport-related research examples;
- identify the range of research methods that can be implemented in ethnography;
- understand and appreciate a 'cut it up and stick it together again' approach to data analysis and interpretation.

Introduction

As a research strategy, ethnography is ideally suited to investigating dynamic and complex activities that we constantly encounter within difference sporting cultures. From aerobics to windsurfing, sport provides us with a broad array of cultural experiences that offer a real insight into how we, as people, act out our day-to-day lives through sport. With the wide acceptance of qualitative research in the field of sport, such methodological diversity allows for a rich range of research to be conducted. To this end, ethnography extends and enhances our understanding as a way towards examining sporting cultures and the people that form these. Only occasionally are students studying sports courses exposed to the practice of ethnography, and regrettably when this does occur this is often late in their studies.

What is ethnography?

Ethnography is a way of doing research into what is going on in our social world; that is to say, why do people do the things they do. By attempting to understand parts of the world (i.e. the sporting world) more or less as they are experienced and understood in the everyday lives of people 'who live them out', the ethnographic research strategy enables the researcher to find out the way people's lives are meaningful to them on their terms.

At the heart of ethnographic research is the ability to observe and listen to people as they go about their everyday lives. This can help us to understand the way in which they behave or think about their lives and the societal structures and customs they function to and within. Ethnographers are, therefore, concerned with studying people in their natural environment rather than in situations that have been artificially created, as with experimental research. This means that ethnography fits into the traditions of constructivism and is typically inductive in nature.

However, in some instances positivist ethnography may be conducted. This may be the case when measurement is necessary, such as the development of codes, diagrams or categories that map the insider's cultural world as a series of inter-related variables. This approach attempts to capture and objectify social meaning rather than interpretively 'telling it like it is'.

Reflection Point 9.1

Brewer (2008, page 6: see further reading) defines ethnography as *the study of people in naturally occurring settings or 'fields' by methods of data collection which capture their social meanings and ordinary activities, involving the researcher participating directly in the setting, if not also the activities, in order to collect data in a systematic manner but without meaning being imposed on them externally.*

Ethnography in sport

Consider why we follow different football clubs – wearing team shirts, spending money to attend matches and travelling around to different stadiums. And why is it that when in those stands, we respond in particular ways to behaviours we see acted out on the pitch – what do we see as acceptable and unacceptable behaviours? And does this change depend on the group we are with or situation we are in? Our acceptance, for example, may be different when with a bunch of like-minded supporters than with our family. Both of these illustrations, one more obvious than the other, are governed by rules, which we have learned and seem natural to us. Ethnography allows us to look more closely at these rules that make our lives meaningful. By centralising the importance of the meanings and cultural practices of people from within the everyday settings in which they take place, we can create a vivid picture of the way that social life, and the impact sport has on it, is assembled and how it influences the way we live our lives.

Ethnography may be particularly appealing for sport research as it can be used for evaluating applied sport interventions, problem solving in sport, or enhancing multicultural understanding. Let's not forget that sport has its own culture and, within that larger culture, each type of sport (e.g. tennis vs. horse-riding vs. golf), as well as each individual sport team, has a unique culture. To this end, ethnography is well suited for investigating sporting cultures acted out on real-life settings. As wonderfully illustrated by Krane (*Journal of Applied Sport Psychology*, 2005, 17: 87–107) and Sands (*Ethnography in Sport*, 2002, Human Kinetics, Champaign IL) the goal of understanding the lived experiences of athletes and exercisers, through greater understanding of sport culture can provide an insight into the behaviours, values, emotions, and mental states that sport creates in our wider culture.

'Hanging out' with a group of football supporters, for example, will allow the ethnographic researcher an opportunity to see how they go about their day-to-day business and how this may impact on their sporting practices. How may this impact on their commitment to a particular team or acceptance of behaviours that any other time would be deemed as socially or culturally unacceptable? The researcher must become finely tuned to the patterns and processes that make up the social 'sporting' world as well as the 'bigger' picture, remembering that sport does not occur in a vacuum. By unravelling socially constructed standards, rules and meanings, the researcher takes an unbiased view about people's behaviour as being determined largely by the culture in which they live.

Research Focus 9.1

In a study by MacPhail et al. (*Leisure Studies*, 2006, 25: 57–74) the objectives were to present evidence that detailed the key characteristics of the 'specialising phase' through young people's involvement at a sporting club. Young people's socialisation into sport follows a general pattern of sampling, specialising and investing. In the sampling phase children participate in a range of sports for fun and enjoyment. The specialising phase involves more sport-specific skill development and a reduction in the range of sport activities. The investment phase signals a focus on one activity and a commitment to intensive training and competitive success.

Over a 21-month period, a range of research methods were implemented. Observations took place during specialised group training, with interviews being conducted with young athletes, parents and coaches. Field notes containing the results of observations were kept and written up afterwards. Although not a member of the sports club, the researcher did train with the club once a week and carried out observations on another evening. As time in the field progressed and the researcher's presence at the club, attending training sessions and weekend competitions grew, athletes, parents and coaches became more open to discussing socialisation processes with specialising groups.

Findings revealed a number of characteristics linked directly to young people's socialisation in sport at this specialising phase of involvement. These included a reduction in the number of sporting activities being pursued, enjoyment and success, the notion of deliberate practice and the influence of family, school and club support on those moving into the specialising phase. The researchers noted that while some of the key features of the sampling phase carried over to the specialising phase there were subtle differences in how they were practised. The authors conclude by stating how the quality of the sporting experience in the specialising years can increase the likelihood that young people will remain involved in sport.

Characteristics of ethnographic research

Doing ethnography usually means that the researcher has spent some time with usually a small number of people, studied in the place where these people live and function. The data they would have collected will contain accounts of behaviour and speech that occurred in that place. This approach would have been taken as the researcher would recognise that to understand why a person does something they need to be studied in the context of their lives as a whole.

Ethnographic research is characterised by three fundamental tasks: i) observing people's behaviour; ii) studying what people say they do, believe, and think; and iii) interpreting what people actually believe and think. The key characteristics of ethnographic research reveal that there is:

- a focus on a discrete location, event or setting;
- a concern with the full range of social behaviour within the location, event or setting;
- a range of different research methods applied that may combine qualitative and quantitative approaches but with an emphasis upon understanding social behaviour and meanings from inside the group;
- an emphasis on analysis that moves from description to the identification of concepts and theories;
- an approach which is unstructured, in that it does not involve following a detailed protocol. This does not mean that the research is unsystematic, simply the data is collected in a raw form as it happens.

The ethnographic research process

Unlike other research strategies, it is somewhat difficult to break the ethnographic research process down into discrete stages. Because of the flexible, rather 'organic' nature of this approach a continual process of 'planning', 'doing' and 'reviewing' occurs. This 'research process' is merely a series of actions that produce the end results. Although the actions are coordinated and planned they do not fit into a tight protocol, but rather blend together in an adaptable way. With the unexpected twists and turns research in a natural environment presents, the ethnographic researcher must adapt and adopt when necessary.

Structuring an ethnographic study

For the researcher undertaking ethnography for the first time, constructing a plan that documents the research strategy will provide an initial framework to the study. Such a strategic plan of the project sets out the broad structure of the research. With ethnographic research, it is not unusual to have last minute flexible amendments or unanticipated changes to the plan, so careful consideration beforehand can ensure that any changes that are needed are smoothly implemented at any time in the process. The overall structure should contain the following considerations (Brewer, 2008, page 58):

- Outline of the topics addressed by the research with inclusion of the research aims(s) and objectives(s).
- The choice of research setting or 'field' and the forms of sampling employed to select the site/field and people.
- Resources available to the researcher, as well as the time availability. The effects the resources are likely to have on the research should be mentioned.
- The sampling of the time and the events to be experienced in the field.
- Method(s) of data collection.
- Negotiating to enter field (to include details of 'gatekeepers' – those that will allow access to people/settings).
- The nature of the researcher's role that will be adopted when in the field and when interacting with the people.
- The form of analysis to be used, particularly if any statistical data analysis methods are to be applied.
- Details relating to the process of withdrawal from the field.
- Ethical considerations.

Research Focus 9.2

In a study by Choi et al. (*Sport Marketing Quarterly*, 2006, 15: 71–79) the purpose was to investigate what an average spectator at a sporting event visually records in a two-hour span. One of the primary questions was whether the sponsored activities at a sporting venue, such as logo placement, product demonstrations, hospitality centres, etc., actually matched with the interests of spectators. The study utilised a visual ethnographic inquiry, specifically in the forms of photo-journaling and interviewing to examine the interests of the participants at the event. By comparing the actual data (the topic of pictures that the participants took), to the activities that the sponsor offered at the venue, the study hoped to indicate which of the sponsored activities, if any, caught the eyes of the sampled spectators. Such findings would allow for evaluation of the effectiveness of sponsorship activation against the sponsor's objectives.

Seventeen adult spectators were recruited, each taking photos over a two-hour period at an action sports championship. They were asked to photograph the 'most interesting or meaningful scenes', limited to a maximum of ten photos each. Following data collection, they shared the photos with the researchers in one-on-one interviews. After gathering all data, categories and themes from the data were constructed. Categories were determined by reviewing the entire set of photos and were compartmentalised based on repetition and relevance to the purpose of the study. Themes that emerged were: cool signs and graffiti; athletes; friends and family; freebies; music and self-identity.

The findings revealed that the majority of activities that had 'sponsor placement' at the event indeed matched the interests of spectators. An example was that all participants took at least one photo of an athlete in competition. Within each photo the sponsor's details could be seen. With sponsorship placement located on or near athletes, visibility of logo was clear. This is the primary reason that sport marketers are so enamoured with the concept of 'more logo visibility' at sporting venues, with the photos providing enough evidence that logo placement at this event was tactically solid and in tune with the interest of the spectators. On the contrary, the authors found that for three separate participants, several pictures captured images that portrayed a sense of 'me' or 'self'. Of special interest was a stone with the inscription of someone's name and a picture of a shadow created by two friends. Although trivial to many, several found meaning from such abstraction. These photos reaffirmed to the authors that the brands that excel in their sport marketing programmes are the ones that know how to connect emotionally and culturally with people with their marketing programmes.

The authors concluded by noting that successful marketing is all about people, how to move them emotionally, and how to connect with them. The study shed light on some new consumer insights that may eventually guide sponsors to pursue unconventional yet meaningful sponsorship programmes.

The ethnographer's role

The researcher has a choice of various roles when in the field, often using different ones for different locations or groups, depending upon the number of fields being studied, the level of role development, and the nature of the data being collected. The roles we develop and the skills that we use are implicit to what we know by the term research methods. We must see 'ourselves' as one of those valuable research tools we have in our toolkit, ready to be used when we need it. Just like when we pilot and refine our questionnaires, interviews and diagnostic tests, we must also be prepared to refine and pilot ourselves. Because ethnographic research requires the researcher to actually participate and engage with a group, we cannot hide behind a piece of paper, laboratory equipment or computer screen, rather the quality of our data will be directly related to the quality of ourselves. There are essentially two levels of participation that can occur. As already mentioned in Chapter 6, the researcher can become a:

- complete participant, thereby becoming a member of the group and concealing the research;
- participant-as-observer, researching the field while becoming fully involved in it.

The first involves being covert: that is to say, hiding the true intent of the research from the group. The second is overt and relates to being open with the group about the research role and the research nature. It is rarely the case in practice though that such distinction occurs and the degree of covert and overt practice very much depends on how open the researcher wishes to be and the how the role develops among the group.

Learning Activity 9.1

Start by making a list of all the research skills you think are important in being an ethnographic researcher. Consider what ethnography is, its characteristics, and the type of activities you may be undertaking. Once you have done this, rank them based on their importance to you. Choosing the top ten, assign a mark out of ten next to each that represents how you would rate yourself at this point in time. So, for example, you may have listed 'note-taking' within your top ten and rated yourself 3/10 on your note-taking skills at the moment. Be honest with yourself! Now that you have rated yourself for all ten, convert each score into a percentage (i.e. (3 ÷ 10) x 100 = 30 per cent). Look down the list and pull out three that have the lowest percentage. These are the ones that you would need to improve straightaway before you embarked on any ethnographic research.

Speak to your tutor or supervisor about how best you could develop these skills and remember to look online and in the library for support. Once you have improved these have a look at the next three down and make these your focus. Try and identify times within your studies when you are using or have used these skills and try and put into practice what you have learned. Before long you will not only have developed the key skills needed to be an effective ethnographer but also enhanced your employability chances.

It is important for the researcher to consider four main points before embarking on ethnographic fieldwork. These are: ethics (as detailed in Chapter 1); role building and trust; data recording; and field withdrawal. It is important to recognise that as the researcher you will be the outsider to start with, hoping to become an insider quickly. How well you build this role and how that is viewed by others can make or break the relationship with the group from the very start.

Role building and trust

Think about trust for a moment. Trust between you and your fellow team-mates, between you and your coach, between you and your fellow students. How important is trust to you? When you have trust in others and they have trust in you, how readily do they open up and give you information? Developing trust in ethnographic research will allow the researcher to develop a role to such an extent that the group will really open up and provide them with the rich life tapestry that the researcher seeks. Trust is based on honesty, communication, friendliness, openness and confidence-building, and growing trust ensures that, over time, the group you are working with begin to accept you as a researcher. This acceptance will enter the researcher into their group (i.e. become an 'insider') and allow them to gain a deeper understanding of the group's rules, expectations, social processes and standards. In effect, do what ethnography is all about! Without such trust, the group would be closed and unwilling to accept them.

Learning Activity 9.2

Building trust with a group is a process that needs to be continually worked at, negotiated, renegotiated, affirmed and repeatedly reaffirmed. The first stage of the process, however, is in recognising the actions – verbal and non-verbal – that build trust.

Think of a time when you entered a new situation: maybe when you started your course, became a new member of a sports team or club, attended your first freshers training camp or sports trials, started a new exercise class or joined a gym. You would have met new people, whether that be lecturers, gym staff, instructors, coaches, students in higher years, or students just like you. At what point did you begin to trust them, in say what they were telling you? Why did you trust them? What were the reasons? Were there any points when you lost trust? What was the cause? At what point did you feel that people started to trust you? What actions and behaviours you exhibited may have led to this?

The speed in which the researcher's role develops can be enhanced by a number of factors. By learning the 'native' language of the group, the researcher can show the group a level of understanding, acceptance and commonality. Take for example cycling. There are a number of terms commonly used in the sport of cycling, but not in day-to-day language. Terms such as 'through-and-off', 'bonk', and 'bit-and-bit' seem strange to the non-cycling fraternity, but are terms used when talking about cycling and when out cycling in a group. Knowing language related to training, bikes, diet and racing can ensure you build trust and acceptance quickly. By thinking about your own sport, you can probably list several terms or words that may be unique to the activity, or even to your group. Think how accepting of an outsider you would be if they had no idea about your sporting 'native' language?

Research Focus 9.3

In a study by Atkinson (*Sociology of Sport Journal*, 2007, 24: 165–86), who investigated the role 'sport supplements' played on male musculinity, trust was built quickly. An opportunistic chat with a fellow gym-user, who happened to share the same interest, lead firstly to a one-to-one interview and then access to other gym-users who were willing to be involved in the research. The researcher himself had been a regular gym-user for a number of years, understood the 'native' language, recognised social and cultural practices, had a historical perspective of supplement use in sport and had also been taking supplements for nearly a decade. Trust and openness had been developed in a short space of time among the researcher and the participants, and because they all shared a common focus and interest, the researcher was acccepted by the particpants.

In a study by Ollis et al. (*Journal of Sports Science*, 2006, 24: 309–22) a much longer time period was needed to firstly develop trust with the participants, and secondly collect the field data. With the focus being to establish how expertise is developed in rugby referees, an 18-month time period was required to firstly develop relationships and refine data collection tools, and secondly collect sufficent data in order to answser the research question. So that the researcher could be accepted by the group, they attended a number of matches, social events and meetings, as well as being involved with training and development sessions. Trust with the participants would have developed gradually allowing the researcher to become more of an 'insider' with the group.

Do some homework on the history of the sport, so, for example, find out about cycling from a 'big picture' perspective: who's Lance Armstrong and what's his story? And who won last year's Tour de France? A visit to the BBC Sports website would fill you in. What about from a local perspective: what's the local cycling scene like? Have there been any races recently? And how many clubs exist locally? Also find out about the basic structure and function of the culture. What do cyclists do when they go training? Do they have any special rituals distinct from other sports? What about their bikes? Most cyclists are obsessed with these so finding out about all of the components, their functions, different wheels and frames would give you a heads-up as to what standards they would come to expect from their machines.

Data recording

Planning for effective data recording in the field is a key priority for any researcher. With the ethnographer often accessing a wide variety of data through a range of research methods, preparation will ensure that vital opportunities to record data are not missed. The ability to effectively data record during the researcher's time in the field comes down to a number of key factors. It is likely that they will use a number of different data collection approaches in order to collect and process the data, so having appropriate time to consider what data collection methods they are likely to use will save time later. Being able to effectively write field notes, conduct focus groups, operate video and audio systems and make detailed observations requires a degree of patience and practice.

Learning Activity 9.3

To help effectively plan the data recording process prior to field entry, making a list of all the data collection methods that can be employed is a valuable activity to undertake. Based on a compiled list, all of the different ways in which the data could be recorded can then be established. By identifying the strengths and weaknesses of each data recording technique linked to each data collection method the researcher can then begin to justify inclusion or exclusion criteria.

Try and consider the amount of time it may take a researcher in implementation of their data collection methods. This may include the set-up and familiarisation time, and the amount of time it could take to document the data afterwards, and what about the analysis required? Consider access to resources and any additional training they may need above and beyond what they have already received.

Withdrawing from the field

This sounds a little strange, considering how the researcher will exit the field before you've entered it, but integrating this into your research plan is important. The reason for this is that it starts you thinking about an appropriate timescale of exposure with the group, the nature and extent of data collection and what processes you plan to implement to ensure a smooth withdrawal. As this is an important part of the research design, consideration must be given to your physical removal from the field as well as any emotional disengagement from the relationships established. For most short-term research projects (i.e. 2–5 months' exposure time) within the field, the complexities of withdrawal are relatively minimal, and in some cases, the researcher continues to work with the group long after the research has finished. What is important in this instance is that the researcher and the participants are clear when the researcher activity has ceased and further support continues. This will prevent any misunderstanding and ensure relationships are maintained.

Very few published ethnographic studies document withdrawal procedures within the methods sections and natural removal seems to occur in most once a certain degree of data has been collected. It is important, however, to ensure that the process and mechanics of withdrawal are documented within any report. Providing details and justifying the point of withdrawal demonstrates an ethically and morally responsible researcher who has considered the impact that group removal may have once the group has left.

Effective data collection techniques

A central feature of any research strategy is the formulation of data collection methods. To access social meanings, observe behaviour and work closely with participants, the correct choice of relevant collection approaches will allow for effective data gathering in the field. As can be seen in Table 9.1, research methods such as participant observation, interviews, focus groups, video and audio-recordings and document analysis provide the researcher with a wide range of techniques and instruments that will enable a full and in-depth understanding of the group's social behaviours.

Analysis and interpretation of ethnographic data

It is important to recognise that data can take many forms for the ethnographic researcher. Whether numerical lists, extracts from field notes, long quotations from interviews, entries from diaries, examples from observations, transcripts from conversations, graphic evidence from photographs, or sound-bytes from audio recordings, bringing data together in some kind of order requires a systematic and logical process to analysis and interpretation.

By bringing order to the data, organising into categories, themes and units, patterns and associations can be discovered. Any analysis should be seen as a process as well as a research method in its own right. As with most research strategies analysis typically occurs following data collection. With ethnography, the analysis of data should be seen as an iterative process and one that occurs simultaneously with data collection. This approach allows for ideas or frameworks to be tested, refined and qualified in the field.

Field collection approaches	Description
Participant observation	This field method is most closely linked to ethnographic research, with observation occurring alone or by both observing and participating. Participant observation always takes place in community settings, in locations believed to have some relevance to the research questions. The method is distinctive because the researcher approaches participants in their own environment rather than having the participants come to the researcher.
Interviewing	To the ethnographer, interviewing is a primary means through which a grasp of the context and content of people's everyday social, cultural, political and economic lives can be gained. The interview can range from a highly structured one-to-one approach to broader group focus meetings. Surveys or questionnaires are further forms of interviewing that can be implemented.
Diaries	The use of diaries as a form of data collection provides the researcher with time-bound detailed personal reflections and perspectives from group members. Typically being factual in focus, centring on events and activities, diaries are guided by the researcher to ensure that content informs the research question.
Photographic evidence	Photography can be used to great success in ethnographic research, providing a different perspective from the oral or written account of reality. This medium of data collection seeks to represent what is seen without interpretation or mediation via words or impressions from the researcher. This approach emphasises the importance of 'here and now', capturing precise moments in time. Taken by the researcher or participants, spontaneous photography can offer a different view of reality sometimes missed by more formal data collection techniques.
Web forums and chat rooms	Virtual environments comprising forums, chat rooms or open-access discussion boards can be a valuable location for data collection. By observing from a distance or participating in virtual communication, an understanding of cultural rituals, standards and rules can be achieved. Making sure that appropriate data recording techniques are applied to capture text for future analysis, virtual environments can provide a rich source of cultural practice where anonymity can reveal the most interesting of findings.

Table 9.1: A range of field-based data collection methods can be applied within ethnographic research.

'Cut it up and stick it back together'

An easy way to conceptualise ethnographic data analysis is to view it as a 'cut it up and stick it back together again' exercise. This way, the task of ploughing through reams of data files in order to find the metaphorical needle becomes less daunting. The three basic steps are:

- reduction (cut up the data into smaller units, themes or categories – these categories or themes may be 'loosely' determined prior to field entry, established during simultaneous data analysis or created following field withdrawal);
- display (sticking the data back together into some format that starts to tell a story, unite commonality or highlight differences – during this stage the researcher should have the research question firmly in the centre of thought);
- conclusion drawing (making sense and meaning from the findings).

Key Point 9.1

Managing ethnographic data can be a daunting task for the novice researcher. Fortunately, a number of computer software packages exist that can help you to handle the large amounts of data likely to be collected during ethnographic research. Packages such as NUD*IST or NVivo may be available to you and provide a way in which inputted data can be more easily categorised, linked and interpreted. It is worth asking your supervisor or seeking assistance from your library support services as to whether you have access to these types of qualitative data packages. Alternatively, you may be able to download demo versions from online sites that may give you sufficient time and functionality so that you can undertake data analysis for your project.

Brewer (2008) recognises data analysis for the researcher as a series of processes, each of which can begin both during and after data collection. The steps are:

- data management (organising the data into manageable chunks);
- coding (indexing the data into categories, themes or units);
- content analysis of any collected documents relating to the field and/or group;
- qualitative description (identifying the key events, people, behaviour, etc.);
- establishing patterns in the data (looking for recurring themes, association between the data);
- examining cases that do not fit within the categories or themes, or are unexpected in the context of the field and/or group.

Interpretation of ethnographic data is no easy feat even for the most accomplished researcher and seeking support from your supervisor would be recommended. Your ability to understand the stories behind the data will to a large extent come down to your own coverage and understanding of the research literature, as well as your prior experiences of data collection, analysis and interpretation. Practising these before you commence your research would be of extreme value to you. It is worth considering a number of key points when it comes to interpretation.

- What goes with what? Try to consider what patterns or clusters you are looking for in the data. Are you attempting to identify patterns or clusters in the data that relate to 'self-identity', 'signs of self-deprecation', or 'negative thoughts', etc., that may reveal an insight into your sporting group?
- What is there? Try counting particular phrases, metaphors, occurrences, or signs. Identifying frequencies may give you an insight into the cultural individualities present in sport.
- What does it mean? Making contrasts and comparisons, sub-dividing themes further and making links can reveal associations between topics otherwise considered unrelated.
- Where do we go from here? Building a logical chain of evidence and developing theoretical/conceptual understanding can lead to coherent and meaningful conclusions that unravel complex social and cultural meanings to behaviours recorded.

Research Focus 9.4

In a study by Burke et al. (*The Sport Psychologist*, 2008, 22: 336–55), the aim was to ethnographically examine how a group of high altitude climbers drew on a range of cognitive principles to interpret their experiences during an attempt to scale Mount Everest.

By becoming an 'insider' with six mountaineers during their preparation, early climbing exposure and following the attempt, the researcher was able to collect data in the form of in-depth interviews captured on videotape and detailed observations recorded as field notes. The generated data was subjected to content analysis, which entailed the researcher sifting through the data several times to immerse themself in it and understand, interpret, and report the participants' experiences from an empathetic position. The first step for the researcher involved reading the interview transcripts and field diary with a view to identifying where, when, and under what circumstances the phenomenon of research interest (i.e. cognitive dissonance) was alluded to in the participants' experiences. Thematic issues that the researcher had identified were:

- situations in which participants became aware of falling short of their expectations of being a capable climber;
- enduring a great deal of physical discomfort without the reward of reaching the summit;
- spending large amounts of money to endure a great deal of physical discomfort;
- placing the personal goal of climbing the mountain before their family.

Next, the identification of similarities in the data was undertaken to examine the ways in which the participants experienced cognitive dissonance and how this related to their sense of self and the situations they found themselves in. Connections across the data were explored in an attempt to identify patterns as they emerged in the participants' accounts of their experiences on the mountain. Emerging themes and categories were noted and analytic memos were used to make preliminary and tentative connections to various processes that had been identified within the participants. These were interpreted and presented with the aim of making sense of the climbers' cognitive dissonance experiences during such physical and psychological extremes.

Learning Activity 9.4

Consider your own hectic day-to-day life for a moment. Let's take yesterday. Just stop and reflect on yesterday. From the point your eyes opened to the point that they closed. Think about all the activities you got up to, the places you went to, the people you met, the things you talked about, the behaviours you exhibited, and the rituals you performed. Based on these, your life can quite simply be broken down into categories or themes and then subdivided even further. Take the category of 'social contact' for example. This could be subdivided into friends, family, acquaintances and strangers. This could be divided further, so for acquaintances there may be subordinates, peers and superiors.

By observing, recording and interviewing you we could start to identify, based on our categories, some of the cultural behaviours, standards, rules and rituals within your own life. How many times did you mention friends and in what context: positive, negative or neutral? Did you repeatedly talk about practical activities that indicate particular behaviours or social customs? Did we observe a particular eating or drinking pattern that may indicate something about you and your cultural standards?

Now your life may not be that interesting, but apply the same principles to a group of snowboarders, windsurfers, female bodybuilders, elderly yoga practitioners, junior coaches or aerobics instructors, and we may find that their lived experiences as athletes, exercisers or coaches offer us a greater understanding of sport culture by providing a real insight into their unique cultural behaviours, values, emotions and mental states.

Writing and presenting ethnographies

The writing of our ethnographies brings together many hours of research planning, field involvement, data collection and analysis. It is unfortunate to say that this is often the part that receives the least attention, but is probably the most significant (particularly in terms of your grade). You would have already written much, in the form of field notes, transcriptions, observation letters and emails, so the point of drawing all the findings together can seem an uphill battle.

It is worth noting at the start of this process that writing ethnographic research centres on the 'truthfulness' of our interpretations and accounts. By undertaking a process of reflection that takes into account credibility of data (i.e. an authentic representation of what actually occurred), transferability of the material (i.e. making what actually occurred intelligible to the reader), dependability of the interpretation (i.e. that an illogical biased position is not presented), and confirmability of the study (i.e. sound methodology that is auditable through the written report), the validation of truth in our research can be upheld.

As with all presented research, sections should relate to the aims and objectives, background to the problem, research strategy, findings and discussion. Details covering the choice of research setting or 'field', sampling techniques, resources used, field-based data collection approaches, the nature of the researcher's role, the form of analysis, details relating to the process of withdrawal and ethical considerations should all be included within the research strategy section.

One of the most straightforward approaches to writing ethnographies is to focus on the emerging categories or themes that have been identified throughout the analysis process. In the study by Choi et al. (2006) (Research Focus 9.2) for example, the emerging themes of: cool signs and graffiti; athletes; friends and family; freebies; music; and self-identity were identified and discussed separately with a final conclusion to make wider social and cultural sense of the data. Through narrative, associations between such themes and their wider cultural meanings can start to be explored. In effect, this approach requires you to go through the categories or themes, summarising, quoting passages, and making sense by sticking the bits back together in an attempt to understand the bigger picture!

As outlined by Pole et al. (2003: see further reading) writing and presenting ethnographic research should contain most, if not all, of the following features.

- A depiction of what the 'story' is about (does the report clearly explain themes, categories and associations?).
- A sense of context, whether that be social, political, economic and/or educational.
- An ability to trace and track the history and the progress of the research (will the reader know when and why the researcher made key decisions and what effect these may have had on data collection and analysis?).
- An illustration as to how and why key insights and concepts emerged (this will be more than a list of methods).
- Data that is clearly presented through a range of textual accounts, quotations, data displays, photographs, etc..
- Conclusions that show connections between themes, categories and concepts in a systematic and organised way allowing for theory development.

Chapter Review

In this chapter we have considered the importance of the ethnographic research strategy to sport and identified that the ethnographer is not merely a conduit for data collection in social life, but an active participant in the construction of social accounts. Ethnography is a unique research approach that offers a wide range of opportunities to those interested in learning more about sporting cultures. By demystifying the research process, providing sport-related research examples and describing methods of data collection, analysis and interpretation, application of this research strategy can result in meaningful research projects as well as the development of important employability skills. By using a range of sport-related research examples throughout this chapter you should now be able to:

❑ define ethnography in the context of sport research and identify how and why this research strategy is distinct from others;

❑ describe the stages of the ethnographic research process;

❑ define the role of the researcher and appraise the factors that will improve data collection;

❑ appreciate the range of field-based data collection approaches and describe the relevance to ethnographic research;

❑ understand a 'cut it up and stick it back together again' approach to data analysis and interpretation.

(Tick when completed)

Further Reading

Brewer, JD (2008) *Ethnography*. London: Open University Press.
For those serious about ethnographic research, this book consolidates on early chapter content by further examining the meaning of ethnography and placing it into a methodological framework.

Sands, R (2002) *Ethnography in Sport*. Leeds: Human Kinetics.
With this being the only book to date solely dedicated to sport ethnography, this is a must-read for those interested in this research approach. It is packed full of excellent sporting examples, real-life case studies and a clear description as to the ethnographic research process.

Pole, C and Morrison, M (2003) *Ethnography for Education*. London: Open University Press.
Don't be put off by the educational emphasis! The authors have informatively presented an engaging book that offers the reader a real insight into the whole approach to ethnographic research. The three sections on analysing, use and writing about ethnography are highly recommended to anyone wanting to undertake ethnographic research.

Crang, M and Cook, I (2007) *Doing Ethnographies*. London: Sage Publications.
This is an excellent research book focusing primarily on the wide range of ethnographic field methods that can be used by the researcher. Building on the data collection approaches outlined in this chapter, the authors present clear examples to assist understanding and application.

Chapter 10
A mixed-research approach to sport

Learning Objectives

By linking your understanding of sport in practice to sport-related research examples, this chapter is designed to help you:

- explain how a mixed-research strategy can be an effective approach to sport research;
- describe uses of the mixed-research approach to sport and show how different research methods can be used in combination;
- appreciate the associated strengths and weaknesses of a mixed approach to research.

Introduction

Research into sport offers a multitude of opportunities that are diverse in topic and broad in approach. As has been covered so far in this book, a number of research strategies and associated research methods exist that allow for the exploration and explanation of sporting behaviour from a range of perspectives. These could be observational if we were interested in coaching behaviour, ethnographical if we wished to examine the socio-cultural functioning of a sports team, or experimental if our questions centred on performance enhancement. Each research strategy can be selected based on the nature of the inquiry and questions that need answering. As in all research, the selection of an appropriate research strategy from a clearly stated research question creates the link between aims and research methods.

Sometimes, however, single or 'mono' strategies alone may limit the researcher's ability to fully explore the topic and explain the meanings of the findings. By using multiple approaches to sport research, we can capitalise on the strengths of each single approach and offset their different weaknesses. It could also provide more comprehensive answers to our research questions, going beyond the limitations of a single research approach. Such 'mixed-research' strategy is most appropriate when we have a specific issue or problem that is best understood through both exploration and explanation.

Case Study 10.1

As part of a unit project, and working in conjunction with the Community Sports Development Office, two students were asked to explore why so many elderly residents from a local area were dropping out of a physical-wellness exercise programme. In addition to this, the Office wished to find out how participation could be increased and maintained. The programme was repeated in six different local venues ensuring a wide target population, and involved a 12-session series provided free of charge, at times that were deemed suitable. At first, in excess of 20 exercisers completed the first three sessions at each location. By the fifth session, however, attendance had dropped for all by up to 75 per cent.

To tackle this problem the students decided to obtain both quantitative and qualitative data so to understand more about the frequency of attendance, intensity of physical activity during sessions, social relationships among the session members and the instructor, reasons for participation and 'outside of session' daily functioning. The students decided to break the project into two distinct parts with phase one taking place at the exercise sessions and the second outside of session time in a more informal venue. The first phase was quantitative in nature and involved two components: (i) 5-point Likert scale physical activity questionnaire; and (ii) session-based observation. Following data collection, basic statistical analyses on the data were performed and a number of themes emerged.

The second phase of the research was qualitative in nature and involved a survey strategy approach whereby a number of informal focus groups with attending and non-attending elderly residents took place. The students used the themes that had emerged from phase one to develop a guide of questions for the groups. In addition, they also undertook semi-structured interviews with the programme instructors.

By employing a mixed-research approach in a sequential manner (i.e. one phase following the next), the students were able to build on exploratory findings determined in phase one to explain the reasons for poor retention. They were also able to recommend strategies that could be deployed to enhance and maintain attendance. Based on their findings, reasons for the drop off in attendance throughout the programme were attributed to: exercises being perceived as too demanding with intensity being too high; instructors having little or no interaction with the group before or after sessions; and no additional advice or support being given on healthy lifestyles for home-based implementation. Feedback from all those interviewed revealed that involvement in the programme could be increased through more effective travel arrangements, a home-based support system that helps the elderly integrate the exercises into their everyday life, and more empathetic and friendly instructors.

Combining methodologies: can paradigms be mixed?

We all know how rich in detail sport can be, and with the interconnected disciplines of the natural and social sciences encountered through our study, it seems logical to assume that many research questions will require the researcher bringing together a range of research approaches. For the researcher wishing to understand the link between exercise and quality of life, group dynamics, leadership and performance achievement, or coaching strategies and player improvement for example, they may need to go beyond a single research approach to fully explore and explain behaviour and meaning. For the researcher interested in understanding more about sporting behaviour and its meanings, combining quantitative and qualitative research and the associated research methods sounds like a good idea and one that may allow for deeper learning and understanding to take place.

To answer questions about sport and exercise through the implementation of research, understanding as to appropriate sources of knowledge (e.g. interviews, observations, experiments), data analytic strategies (e.g. quantitative and/or qualitative), underlying philosophies of various research methodologies, and the development of alternative paradigms needs to occur. While several of these have influenced the field of sport research, there is still a need to develop and accept alternative ways of examining human behaviour within sport. By adopting a mixture of approaches, concepts, tools and methods the researcher can extend current practices and uncover discoveries about how sport impacts on our life from a physical and social perspective.

Key Point 10.1

A paradigm is a term that is used to describe a cluster of beliefs and dictates for scientists in a particular discipline what should be studied, how research should be done, and how research should be interpreted.

(Bryman, 2008, p 446)

Bryman (2008) recognises two different positions that are linked to the debate on whether or not a mixing of approaches should be formed by combining quantitative and qualitative research. The first is an epistemological view, namely that each paradigm is unique and therefore incompatible. Because of the contrasting ontological and epistemological assumptions (see Chapter 1), the nature of mixing research would be considered not possible. The second position is the technical one, where the focus is on the strengths of data collection and data analysis techniques rather than the philosophical assumptions governing each. As can be seen throughout the book and particularly in Table 2.1, research methods should not be seen as being bound to each paradigm (i.e. quantitative versus qualitative), but rather viewed as 'free-agents' that can operate across boundaries. Taking a technical position provides the researcher with a more pragmatic or practical approach to their research, opening the gateway to mixed-research approaches.

Research Focus 10.1

In two connected studies, Gould et al. (*The Sport Psychologist,* 1996, 10: 322–66) examined 'burnout' in competitive junior tennis players. The researchers selected a sequential mixed-research approach that involved two distinct phases of study. Both phases applied the survey research strategy, but with each being linked to either qualitative or quantitative methodological paradigms.

The first phase of the research was quantitative in nature and involved the completion of a psychological assessment by a range of junior players who had or had not experienced 'burnout'. By recording numerical scores on a 7-point Likert scale, findings revealed that 'burned-out' players significantly differed from the comparison 'non-burned-out' group on a variety of social, psychological and demographic measures, including input into training, motivation, burnout, perfectionism and coping strategies.

The second phase of the research was qualitative in nature and involved two linked components. Firstly, interviews were conducted with ten players who were identified as being most burned-out in the quantitative phase of the research. Content analyses were further conducted on the transcribed interviews to identify mental and physical characteristics of burnout, as well as reasons for burning-out.

By applying a quantitative approach to identify key differences between players who had experienced burnout to those who had not, the researchers were able to next implement a qualitative approach to identify the characteristics or symptoms of burnout. A number of varied symptoms were identified, ranging from increased aggressiveness on and off the court to feelings of embarrassment and shame. The most frequently cited characteristics included: (i) a lack of motivation; (ii) frustration; (iii) being moody and irritable; and (iv) physically lacking energy.

A multi versus mixed approach to research

As can be read throughout the preceding chapters, a wide range of research studies have been described that use different research methods of data collection and analysis within a single research paradigm. For example, Choi et al. (2006; see Research Focus 9.2) conducted an ethnographic qualitative study in which they collected photographic evidence from participants as well as conducting unstructured interviews. In the quantitative study conducted by Bressel et al. (2007; see Research Focus 4.2) a range of physiological and performance measures were recorded during a performance assessment, while afterwards the performers completed a questionnaire. As is evident from the approach taken in each of these two studies, the application of selected research methods is broadly compatible to either the qualitative or quantitative paradigm. This can be known as a multi approach to research and is the most typical form of research encountered.

Learning Activity 10.1

Select two research articles from the same topic area but with contrasting research perspectives (i.e. qualitative and quantitative). For example, they may be two articles about anxiety and sporting performance in football, cardiovascular benefits of exercise in the elderly, or gifted and talented in youth sport. Focus only on the research strategy (i.e. research design and methods) for each. Make a list of the research method(s) used: try and think about the nature of the data collected, how it was collected and the type of analysis performed.

Next, consider whether combining these studies would have improved our understanding of the topic. Would a mixture of the perspectives be of any benefit? Try and consider why. How may they have been combined? Could one be viewed as exploratory and the other explanatory? Do their findings complement each other? What may limit the combination of the two research strategies? What problems do you see existing by combining them?

An alternative is mixed-approach studies that attempt to bring together methods from different paradigms. In a mixed-approach study the researcher may choose to conduct a series of semi-structured interviews with a small number of performers, combined with a large-scale survey. This kind of integration of qualitative with quantitative approaches is also referred to as a mixed-research strategy.

What is a mixed-research strategy?

A mixed-research strategy is one where the researcher mixes or combines quantitative and qualitative research approaches, concepts, techniques, and methods into a single study. As indicated above, the term mixed research could be viewed as being synonymous with the popularised term 'mixed methods'. The label 'mixed research', however, in this context is broader, more inclusive and clearly paradigmatic. A mixed-research strategy is more than just a mixture of methods, rather a mixture of ontological and epistemological positions that do not compete, but complement each other. Philosophically, mixed research makes use of the pragmatic paradigm and system of philosophy. Its logic of inquiry includes the use of induction (or discovery of patterns), deduction (testing of theories and hypotheses), and abduction (uncovering and relying on the best of a set of explanations for understanding one's results).

Key Point 10.2

A *mixed-research strategy* combines quantitative and qualitative research approaches, concepts, techniques and methods into a single study.

Purposes of mixed research in sport

There are four key reasons why a mixed-research approach to sport is of value. These are expansion, triangulation, complementarity, and development. Expansion refers to the growth of knowledge by applying different research approaches to assess sporting phenomena in order to expand the scope and range of research studies. Triangulation relates to the way in which the researcher applies different research strategies to measure the same sporting phenomenon, thereby increasing confidence in the conclusions reached. Complementarity relates to strategies, which are used to investigate different aspects or dimensions of the same sporting phenomenon in order to deepen and broaden the interpretations and conclusions from a study. Finally, development refers to how results from one research approach can be used to inform the development of the other (e.g. instrument development).

In areas of applied sport and exercise psychology, coaching science, education in sport, sport management and business, and long-term athlete development, to name but a few, research excellence has led us to understand much about how we act, perform, respond and develop as individuals and groups through our sporting endeavours. There is still, however, much we do not know about social interactions, behaviours and their deeper meanings acted out through sport. By mixing strategies through the implementation of different research approaches, the researcher positions themselves well to develop new instruments and techniques, evaluate method compatibility and suitability and expand research studies through the growth of new questions that may reveal new and exciting knowledge about our social and personal functioning within sport.

Developing a 'pragmatic' approach to mixed research in sport

The application of a mixed-research strategy to sport attempts to legitimise the use of multiple approaches in answering research questions, rather than restricting or constraining researchers' choices. Sport is after all a complex milieu of natural and social phenomena. In appreciating this, the mixed-research approach to sport should be inclusive and complementary, accepting that a wide- ranging approach to research strategy and method selection can provide a vehicle for broader sporting inquiry. As has been a common theme throughout this book, the most fundamental aspect for research success is question formulation; research strategies should follow research questions in a way that offers the best chance to obtain useful answers. Many research questions emerging in sport are therefore best and most fully answered through mixed-research solutions.

The pragmatic researcher, put simply, refers to one who opts for strategies and associated methods that are more useful within specific sporting contexts (e.g. answers to practical problems), not those that necessarily are tied into single paradigmatic positions. As has been emphasised throughout this book, the researcher's quest for knowledge and the evolvement of research questions should lead to the most appropriate research strategies, rather than lead to a dogmatic view of research and its associated assumptions.

Characteristics of mixed research

In order to mix research in an effective manner, the researcher first needs to consider all of the relevant characteristics of quantitative and qualitative research. For example, the major characteristics of traditional quantitative research are a focus on deduction, confirmation, theory/hypothesis testing, explanation, prediction, standardised data collection, and statistical analysis (see Table 1.2 in Chapter 1). The major characteristics of traditional qualitative research are induction, discovery, exploration, theory/hypothesis generation, the researcher as the primary 'instrument' of data collection, and qualitative analysis (see Table 1.3 in Chapter 1).

Research Focus 10.2

In a study by Giacobbi et al. (*Adapted Physical Activity Quarterly*, 2008, 25: 189–207) the purpose was to examine links between physical activity and quality of life experienced by individuals with physical disabilities recruited from a wheelchair users' basketball tournament. This mixed-research approach involved an integrated survey and ethnographic research strategy, combining quantitative and qualitative methodologies. Such approach was deemed necessary to evaluate the frequency and intensity of physical activity behaviours, social relationships, and daily functioning in a manner consistent with quality of life literature previously reviewed by the authors.

Through a parallel mixed-research approach, which involved the collection of quantitative and qualitative data simultaneously, adapted physical activity questionnaires alongside semi-structured interviews were administered to a range of physically impaired performers. The physical activity scale questionnaire, specifically designed for individuals with physical disabilities (PASIPD), consisted of five subscales: home repair/lawn and garden work; housework; vigorous sport and recreation; moderate sport and recreation; and occupational activities. The instrument scoring system produced a mathematically maximum score and an estimated metabolic equivalent or MET value (e.g. energy expenditure) for each of the five factors and a total score. This numerical data could then be subjected to statistical analysis methods. The interviews were semi-structured in nature and based on a pre-determined guide of questions focusing on the: (i) nature of the participants' disabilities; (ii) occupational or school-related activities of daily living; (iii) perceived benefits of physical activity; (iv) motives that sustain involvement in physical activity; and (v) evaluations about one's life.

With the purpose of this mixed-research study being to explore the role that physical activity plays in the quality of life for individuals with physical disabilities, the researcher's findings revealed that descriptions of the physical activity experiences, perceived benefits, and motives for participation highlighted several themes of importance: psychological benefits; physical health benefits; social opportunities; social influences; and increased overall quality of life.

Gaining an understanding into the strengths and weaknesses of quantitative and qualitative research puts a researcher in a position to mix or combine strategies and collect multiple data using different strategies, approaches, and methods in such a way that the resulting mixture or combination is likely to result in complementary strengths and non-overlapping weaknesses. As illustrated in Table 10.1, combining quantitative and qualitative research approaches presents the researcher with both strengths and weaknesses to this strategy that they must be aware of before embarking on a mixed-research study.

Effective use of this approach is a major source of justification for mixed research because the end result can be superior to studies where a single methodology is followed. For example, adding qualitative interviews to experiments as a manipulation check and perhaps as a way to discuss directly the issues under investigation and tap into participants' perspectives can enrich the study and provide more meaningful answers.

Learning Activity 10.2

Try and summarise the key strengths and weaknesses of a mixed-research strategy. If you were to use this approach then it is important you are able to justify its value over a single strategy study.

Design of mixed-research study

The designing of a mixed-research study can be loosely based on three key decisions (Creswell, 2008).

1. What order does the researcher want the quantitative and qualitative research methods to appear in the study?
2. What priority will the researcher give to the quantitative and qualitative data collection and analysis procedures?
3. At what stage will the researcher want the quantitative and qualitative findings to be combined?

Each of these should be dictated by the nature of the research question and not familiarity and confidence in using particular research approaches. The decision as to the order, priority and

Strengths

– Words, pictures, and narrative can be used to add meaning to numbers.
– Numbers can be used to add precision to words, pictures, and narrative.
– Can provide quantitative and qualitative research strengths (i.e. see strengths listed in Tables 1.2 and 1.3).
– Researcher can generate and test a developed theory.
– Can answer a broader and more complete range of research questions because the researcher is not confined to a single method or approach.
– The specific mixed *research designs* discussed in this chapter have specific strengths and weaknesses that should be considered (e.g. in a two-phase sequential design, the results from phase one can be used to develop and inform the purpose and design of the phase two component).
– A researcher can use the strengths of an additional method to overcome the weaknesses in another method by using both in a research study.
– Can provide stronger evidence for a conclusion through convergence and corroboration of findings.
– Can add insights and understanding that might be missed when only a single method is used.
– Can be used to increase the generalisability of the results.
– Qualitative and quantitative research used together produce more complete knowledge, necessary to inform theory and practice.

Weaknesses

– Can be difficult for a single researcher to carry out both qualitative and quantitative research, especially if two or more approaches are expected to be used concurrently; it may require a research team.
– Researcher has to learn about multiple methods and approaches and understand how to mix them appropriately.
– Methodological purists contend that one should always work within either a qualitative or a quantitative paradigm.
– More expensive.
– More time consuming.
– Some of the details of mixed research remain to be worked out fully by research methodologists (e.g. problems of paradigm mixing, how to qualitatively analyse quantitative data, how to interpret conflicting results).

Table 10.1: Strengths and weaknesses of a mixed-research approach (extracts from Johnson et al. 2004).

integration of data collection and analysis should be explicitly stated in any research plan or protocol before the collection phase(s) begin. Integrated into the overall design plan, the researcher's decisions should be considered carefully to ensure that data collection and analysis is relevant and implemented at the right time.

Mixed-research designs can occur in one of two ways. The first is known as a 'parallel-design' and relates to the mixing of qualitative and quantitative approaches within the same stage of the research process (i.e. one phase). Take for example a researcher who may wish to evaluate the effectiveness of a new physical training aid during dance performance. By implementing a parallel design they could collect physiological and movement data, in addition to simultaneously recording the participant's verbal description of effort or their subjective likes and dislikes about the aid. In this instance, the researcher is therefore able to concurrently collect both quantitative and qualitative data at the same time in the study and the implementation is simultaneous.

The alternative approach is known as a 'sequential-design', with qualitative and quantitative approaches occurring in a sequence with one phase of collection happening before the next. If a researcher wished to explore professional coaches' opinions on the value of volunteer coaching, the first phase (qualitative) may involve several small-scale focus groups to explore the topic and develop some emerging themes. The second phase (quantitative) may then involve the development and deployment of a closed-question survey to a much larger number of coaches that were typically representative of the professional coaching fraternity.

Most sequentially designed mixed-research studies consist of two phases. The order in which these phases occur (i.e. quantitative and qualitative) will depend on the nature of the question. Two key questions the researcher may wish to ask are: (i) what information needs to be emphasised/established first in the study: quantitative or qualitative?; and (ii) will theory be built, tested and explained (induction > deduction > abduction) or tested and deconstructed and then explained (deduction > induction > abduction)? In addition to the order in which quantitative and qualitative approaches will occur, there is also the question as to the dominance of each. Will each approach be of equal weighting in the study or will one be considered a major approach and the other a minor?

Associated with each design approach comes the way in which the collected data will be combined for analysis. For the researcher, the term 'combined' simply refers to the stage of the research process where quantitative and qualitative data will be mixed, analysed and then interpreted. Take for example the parallel-design study illustrated above. Because the data was collected simultaneously during a single phase of collection, the combination of data will occur during the interpretation stage of research. For the sequential-design example provided, combining of data collected from professional coaches may occur during data collection, data analysis, data interpretation or a combination of all three. For phase one of the study, qualitative data recorded during the focus groups could be transformed into numerical codes during analysis. For phase two, the survey administered to the coaches may be a combination of open and closed-questions, therefore eliciting qualitative and quantitative data.

Learning Activity 10.3

By applying the description above to the three published research studies found within this chapter (see Research Focus 10.1, 10.2 and 10.3), try to answer the following questions:

1. Is the study a 'parallel' or 'sequential' design?
2. In what order do the quantitative and qualitative approaches appear?
3. Are the approaches of equal weighting or does it seem that one is more dominant that the other?
4. At what point are the findings combined?

Data analysis in mixed research

There are a number of approaches the researcher can implement when it comes to data analysis within mixed research. As reviewed in Table 10.2, a broad range of approaches to data analysis can be implemented within a mixed-research strategy. By administering different collection instruments and procedures within the mixed-research strategy (e.g. focus groups, interviews, observations, clinical measurements, diagnostic tests, questionnaires, photography and content analysis), data analysis will occur by way of quantitative (descriptive and inferential numeric analysis) and qualitative (description and thematic text or image analysis) techniques. The relationship between each analysis technique can be broadly categorised into five approaches: data transformation; multiple level examination; outlier exploration; instrument development; and data separation. The approach selected will be governed by both the research design and the research question.

Learning Activity 10.4

Key questions that the researcher may wish to ask when designing a mixed-research study.

- Has a definition of mixed research been clearly stated?
- Has the selection of a mixed-research approach been justified?
- Are the criteria for selecting a mixed-research strategy identified?
- Are both quantitative and qualitative research methods stated and justified?
- Are sampling strategies for both quantitative and qualitative data collection mentioned?
- Is an explanation as to how these relate to the mixed-research strategy given?
- Are specific data analysis procedures indicated?
- Are procedures for validating both quantitative and qualitative data discussed?

Data analysis approach	Design type	Description and example
Data transformation	Parallel-design	This approach involves transforming qualitative into quantitative data or vice versa (e.g. unstructured interviews with several fitness centre managers resulted in the theme 'recession' being mentioned 17 times).
Multiple level examination	Parallel-design	This approach involves collecting quantitative data at one level (e.g. survey with a sports team) while at the same time collecting qualitative data at another level (e.g. interview data with individual players to explore the role of players within that team).
Outlier exploration	Sequential-design	In this approach, phase one quantitative analysis could highlight outliers that phase two qualitative research could investigate (e.g. tachycardia recorded in a participant could lead to follow-up interview).
Instrument development	Sequential-design	This approach can allow for the development of categories or themes from qualitative data collection that can be used to create quantitative surveys (e.g. a focus group with children could lead to the development of a PE observation sheet).
Data separation	Both	This approach involves qualitative and quantitative data being analysed separately where one does not inform or influence the other (e.g. isokinetic data of lower limb bilateral strength and interview data examining training history).

Table 10.2: Five broad approaches to data analysis in a mixed-research strategy (extracts from Creswell, 2008).

Research Focus 10.3

In a study by Smith et al. (*Journal of Sports Sciences*, 2006, 24: 355–66) the aim was to use a mixed-research approach to examine the coaching behaviour of professional youth soccer coaches during games. The researchers recognised that continued investigation into the knowledge and strategies that expert coaches use, which in fact underpins their behaviour, could provide useful information for improving coach education. As a consequence, they felt that an interpretative investigation to enable a deeper understanding of the factors that coaches believe explain their performance would seem necessary. For this reason, and to aid the interpretation and understanding of coaches' behaviour, rigorous application of quantitative methods (e.g. observational techniques) complemented with sound interpretations of qualitative data (such as obtained from interviews) would offer insight.

Conducted in a sequential manner, the researchers firstly undertook an observational research strategy, becoming complete-observers in order to produce a quantitative description of the instructional behaviours of the coaches during games. The second stage focused on selecting a survey research strategy and employing structured and unstructured one-to-one interviews with the coaches. Such interpretive interviews allowed the researchers the chance to examine the experiential, situational and contextual factors that impacted the coaches' instructional behaviour in the competitive environment. The aim of combining a systematic observation method (observational strategy) with the interview method (survey strategy) was to produce data whereby the qualitative findings would offer explanation and meaning to the quantitative research.

Findings indicated the demonstration of conscious and well-thought-out patterns of behaviour: silently monitoring, interspersed with clips of instruction coupled with praise and encouragement. The interviews exposed three themes underpinning this behaviour: developing game understanding; support and encouragement; and coaches' role and influences. The use of silence was the largest single behaviour, the efficacy of which was considered in light of theories of experiential and discovery learning.

Chapter Review

In this chapter we have examined the benefits and limitations of the mixed-research approach to sport. Mixed research can be seen as a combination of quantitative and qualitative methodologies for the purpose of gaining a greater understanding of sport behaviour and its associated meanings. By developing research designs combining research methods in a number of possible ways, we can start to implement a mixed-research strategy to examine a much wider perspective of sport. Through the use of sport-related research examples you should now be able to:

❑ describe how a mixed-research strategy can be of benefit to sport research;
❑ list a wide range of strengths and weaknesses associated with the mixed-research approach and justify its use in sport research;

❏ design a mixed-research study that considers order, priority and combination of findings;

❏ recognise sport-related research that has implemented a mixed-research approach.

(Tick when completed)

Further Reading

Creswell, JW and Plano, VL (2006) *Designing and Conducting Mixed Methods Research*. London: Sage Publications.

Bryman, A (2008) *Social Research Methods*. 3rd edition. Oxford: Oxford University Press.

Creswell, JW (2008) *Research Design: Qualitative, Quantitative and Mixed Methods Approaches*. 3rd edition. London: Sage Publications.

These three books will provide extended notes on the combining paradigms debate: quantitative versus qualitative, as well as a detailed perspective as to mixed-research design. Although not linked particularly well to examples, concepts are clearly stated and easily transferable to sport.

Giacobbi, P, Poczwardowski, A and Hager, P (2005) A pragmatic research philosophy for applied sport psychology. *Sport Psychologist*, 19, 1–31.

For the interested reader, this excellent article provides a well-resourced guide to the application of pragmatism to the area of sport psychology. Arguing the case for a mixed-research paradigm within sport research, this should be read once you have a firm grip of the key concepts covered in Chapter 1.

Teddlie, C and Tashakkori, A (2008) *Foundations of Mixed Methods Research*. London: Sage Publications.

Further supporting key concepts and practical aspects of this chapter, this handbook offers the reader an extended coverage of mixed research within social sciences. It also expands on design types and analysis processes, which may be of value when planning a mixed-research study.

Glossary

Action research: An approach that attempts to improve the social situation under investigation whilst at the same point generating knowledge about it.

Association: Any relationship between two measured variables that renders them statistically dependent.

Attributes: Properties possessed by one or more persons or objects. By measuring and comparing attributes the researcher can establish patterns within or between groups.

Attrition: The tendency for participants in the study to drop out through illness, injury, or refusal to continue to be involved.

Between-group design: An experimental approach where two or more different groups of participants are subject to different experiences or treatments.

Case study research: A research strategy that involves the detailed and intensive analysis of a single case. The term can be extended to include multiple-case research whereby two or more cases are compared.

Case: An individual unit being studied. A case could be a person, a team, a school, a club or an organisation.

Causation: A concern with establishing causal connections between variables, rather than mere relationships between them.

Closed questions: A question employed within a survey that presents the respondent with a set of possible answers to choose from (as opposed to *open questions*).

Cluster sampling: A procedure in which at an initial stage the researcher stages areas (i.e. clusters) and then samples units from those clusters, usually using a *probability sampling* technique.

Cohort: A group of persons sharing a particular statistical or demographic characteristic (e.g. all the participants live in the same postcode area).

Comparative design: A research design that involves identifying differences and similarities between two or more cases in order to establish theoretical insights.

Confounding variable: A variable that is not controlled in an experiment and may affect the dependent variable.

Constant: An attribute that does not change or vary throughout the course of a study.

Constructivism: An ontological position that asserts that social phenomena and their meaning are constructed and do not necessarily reflect external realities. From this perspective, knowledge is dependent on social experience, human perception and social conventions.

Content analysis: A method by which textual and visual documents are analysed and categorised in a systematic and reliable manner in order to produce quantitative data. The term can also be applied to qualitative content analysis.

Control group: Used to try to establish whether any effect found in the intervention group is due to the intervention or would have occurred anyway.

Convenience sampling: A procedure that selects a sample based on their availability to the researcher.

Correlation co-efficient: A measure of the strength and direction of the relationship between two variables. This approach is applied when the two variables are both measured at the interval or ratio level of measurement.

Correlational research: A research strategy that involves the analysis of relationships between variables.

Counterbalancing: A process of controlling for order effects in a repeated measures design by either including all order of treatment presentation or randomly determining the order for each participant.

Covert research: An approach by which those that are being researched are not aware, or not fully aware, of the researcher's identify and/or role.

Cross-sectional design: A research design that involves collecting data from a sample at one point in time.

Curvilinear relationship: A relationship between two or more variables, which is depicted graphically (i.e. scatter plot) by anything other than a straight line.

Data analysis: A process of gathering, organising and synthesising data with the goal being to highlight useful information.

Data collection: The period within the research process that involves preparing for and collecting data by engaging with a target sample or population.

Data: Material that is either numerical or textual, which is generated and collected in the research process for the purpose of analysis. Data is the product of the research itself and is determined by the research process.

Deduction: An approach to research by which a conclusion is reached from previously known premises. For example, a conclusion may be reached by deduction from the combination of a theory and some facts about a specific case (as opposed to *induction*).

Dependent variable: A variable that is causally influenced by another variable (i.e. the *independent variable*).

Descriptive statistics: An approach that is used to describe or summarise the characteristics of a sample.

Ecological validity: The degree to which behaviours that are observed and recorded in a study reflect the behaviours that occur in a natural setting.

Empiricism: An approach that uses observations to answer questions about the nature of behaviour.

Epistemology: The branch of philosophy that concerns the theory of knowledge, that is, what is true and how we come to believe its truth.

Ethics: A theory or system of moral values, such as what is right and wrong.

Ethnographic research: A research strategy that involves the researcher immersing themselves in a social setting for an extended period of time, utilising a wide range of research methods.

Exercise science: A discipline that studies the application of scientific principles and techniques with the aim of enhancing or maintaining physical fitness and overall health.

Experimental research: A research strategy that involves the testing of a hypothesis, usually through the manipulation of an independent variable to measure the changes in the dependent variable. Typically involves an intervention and control condition/group.

External validity: The extent to which the research findings can be generalised to the population and different social settings.

Extraneous variable: Any variable other than the dependent and independent variable that may influence the relationship between the two. In true experiments all possible extraneous variables are controlled.

Falsification: The process of trying to disprove a proposition, hypothesis or theory.

Field notes: A description of events observed during field research in a social setting and recorded at observation, or shortly afterwards.

Field research: Research carried out in a naturally occurring setting rather than in a controlled setting such as the physiology or biomechanics laboratory.

Focus group: A form of group interview in which several participants, in addition to a moderator/facilitator, explore a range of topics with the aim of generating a range of opinions.

Gatekeeper: Persons within research process, whose assistance enables the researcher to access those they wish to research: for example, a coach of a football team or a manager of a fitness centre.

Generalisability: The extent to which findings from the researcher's sample can be claimed to accurately reflect the characteristics of a wider population than that from which the researcher sampled from.

Haphazard sampling: A procedure that involves selecting participants in a haphazard manner, usually based on their availability.

Hypothesis: An informed speculation, which is set up to be tested, about the relationship between two or more variables.

Independent variable: A variable that has a causal impact on another variable (i.e. the dependent variable).

In-depth interview: A method of data collection that is often open and unstructured in nature that explores a topic in significant detail from the interviewee's perspective.

Induction: An approach to research by which generalisations are generated by seeking commonality in cases. In social research, this approach generates theory from evidence (as opposed to *deduction*).

Inference: The act or process of deriving logical conclusions from premises known or assumed to be true.

Inferential statistics: Statistics that allow the researcher to make inferences on the likelihood of the sample findings being replicated in the population.

Informed consent: A process whereby participants provide consent to become involved in the research, being made fully aware of the implications of his or her involvement.

Internal validity: The extent to which data collected accurately reflects the reality of beliefs or behaviours of those from whom the data was collected.

Interpretivism: An epistemological position that requires the researcher to grasp subjective meaning of social action (see *qualitative research*).

Intervention group: A group that receives an intervention.

Interview guide: Relates to a list of themes, topics or categories to be covered during the interview. Often synonymous with the term interview schedule that provides a framework of linked questions/prompts for the interviewer.

Interview: An approach that requires a face-to-face talk in order to generate data. Interviews may be one-to-one or conducted as *focus groups*.

Interviewer effect/bias: The potential for the researcher to distort the behaviour of the interviewees based on their own social characteristics, opinions and expectations.

Level of measurement: A term used to describe the varying mathematical scaling of numerical variables that can be recorded by the researcher. These include nominal, ordinal, interval and ratio levels of measurement.

Likert scale: A scale used to gauge respondent's attitude to a particular question. Involves the construction of a scale (i.e. 1 to 5) where the respondent scores based on their preference (e.g. 1 = strongly disagree, 5 = strongly agree).

Longitudinal design: A research design in which data are collected on a sample on at least two separate occasions.

Mail survey: A self-completion questionnaire that is distributed via a postal service.

Measurement: The process of obtaining the magnitude of a quantity, such as length or mass, relative to a unit of measurement, such as a metre or a kilogram.

Methodology: A position concerned with the logic, potentialities and limitations of research methods.

Mixed research: A research strategy that involves mixing or combining quantitative and qualitative research approaches, concepts, techniques, and methods into a single study (also see *triangulation*).

Multi methods: An approach that utilises two or more research methods positioned within the paradigm into a single study (e.g. the use of social observation and focus groups).

Narrative analysis: The process of deconstructing narrative to identify sequences, patterns and interactions within the text.

Narrative: the construction of process/sequence within the text. Often relates to the tale or story found within the text.

Naturalistic: Research that takes place outside of controlled conditions (e.g. within the setting of a school).

Negative relationship: A relationship between two variables whereby one increases and the other decreases.

Neutral relationship: A relationship between two variables whereby change in one variable is unaccompanied by change in another variable.

Non-equivalent control group: A quasi-experimental research design in which participants are allocated into an experimental and control group according to naturally occurring features.

Non-experimental research: An approach to research that does not adhere to an experimental strategy that originated from the natural sciences.

Non-probability sampling: A procedure that does not select participants using a random sampling approach (as opposed to *probability sampling*).

Objectivism: An ontological position that asserts that social phenomena and their meanings are not dependent on any features of the particular subject who studies it.

Observation: A form of data collection method that is used to record observable behaviours. These may be both verbal and non-verbal in nature.

Observational research: A non-experimental research strategy that involves the direct observation and measurement of behaviour that may occur in a range of settings.

Ontology: A branch of philosophy concerned with questions of what exists, and how we view reality.

Open-ended question: A question employed within a survey that does not require the respondent to choose between a prescribed set of answers (as opposed to *closed questions*).

Outlier: an extreme value in a distribution, that is either very high or low compared to the average.

Paradigm: A term describing a cluster of beliefs that in the context of research dictates what should be studied, how research should be done, and how results should be interpreted.

Participant observation: A research design in which the researcher immerses themselves in a social setting for an extended period of time, observing and recording behaviour (see ethnographic research).

Participant: A person or group of people who participate in the research project.

Pearson's r: A measure of association (i.e. strength and direction) used to explore the association between two variables.

Pilot/piloting: A procedure that involves pre-testing of research methods (i.e. instruments and procedures) in order to identify weaknesses in data collection approach.

Population: The universe of units from which a sample is drawn.

Positive relationship: A relationship between two variables, whereby as one variable increases the other also increases.

Positivism: An epistemological position that emphasises the use of natural approaches (i.e. experimental research) to study social reality.

Pragmatic: In a mixed-research approach, a pragmatic view sets aside paradigm or position differences between research methods used, and rather priority is given to the research question and process.

Prediction: A statement made about a future occurrence that can be tested in a rigorous form (i.e. hypothesis testing).

Probability sampling: A procedure that selects participants using a random sampling approach (as opposed to *non-probability sampling*).

Purposive sampling: A procedure that involves selecting a sample on the basis of particular characteristics or an identified variable (e.g. all those that started swimming at a local pool within the last three months).

Qualitative: A methodological position that emphasises words rather than quantification (i.e. numbers) in the collection and analysis of data (as opposed to *quantitative*).

Quantitative: A methodological position that emphasises quantification (i.e. numbers) rather than words in the collection and analysis of data (as opposed to *qualitative*).

Quasi-experiment: A research approach that is close to being an experiment except that participants are not randomly assigned to groups but rather selected based on naturally occurring features.

Questionnaire: A question-based data collection instrument designed to be distributed and filled in by a respondent in the absence of a researcher (i.e. self-completion questionnaire).

Quota-sampling: a procedure that involves the non-random allocation of participants into different categories.

Randomisation: The process of controlling for all extraneous variables by ensuring that the variables operate in a manner determined by chance.

Random sampling: A procedure based on the random selection of units from a sampling frame.

Relationship: An association between two variables whereby the variation in one variable coincides with the variation in another variable.

Reliability: The degree to which a measure is considered stable.

Repeated measures design: A research design that involves the same participants being studied at different times or under different conditions.

Representative sample: A sample that reflects the characteristics of the population from which it was drawn.

Research design: The term employed in this book to refer to the logical and systematic structure or plan by which data collection can take place.

Research method: The term employed in this book to refer to the execution of the study (incorporating the implementation of instruments, techniques and procedures used to collect data).

Research objective: The purpose for which the research is being carried out (e.g. to describe, to understand, to explain, to evaluate).

Research question: The overarching question that focuses the topic and defines the scope, scale and conduct of the research study.

Research strategy: The term employed in this book to refer to logic of inquiry (set of ground rules/principles that shape the decisions we make when selecting and implementing our research design and methods).

Sample bias: Bias occurs when the sample characteristics are different from that of the population.

Sample: A segment of the population that is selected for the research study. The method of selection is known as *probability* and *non-probability sampling*.

Sampling frame: The listing of all units within a population from which a research sample is selected.

Sampling variability: A term used to refer to degree of variation shown in a sample when compared to the population from which it was drawn.

Scatter plot: A graphical representation of the relationship between two measured variables.

Semi-structured interview: A data collection procedure that involves the interviewer developing a series of questions that is in the general form of an *interview guide*. This procedure offers the interviewer some degree of flexibility in the interview structure.

Snowball sampling: A procedure that involves the researcher making initial contact with participants who then use their contacts to establish more research participants (see *non-probability sampling*).

Spearman's rank order correlation: A measure of association (i.e. strength and direction) of the relationship between two ordinal variables.

Sport science: A discipline that studies the application of scientific principles and techniques with the aim of improving sporting performance.

Statistical significance: A concept that allows the researcher to estimate, by way of statistical tests, how confident they can be that the results derived from a study based on a randomly selected sample are generalisable to the population from which the sample was drawn.

Stratified sampling: A procedure that involves randomly assigning units to a sample based on categories (i.e. strata).

Structured interview: A data collection procedure that involves the interviewer asking all participants exactly the same questions in order, with the aid of a rigid interview guide.

Survey research: A research strategy that involves describing the characteristics of a population. Whether that is another group, organisation or community, the approach allows the researcher to find out how the population distribute themselves on one or more variables.

Systematic review research: A research strategy that involves the identification, evaluation and interpretation of all available research (i.e. primary and secondary evidence) relevant to a particular research question, topic area, or phenomenon of interest.

Time sampling: A sampling technique that involves using a criterion for deciding when measurement (e.g. observations or interviews) will take place.

Triangulation: The use of more than one research method within a study so that the validity of the findings can be cross-checked.

Unobtrusive research: An approach that does not involve making the participants aware of the research, therefore reducing their reactivity to the project.

Unstructured interview: An informal data collection procedure that involves the interviewer having a list of topics/issues that are used to explore the participants' understanding.

Validity: A concept concerned with the integrity of the conclusions generated from research (see *external* and *internal validity*).

Variable: An attribute that stands for a value that may vary (see *dependent* and *independent variable*).

Within-group design: An experiment approach where all participants test (and respond to) all treatment combinations (as opposed to a *between-group design*).

References

Abbiss, CR and Laursen, PB (2005) Models to explain fatigue during prolonged endurance cycling. *Sports Medicine*, 35: 865–98.

Atkinson, M (2007) Playing with fire: masculinity, health, and sports supplements. *Sociology of Sport Journal*, 24: 165–86.

Blaikie, N (2009) *Designing Social Research*. 2nd edition. Cambridge: Polity Press.

Blaxter, L, Hughes, C and Tight, M (2001) *How to Research*. 2nd edition. Maidenhead: Open University Press.

Bressel, E, Yonker, JA, Kras, J and Heath, EM (2007) Comparison of static and dynamic balance in female collegiate soccer, basketball, and gymnastics. *Athletes Journal of Athletic Training*, 42: 42–46.

Brewer, JD (2008) *Ethnography*. Maidenhead: Open University Press.

Brown, AG, Wells, TJ, Schade, ML, Smith, DL and Fehling, PG (2007) Effects of plyometric training versus traditional weight training on strength, power, and aesthetic jumping ability in female collegiate dancers. *Journal of Dance Medicine and Science*, 11: 38–44.

Brunner, F, Schmid, A, Sheikhzadeh, A, Nordin, M, Yoon, J and Frankel, V (2007) Effects of aging on type II muscle fibers: A systematic review of the literature. *Journal of Aging and Physical Activity*, 15: 336–48.

Bryman, A (2008) *Social Research Methods*. 3rd edition. Oxford: Oxford University Press.

Burke, SM, Sparks, AC and Allen-Collinson, J (2008) High altitude climbers as ethnomethodologists making sense of cognitive dissonance: Ethnographic insights from an attempt to scale Mt. Everest. *The Sport Psychologist*, 22: 336–55.

Burns, RB (2000) *Introduction to Research Methods*. London: Sage Publications.

Carek, PJ and Mainous III, A (2002) The pre-participation physical examination for athletics: A systematic review of current recommendations. *British Medical Journal*, 2: 661–64.

Centre for Reviews and Dissemination (2009) *Systematic Reviews: Guidelines for Undertaking Reviews in Healthcare*. York: York Publishing Services.

Choi, A, Stotlar, DK and Park, SR (2006) Visual ethnography of on-site sport sponsorship activation: LG Action Sports Championship. *Sport Marketing Quarterly*, 15: 71–79.

Christensen, LB (2006) *Experimental Methodology*. 10th edition. London: Pearson Education.

Cohen, L, Manion, L and Morrison, K (2003) *Research Methods in Education*. 5th edition. London: Routledge.

Crang, M and Cook, I (2007) *Doing Ethnographies*. London: Sage Publications.

Creswell, JW (2008) *Research Design: Qualitative, Quantitative and Mixed Methods Approaches*. 3rd edition. London: Sage Publications.

Creswell, JW and Plano VL (2006) *Designing and Conducting Mixed Methods Research*. London: Sage Publications.

Creswell, SL and Eklund, RC (2007) Athlete burnout: A longitudinal qualitative study. *The Sport Psychologist*, 21: 1-20.

Crozby, PC (2009) *Methods in Behavioural Research*. 10th edition. Maidenhead: McGraw Hill Higher Education.

Dale, GA (2000) Distractions and coping strategies of elite decathletes during their most memorable performances. *The Sport Psychologist*, 14: 17–41.

Dorgo, S (2009) Unfolding the practical knowledge of an expert strength and conditioning coach. *International Journal of Sports Science and Coaching*, 4: 17–30.

Eisenhardt, KM (1989) Building theories from case study research. *Academy of Management Review*, 14: 532–50.

Field, A (2009) *Discovering Statistics using SPSS*. 3rd edition. London: Sage Publications.

Fink, A (2008) *How to Conduct Surveys*. 4th edition. London: Sage Publications.

Fisher, A (2001) *Critical Thinking: An Introduction*. Cambridge: Cambridge University Press.

Foster, C, Hillsdon, M and Cavill N (2005) *Understanding Participation in Sport: A Systematic Review*. London. Sport England.

Fraenkal, JR and Wallen, NE (2003) *How to Design and Evaluate Research in Education*. 5th edition. Maidenhead: McGraw-Hill Higher Education.

Frankfort-Nachmias, C and Nachmias, D (1996*) Research Methods in the Social Sciences*. 5th edition. Chapter 12. London: Arnold Publications.

Gearing, J (2006) *Case Study Research: Principles and Practice*. Cambridge: Cambridge University Press.

Giacobbi, P, Poczwardowski, A and Hager, P (2005) A pragmatic research philosophy for applied sport psychology. *Sport Psychologist*, 19: 1–31.

Giacobbi, PR, Stancil, M, Hardin, B, and Bryant, L (2008) Physical activity and quality of life experienced by highly active individuals with physical disabilities. *Adapted Physical Activity Quarterly*, 25: 189–207.

Glaszious, P, Irwing, L, Bain, C and Colditz, G (2005) *Systematic Reviews in Health Care: A Practical Guide*. Cambridge: Cambridge University Press.

Goodger K, Gorely T, Lavallee D, et al. (2007) Burnout in sport: A systematic review. *The Sport Psychologist*, 21: 127–51.

Gould, D, Udry, E, Tuffey, S and Loehr, JE (1996) Burnout in competitive junior tennis players: I. A quantitative psychological assessment. *The Sport Psychologist*, 10: 322–66.

Grandjean, BD, Taylor, PA, and Weiner, J (2002) Confidence, concentration, and competitive performance of elite athletes: A natural experiment in Olympic gymnastics. *Journal of Sport and Exercise Psychology*, 24: 320–27.

Grix, J (2002) Introducing students to the generic terminology of social research. *Politics*, 22: 175–86.

Hare, R, Evans, L and Callow, N (2008) Imagery use during rehabilitation from injury: A case study of an elite athlete. *The Sport Psychologist*, 22: 405–22.

Hitchcock, G and Hughes, D (1995) *Research and the Teacher*. 2nd edition. London: Routledge.

Johnson, RB and Onwuegbuzie, AJ (2004) Mixed methods research: A research paradigm whose time has come. *Educational Researcher*, 33: 14–26.

Keeble, S (1995) *Experimental Research 1: An Introduction to Experimental Design*. The Open Learning Foundation, Churchill Livingstone.

Keeble, S (1995) *Experimental Research 2: Conducting and Reporting Experimental Research*. The Open Learning Foundation, Churchill Livingstone.

Krane, V (2005) Using ethnography in applied sport psychology. *Journal of Applied Sport Psychology*, 17: 87–107.

Lee, RM (2000) *Unobtrusive Methods in Social Research*. London: Open University Press.

Lindsay, FH, Hawley, JA, Myburgh, KH, Schomer, HH, Noakes, TD and Dennis, SC (1996) Improved athletic performance in highly trained cyclists after interval training. *Medicine and Science in Sports and Exercise*, 28: 1427–434.

Lofland, J, Snow, DA, Anderson, L and Lofland, LH (2006) *Analysing Social Setting: A Guide to Qualitative Observation and Analysis*. 4th edition. Andover: Wadsworth Cengage Learning.

Lubans, DR, Morgan, PJ, Collins, CE, Boreham, CA and Callister, R (2009) The relationship between heart rate intensity and pedometer step counts in adolescents. *Journal of Sports Sciences*, 27: 591–97.

Machotka Z, Kumar S and Perraton LG (2009) A systematic review of the literature on the effectiveness of exercise therapy for groin pain in athletes. *Sports Medicine, Arthroscopy, Rehabilitation, Therapy and Technology*, 1: 5.

MacPhail, A and Kirk, D (2006) Young people's socialisation into sport: Experiencing the specialising phase. *Leisure Studies*, 25: 57–74.

Mankad, A, Gordon, S and Wallman, K (2009) Perceptions of emotional climate among injured athletes. *Journal of Clinical Sports Psychology*, 3: 1–14.

McDermott BP, Casa DJ, Ganio MS, et al. (2009) Acute whole-body cooling for exercise-induced hyperthermia: A systematic review. *Journal of Athletic Training*, 44: 84–93.

Mesquita, I, Sobrinho, A, Rosado, A, Pereira, F and Milistetd, M (2008) A systematic observation of youth amateur volleyball coaches' behaviours. *International Journal of Applied Sports Science*, 20: 37–58.

Mulrow, CD (1994) Rationale for systematic reviews. *British Medical Journal*, 309: 597–99.

Nesser, TW and Lee, WL (2009) The relationship between core strength and performance in division I female soccer players. *Journal of Exercise Physiology Online*, 12: 21–28.

Nieuwenhuys, A, Hanin, YL and Bakker, FC (2008) Performance-related experiences and coping during races: A case of an elite sailor. *Psychology of Sport and Exercise*, 9: 61–76.

Ntoumanis, N (2001) *A Step-by-Step Guide to SPSS for Sport and Exercise Studies*. London: Routledge.

O'Leary, Z (2004) *The Essential Guide to Doing Research*. London: Sage Publications.

Ollis, S, Macpherson, A and Collins, D (2006) Expertise and talent development in rugby refereeing: An ethnographic enquiry. *Journal of Sports Sciences*, 24: 309–22.

Pate, RR, Mciver, K, Dowda, M, Brown, WH and Addy, C (2008) Directly observed physical activity levels in preschool children. *Journal of School Health*, 78: 438–44.

Petticrew, M and Roberts, H (2005) *Systematic Reviews in the Social Sciences: A Practical Guide.* Oxford: WileyBlackwell.

Pole, C and Morrison, M (2003) *Ethnography for Education.* London: Open University Press.

Priest, N, Armstrong, R, Doyle, J and Waters, E (2007) Interventions implemented through sporting organisations for increasing participation in sport. *Cochrane Database of Systematic Reviews*, 2: www.cochrane.org.

Rollo, I, Williams, C, Gant, N and Nute, M (2008) The influence of carbohydrate mouth rinse on self-selected speeds during a 30-min treadmill run. *International Journal of Sport Nutrition and Exercise Metabolism*, 18: 585–600.

Sands, R (2002) *Sport Ethnography.* Champaign, IL: Human Kinetics.

Smith, M and Cushion, CJ (2006) An investigation of the in-game behaviours of professional, top-level youth soccer coaches. *Journal of Sports Sciences*, 24: 355–66.

Sport England (1999) *Best Value Through Sport: Case Studies.* London. Sport England.

Teddlie, C and Tashakkori, A (2008) *Foundations of Mixed Methods Research.* London: Sage Publications.

Thacker SB, Gilchrist J, Stroup DF, et al. (2004) The impact of stretching on sports injury risk: A systematic review of the literature. *Medicine and Science in Sports and Exercise*, 36: 371–78.

Thompson, DC, Rivara F and Thompson R (2006) Helmets for preventing head and facial injuries in bicyclists. *Cochrane Database of Systematic Reviews*, 4: www.cochrane.org.

Vaus de, D (2001) *Research Design in Social Research.* London: Sage Publications.

Vaus de, D (2008) *Surveys in Social Research.* London: Routledge.

Vila, H, Ferragut, C, Argudo, FM, Abraldes, JA, Rodriguez, N and Alacid, F (2009) Relationship between anthropometric parameters and throwing velocity in water polo players. *Journal of Human Sport and Exercise*, 4: 57–68.

Walliman, N (2005) *Your Research Project.* 2nd edition. London: Sage Publications.

William, C and Wragg, C (2006) *Data Analysis and Research for Sport and Exercise Science: A Student Guide.* London: Routledge.

Yin, RK (2008) *Case Study Research.* 4th edition. London: Sage Publications.

Index

Note: Page references in **bold** refer to terms in the Glossary